In Search
of
Owain Glyndŵr

In Search of
Owain Glyndŵr

Chris Barber

Blorenge Books

First Published 1998
New Edition 2004

ISBN 1 87 2730 33 7

© Chris Barber 2004

Photography by Chris Barber FRGS

Blorenge Cottage, Church Lane, Llanfoist,
Abergavenny, Monmouthshire NP7 5LP
Tel: 01873 856114

Printed by MWL Print Group Ltd.,
Units 10/13, Pontyfelin Industrial Estate,
New Inn, Pontypool, Torfaen NP4 0DQ.
Tel: 01495 750033

CONTENTS

WALES IN THE TIME OF OWAIN GLYNDŴR

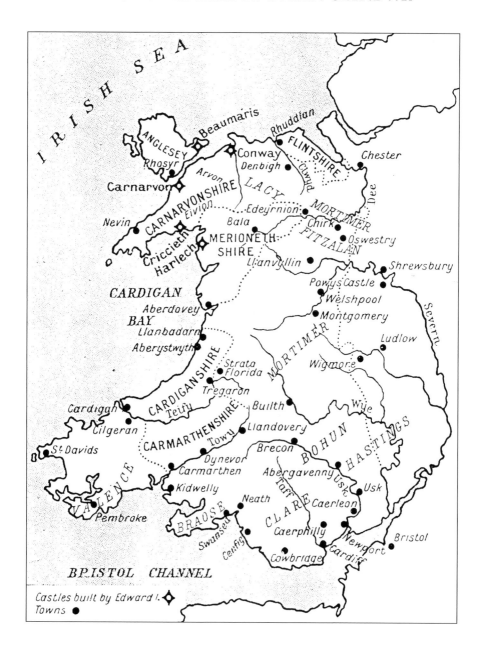

For the Welshmen of all subsequent ages, Glyn Dŵr has been a national hero, the first, indeed, in the country's history to command the willing support alike of north and south, east and west, Gwynedd and Powys, Deheubarth and Morgannwg. He may with propriety be called the father of modern Welsh nationalism.

Prof. J. E. Lloyd 1931

The River Dee at Glyndyfrdwy from which Owain Glyndŵr took his name

FOREWORD

It is only proper that the people of Wales should honour as their national hero a figure whose memory is inextricably entangled with myth and wishful thinking. A nation which is not a State, a community without sovereignty, a people whose higher instincts have traditionally been expressed in music, poetry and story-telling – no Nelson, Napoleon, Washington or Garibaldi would satisfy the sensibilities of the Welsh. They need a champion, mistier, wilder, less exactly defined: and 600 years ago they found one in the person of Owain Glyndŵr, at once the subject and inspiration of this book.

Owain was of course an historical figure, much the most formidable of the Welshmen who have challenged English supremacy since Edward I's conquest of Wales in the 13th century. Nobody else has defied the English as he did – setting himself up as an independent Prince of Wales, defying the imposed authority of London, allying himself with England's historic enemies, the French, summoning a Welsh parliament to legislate on Welsh affairs. Not for another six centuries, until the devolution proposals of the late 20th century, did the Welsh come anything like so near to running their own affairs. That Owain was a thoroughly Anglicized Welshman, who had been educated in London and had borne arms in his time for the King of England, was not inapposite either: for one of the constants of the Welsh condition, in his day as in ours, was an ambivalent hybrid state, at once fascinated and repelled by the English example, eager to be independent yet ready to be seduced. Almost nothing is black and white about the matter of Wales, and not much was simple about Glyndŵr either.

In his lifetime all manner of mystery surrounded him. He was said to have magical powers, able to summon the very weather of Wales to disconcert his enemies, and this dark and alluring reputation was as current among the English as it was among his own besotted supporters – Shakespeare might make fun of Owain's skimble-skamble pretensions, but his portrait of the Welshman in *Henry V Part One* is wonderfully potent all the same. Glyndŵr was undoubtedly a *star*. Chris Barber calls him the greatest Welshman who ever lived, and in death as in life he is certainly one of the most charismatic.

In death, perhaps, especially, for it would have been a sad anticlimax if Owain had died just like the rest of us, whether in battle or in bed, to be placed beneath a gravestone in a churchyard somewhere. But nobody really knows where he died, where he is buried, or indeed if he died at all. In the way of mythological heroes, he simply evaporated, to be pursued by archaeologists, poets, patriots, mystics and romantics from that day to this. Sometimes his memory is confused with other great heroes of long ago. Sometimes he is claimed to have ended his life as a reclusive poet. His name is commemorated in scores of caves, gulleys, battlefields or mounds, places forever linked with him in folk-memory, where he is variously supposed to have won a battle, escaped his enemies, or hunkered himself down with his warriors, sleeping on their shields, to await the call of his nation once again.

The nation has often called him, too, especially since the romantic eruption of Welsh patriotism in the 19th century, and so far he has not let us down. His rising was a failure, and left behind it a Wales ravaged and forlorn, but all down the centuries since then the Welsh identity has survived, against overwhelming odds; and perpetually linked with it in the minds of patriots is the example of old Glyndŵr. Scholars have meticulously identified the historical facts of Owain's story, but I doubt if we shall ever see all its edges clarified, all its mists dispersed – the power of myth will see to that. What Chris Barber has done, in text and photograph, is to bring its poignant and heroic mystery closer to us, to set it against its background in a way that makes it no less strange, but rather more intimate. Owain Glyndŵr died in places familiar to us all: I can imagine nothing more fascinating than to join in Chris Barber's search, this book in hand, for that grand elusive shadow.

Jan Morris
July 1997

PROLOGUE

Moel Hebog loomed impressively above me as I slowly made my way up the hillside above Beddgelert. Following a line of cairns up a steep shoulder and keeping some cliffs on my right, I scrambled up to the summit. The scent of the heathery hill was in my nose as I stood there for a moment savouring the absolute silence in the still air of that mid-July evening.

As I descended the northern slope I took in the view across to Snowdon, and saw its craggy summit tinged with gold as the sun began to drop towards the horizon. Turning around, I then picked out a narrow gully rising through the cliff of Clogwyn yr Ogof Owain Glyndŵr.

Below the gully, which is known variously as Simnai Foel Hebog, Pursuers' Folly and Glyndŵr 's Ladder, I sat on a rock and delved into the depths of my rucksack for a flask. After taking a few sips of the hot coffee I put the mug down to cool. Then, not for the first time, I opened the climbing guide to the appropriate page and once more read the description of the route up this gully.

> *Glyndŵr's Gully – 230 feet. First Ascent Owain Glyndŵr, circa 1400.*
> *Easy. The gully offers a few short pitches interspersed with noisy scree*
> *and good rock scenery.*

As I drank my coffee, I recalled the story of Owain Glyndŵr, a famous Welsh patriot who rose in rebellion against the English King, Henry IV, in 1400. It would seem that at some unknown period Glyndŵr spent time in this valley seeking supporters for his cause. He stayed for a while with his friend Rhys Goch Eryi, a gentleman of means, who lived at Hafod Garegog, an ancient house which still stands near the mouth of the Nanmor stream.

It is said that Owain's presence in this locality was revealed to his enemies and an armed force was sent to capture him. On receiving a warning of its approach Owain ran from the house towards the River Glaslyn, which in those days was tidal as far as Aberglaslyn. It was full tide when he reached the water's edge, and he swam across to the other side to make his way up the lower slopes of Moel Hebog with the English soldiers in hot pursuit.

Crossing the steep hillside below Moel Hebog ('Bare Hill of the Hawks') he found himself below Simnai y Foel, a narrow gully in the middle of the continuous line of cliffs. His pursuers were now hard on his heels, so in

Clogwyn yr Ogof on Moel Hebog near Beddgelert

a desperate attempt to avoid capture Owain entered the gully and scambled upwards. The English soldiers reached the bottom of the gully and lacking Owain's courage, decided to look for an alternative way up to the ridge. Their route was certainly easier but it took them much longer, for they had to skirt the edge of the cliffs and then ascend the steep hillside. By the time they reached the top, there was no sign of Owain, so, quite naturally assuming that he must have descended into Cwm Pennant, they headed down in that direction, hoping to catch up with him.

Owain in fact had climbed the long rocky cleft in safety and then raced across to Moel yr Ogof, where he made an airy traverse along an exposed ledge into a cave, which provided him with an ideal hiding place. This has since become known as 'Owain Glyndŵr 's Cave.' According to one story he is said to have spent several weeks living in this lonely cave and was supplied with food by a monk from Beddgelert Monastery. To the north of Moel Hebog summit is a spring still shown on the Ordnance Survey map as 'Ffynnon Owain Glyndŵr', where he is supposed to have obtained his daily drinking water during his long period of concealment on this hillside.

Glancing at my watch, I calculated that within an hour it would be dark and I needed to make a decision on where I was going to spend the night. I smiled as a glimmer of an idea came into my mind. Yes that's it, I'll make an ascent of Glyndŵr's Gully and traverse into the cave to bivouac in his eyrie. I always enjoy a bivouac in an unusual place and this one would certainly provide a good view to wake up to in the morning.

Repacking my rucksack I made my way across to the gully and began my ascent. It was quite easy and within ten minutes I had reached the top of the gully. From there I first made my way up to the summit of Moel yr Ogof to enjoy a brilliant sunset and then, in the failing light, I descended to a col below the summit and delicately followed a diagonal traverse around to the cave. To call it a cave is not really accurate for it is really more of a rock shelter, quite small and damp, but certainly well concealed.

Opening my rucksack I pulled out my bivouac gear – consisting of a large polythene bag and a lightweight sleeping bag and spread them out with the feet end towards the entrance – so that I could look out at the stars and, in the morning, wake up to a good view of Snowdon.

That done, I then took out my pint flask of water and lit the small lightweight gas stove that I generally carry on these adventures. Before long, I was lying cosily in my bag sipping coffee and looking out at the stars. Very slowly, very gently, the sunset faded and darkness enshrouded me. I always enjoy lying in a sleeping bag, out of doors, in a place where I can watch the stars glinting in the night sky, which is never more beautiful than when it is seen from a hill.

To bivouac on your own in a high and lonely place in constant view of the stars, is to be at one with the night and the mountains. With no companion to make needless remarks, the Snowdonia summits and the star studded sky were mine alone. This was the true meaning of silence, an absolute and complete silence.

Lying there snug in my bag, I savoured a sense of history, thinking about the unity and continuity of life, a ceaseless rhythm that sends men and women on their way. The past, the present and the future became united in the calm and silence which was emphasised by the knowledge that across the valley was Snowdon. A slumbering giant that has seen so much, yet apart from erosion caused by countless feet, has changed so little through the passing centuries.

Time to get some sleep, I thought, as I succumbed to the weariness of my long day in the hills, walking and scrambling over many miles of rough country. I drifted gently into the depths of timeless oblivion and began to dream of another age.

Through that night I rode with Owain Glyndŵr, through the mountains and valleys of Wales. He was the valiant leader of a huge army of supporters who had proclaimed him Prince of Wales. Fighting many bloodthirsty battles, storming castles and putting the enemy to flight, I experienced both triumph and disaster.

I awoke from my deep slumber as the first rays of sunshine flooded into the cave and as I gazed across the sunlit valley at Snowdon the dreams of the night were still vivid in my mind. It was as if Owain Glyndŵr had been with me in the cave through the long lonely night. I immediately sensed a strong and determined urge to look deeply into Glyndŵr's life and follow the story of his bold uprising to the bitter end. "Yes," I thought to myself, "I will research and write a book about Owain Glyndŵr, the self proclaimed Prince of Wales."

Chris Barber
Llanfoist 1998

One

Not in the Roll of Common Men

And all the course of my life do shew I am not in the roll of common men.

William Shakespeare, Henry IV Part I

For centuries the name of Owain Glyndŵr has been a symbol of the spirit of Wales and its long history of resistance to tyranny. His story is comparable with an Arthurian romance and in four of Shakespeare's plays he is mentioned no less than twenty-four times. Claiming descent from the last of the Welsh princes, he was in his time the wealthiest landowner in Wales. In 1400 he was one of the very few Welshmen who, as Tenants in Chief holding land directly from the crown, controlled areas over which their ancestors had ruled as princes.

English writers over the years have distorted Glyndŵr's name by spelling it in many different ways, such as Glendower, Glendour, Glendore, Glyndour and Glyndowdry. His own countrymen referred to him as Owain Glyndyfrdwy and from this is derived the contracted name of Glyndŵr, which means Owain of the Glen of water. This being a reference to the family estate of Glyndyfrdwy (Glen of the Water of Dee).

But Owain's true name was Owain ap Gruffydd, and his father, Gruffydd Fychan (the Younger) was tenth in lineal descent from Bleddyn ap Cynfyn – Prince of Powys and head of one of the royal tribes of Wales. Owain's great-great-grandfather was a previous Gruffydd Fychan, who fought with Prince Llywelyn ap Gruffydd in the war of 1277 and also for Wales in 1282. He was later pardoned by Edward I, for his part in this rebellion and given land at Glyn Dyfrdwy.

In 1283, at the request of John, Earl of Warren, the King confirmed the lordship of Glyndyfrdwy to Gruffydd Fychan, as we learn from the following charter:

> The king to all his bailiffs and faithful, etc. Know, that at the requisition of our Gruffudd Fychan, son of Madog, permission to hold the territory of Glyndyfrdwy from us during our pleasure. But that the said Gruffudd Fychan shall make out for us his letters patent, by which he shall assert that he holds those lands by no other right than our pleasure. Given at Rhuddlan, Feb 12, 1283, Edw. I.

This territory was inherited by Gruffydd ap Madog ap Gruffydd, who in turn passed it on to his son Gruffydd Fychan, who married Elen Goch, the daughter of Thomas ap Llywelyn ap Rhys. He was a descendant of the great House of Deheubarth and owned land in north Pembrokeshire and South Cardiganshire. Helen Goch, who gave birth to Owain Glyndŵr, was the great-grand-daughter of Catherine the daughter of Prince Llywelyn the Last. Her father, Thomas ap Llewelyn ap Rhys, was Lord of Trefgarn.

It thus becomes obvious that Owain Glyndŵr was of very noble birth. He was a representative of the House of Gwynedd and also the House of Powys, being descended on his mother's side from Llywelyn the Last, Prince of Wales, and on his father's side from Bleddyn ap Cynfyn, Prince of Powys and Gwynedd. Owain's aunt, Margaret, the sister of Elen Goch, married Gwilym ap Gruffydd of Mawddwy and on his death, she later married Tudur ap Gronw of Penmynydd. From this Anglesey estate later came Owen Tudor, the founder of the great Tudor dynasty, from which the British royal family is descended.

Owain Glyndŵr is said to have been born on 28 May, 1354. However, there are varying statements that he was born in 1349, 1348 and 1359. But he is also said to have been 61 years of age at his death in 1415, so it would seem that 1354 is probably the correct date for his birth.

In common with other eminent Welsh and English heroes, uncanny events are supposed to have occurred at the time of Owain's birth.

> Strange wonders happened (as men reported) at the nativitie of this man, for the same night, he was borne his father's horses in the stables were found to stand in blood up to their bellies.
>
> Raphael Holinsted
> (Elizabethan Chronicler)

It is of interest that an earlier chronicler used this same story in connection with an account of the birth of Edmund Mortimer, who was to become Owain Glyndŵr 's son-in-law. It is strange that the story should be told of both men, but we can safely assume that it was originally told in connection with the birth of Owain Glyndŵr and may be a reference to a stampede in the stables. A number of hefty kicks from savage hooves could certainly rip fetlocks and tear flanks to create quite a bloody scene, which was later exaggerated.

Just like Homer, Glyndŵr was a man with several possible birth-places. Some writers maintain that he was born at Glyndyfrdwy in the Valley of the Dee, near Llangollen, while others say that the birth took place at Sycharth in Powys. On the other hand there is also a strong case for his being born at Trefgarn in Dyfed.

The farm house of Trefgarne Owaine in the parish of Brawdy is also called West Trefgarn and Trefgarn Castle. The original building on the site passed by marriage to Llywelyn ab Owen and, on his death in 1309, to his son Owen, from which it took its name. Owen ap Llywellyn was a lineal descendant of the Lord Rhys and he died without issue. But he had two nieces, children of his brother Thomas. The daughter who inherited the property married William of Mawddwy and she was the aunt of Owain Glyndŵr. It is possible that Owain Glyndŵr was born here when his mother Elen was visiting her parents, her father being Thomas ap Llywelyn. We may conjecture that, at the time of the birth, her husband Gruffydd Fychan may have been in France with the army of the Black Prince. During his absence Elen may have been staying with her parents and during that time, gave birth to her son Owain at their house. We shall probably never be certain of the truth of this matter.

Little Treffgarne, the supposed birthplace of Owain Glyndŵr

Gruffydd Fychan, Owain's father, was dead by 1370, and Owain at the age of about twelve was made a ward of Robert Fitzalan the Earl of Arundel, who held the Castle of Dinas Bran, not far from Glyndyfrdwy. From his father Owain inherited the two estates of Glyn Dyfrdwy and Cynllaith Owain which lie on opposite sides of the Berwyn range, and from his mother, lands in Cardigan and Pembroke.

Young Owain became a page at Chirk Castle, which was the main home of the Earl of Arundel, and it was here that he began his training as a soldier. When Robert Fitzalan died in 1376, his son Richard may have assumed the wardship, although Owain was probably an adult by this time. He received a good education and his natural ability as a scholar who could speak Latin, French, English and Welsh, brought him to London to study law at the Inns of Court and he was probably called to the Bar.

> For I was train'd up in the English Court
> Where, being but young, I trained to the harp
> Many an English ditty lovely as well
> and gave the tongue an helpful ornament.

> (Glyndŵr talking to Hotspur)
> William Shakespeare

The Inns of Court was a university for the sons of important landowners and it was in the courts, that Owain met his future wife, Margaret, the daughter of Sir David Hanmer, one of the Justices of the King's Bench. The wedding probably took place in 1380 when Owain was just 21 years old.

In 1384, Owain and his younger brother Tudur served in military service with Sir Degory Sais, a Welsh captain who was in command at Berwick-on-Tweed. In 1385, Owain went with King Richard II to the French wars as his scutifer or shield-bearer, 'bartering his gown for a coat of mail, his flowing wig for a helmet, and his pen for a sword.' Later that year Owain and his brother Tudur followed Richard to Scotland, and fought the Scots under the command of John of Gaunt. Owain's skill and valour as a soldier was praised by the king. It is recorded that Owain fought bravely, wearing a red feather in his helmet and that (according to the bard Gruffydd Llwyd) in one particular skirmish he managed to un-horse an opponent and fight him with a broken lance, using the stump as a dagger to drive the Scots before him *like wild goats*. King Richard was impressed with Owain's bravery and made him a knight under the title Sir Owen de Glendore. It is interesting, however, that Owain does not seem to have adopted his equestrian honour on his return to Wales and it seems to have been generally discarded.

In a certain document (mentioned in Collins' Peerage Vol VII P.507) there is a record that Owain Glyndŵr was present at Chester Court on Sept 3, 1386. It was a record of proceedings at a trial which was held to settle a dispute between Sir Richard le Scrope of Bolton and Sir Robert le Grosvenour of Hulme, concerning the ownership of a coat of arms. During Richard II's expedition to Scotland in 1385, it had been found that three knights bore the same coat of arms. The king ordered a court to settle the dispute between Carminow of Cornwall, Scrope of Yorkshire and Grosvenor of Chester. The court of Chivalry, presided over by the Duke of Gloucester as Constable of England to adjudicate upon these rival claims, sat on and off for nearly five years. Among those who gave evidence on behalf of Grosvenor was 'Oweyn Sire de Glendore' but Scrope won the verdict. Owain, aged 27 years at this time, testified that he had 'seen Grosvenor bear arms in dispute on the last expedition of his present majesty to Scotland" and that in the counties of Chester and Flint and the neighbouring regions they were generally reckoned to be his. Owain's brother 'Tudu de Glendore', 3 years younger, also testified in the same fashion.

In 1387 Owain became a retainer of Richard Fitzalan the new Earl of Arundel and was eighth among his twenty-eight esquires. Tudur Glyndwr was numbered twentieth. The following year Owain was acting as a squire to Henry Bolingbroke at the battle of Redcote Bridge. Henry was the son of John of Gaunt, Duke of Lancaster, the uncle of Richard II and he was known as Bolingbroke because that was his place of birth.

Few of John of Gaunt's many children lived and Henry was the eldest son to survive. In his youth he won a high reputation for courage and enterprise. His skill in all martial exercise was quite outstanding. He bore the titles Earl of Derby and Duke of Hereford, but he is remembered by most historians as Bolingbroke. A bold and unscrupulous man, he no doubt felt himself better qualified to rule England than his feeble and capricious cousin, Richard.

Early in 1399, John of Gaunt died at the age of fifty-nine, and his son Henry then succeeded to the dukedom of Lancaster. This royal House was so-named because in 1359 John of Gaunt married Blanche, heiress of the great Lancastrian inheritance, and in 1362 John was created Duke of Lancaster.

Henry's cousin, Richard, was the son of the Black Prince and he had been created Prince of Wales in 1376, the year of his father's death. On Christmas Day the following year, Edward III ordered his eleven year old grandson to sit at the king's table above his uncles John of Gaunt, Duke of Lancaster, and Edmund Langley, Duke of York. Edward must have had a premonition that his time was running out, for he died the following year.

Richard, son of the Black Prince, Prince of Wales, became King Richard II in 1377

For twenty years Richard struggled with his barons, who gave him considerable trouble. His most difficult opponents were Fitzalan, Earl of Arundel, and Bolingbroke, Duke of Hereford. On the other hand he was popular with his people, having inherited their respect for his father, the Black Prince.

Richard's first wife was Anne of Bohemia, daughter of the Emperor Charles IV. They were married at St Stephen's Chapel, Palace of Westminster, on 20 January, 1382. The coronation of the queen took place a few days after the wedding, at Westminster Abbey.

In 1387 Arundel was brought to trial as a traitor and executed. His son Thomas was placed in captivity, but he escaped to the Continent where he was soon joined by Henry Bolingbroke who was banished for a period of ten years for refusing to allow his cousin Richard, the king, to take possession of the lands owned by Henry's father, John of Gaunt, on his death.

Queen Anne was struck down by the plague in June 1394 and died within a few hours at Sheen Palace. She was buried in Westminster Abbey, where her tomb can be seen. Two years later, on 1 November 1396, Richard married Isabella of France at Calais. She was crowned at Westminster Abbey on 8 January 1397. He was twenty-nine and she was seven. They were married in the church of St. Nicholas at Calais on All Saint's Day. The marriage was arranged to cement peace with France. However, it proved to be an unconsummated marriage and Isabella lived mainly at Windsor Castle, where Richard visited her on frequent occasions.

In May 1399, Richard marched with his army from Windsor to Bristol and then on to Milford Haven. From there he sailed in September with his force to Ireland with the intention of quelling the insurrection of an Irish chief called MacMurrogh and to avenge the death of his kinsman Edmund Mortimer, the Lieutenant of Ireland, who had been killed in a skirmish with some rebels there. It proved to be a disastrous expedition.

Richard took with him his young cousins, Henry of Monmouth and Humphrey of Gloucester (whose father was the ill-fated Thomas of Woodstock and his mother the elder sister of Mary de Bohun). They landed at Waterford on 31 May and on the morning of St. John's Eve they marched against MacMurrogh and his followers. However, the Irish retreated into the woods, so Richard ordered his men to burn the nearest village.

From there, he proceeded to Dublin, where in July he received the news that his cousin Henry Bolingbroke had sailed from Boulogne and, accompanied by Archbishop Thomas Arundel, had landed at Ravenspur on the Humber, near Bridlington, to claim his inheritance. He had brought a small force of about fifteen lances and forty to sixty men-at-arms. He was met by the Percys and other nobles who encouraged him to seize the throne.

From there he travelled via Pickering, Knaresborough, Pontefract and Doncaster where the castles all opened their gates to him. Many friends were also riding to his standard including the Earl of Northumberland, head of the powerful Percy family and Ralph Neville, Earl of Westmorland.

Bolingbroke made it known that he had returned to claim his own property, the lands that Richard had stolen, and to reform the government. As Edmund Mortimer, the six-year-old heir apparent, was alive, Bolingbroke could not seek the throne openly.

Richard's first action was to send the Earl of Salisbury back to England, but he did not leave Ireland himself for another three weeks. Just before he left Dublin, Richard called young Prince Henry to him and said, "Henry, my boy, see what thy father hath done to me! He hath invaded my land and put my subjects to death without mercy. I am very sorry for thee, since on these unhappy doings thou wilt perchance lose thy inheritance."

Henry was just a boy but we are told that he replied very wisely to his uncle. "In truth, my gracious lord and king, I am greatly grieved at these rumours. But I believe your lordship understands that I am innocent of my father's deed".

"Yes," answered Richard, "I know that thou hast no part in thy father's crime, and therefore don't hold thee accused of it."

Richard was obviously fond of Prince Henry for he gave him an income of £500 a year, which was no mean sum in those times. Richard was also fond of reminding people of an ancient prophecy which foretold that a prince called Henry 'will be born in England, who, through the nobility of his character and the splendid greatness of his achievements, will illumine the whole world with the rays of his glory'. He would then add, glancing at the young prince, "And verily do I believe that young Henry will be he."

When Richard departed, Henry and his cousin Humphrey were sent to the castle of Trim in Meath for safe custody.

Richard landed back at Milford Haven on 22 July and made his way to the northern part of his principality and his earldom of Chester. He sent Thomas Despenser to stir up his men of Glamorgan to come to his help, but they proved unco-operative. Meanwhile, Henry Bolingbroke and his followers were travelling via Bristol, Hereford and Shrewsbury to Flint.

With only thirteen people in attendance, Richard travelled through the night to arrive at Conwy, some thirty hours later. Soon after he arrived, a horseman came riding hard from Milford Haven with the disturbing news that the king's army had disbanded due to the treachery of its chief officers.

Richard, feeling very alarmed and confused by the news, then proceeded to wander around North Wales like a hunted hare, doubling backwards and forwards from castle to castle. First he travelled to Beaumaris, a journey of about ten miles. From there he went to Caernarfon Castle, but left after five nights, for there was a lack of food and furniture there and his bedding was no more than bare straw.

He then returned to Conwy and it is probable that on this journey a coin was dropped near Carreg Fawr, Llanfairfechan. It was dug up in a garden in 1894 by a local man, Richard Williams, and found to be a gold half noble bearing the inscription:-

'Richard DI REX. ANGL. 2. F. DNS. HIB. 2. A.'

It also bears a design consisting of the king (crowned and in armour) standing in a ship, with a flag at its stern, ornamented with lions and lis, with a sword in his right hand, and in his left a shield bearing the arms of England and France quarterly. On the 'reverse,' which was from Edward III's die, with 'E' in the centre, is a treasure of eight curves with a beaded interior, and with trefoils in the outer angles, and containing a cross fleuree leaded with a fleur-de-lis at the end of each limb of the cross. In each quarter is a lion under a crown, and centrally placed is a four-leaved rose, pointed with as many trefoils containing the letter 'E.' The 'reverse' inscription reads:-

'DOMNINE : NE : FVORE : TVO : ARGVAS : ME.'

Meanwhile, Henry Bolingbroke rode to Chester, and following the advice of the Archbishop of Canterbury, he sent the Earl of Northumberland to Conwy. He undertook to return with King Richard by reason or by craft. At Penmaenrhos, under the rough and lofty cliffs of a rock, Northumberland placed his men in ambush, while he and five others went as envoy to Conwy Castle. Here he was received by Richard and he told him that Henry Bolingbroke would sue for pardon and make peace on the condition that the king restored him (Bolingbroke) as Chief Judge of England.

Asking Northumberland to withdraw, Richard then spoke to his Council. He told them that he would grant the petition, for he saw no alternative. Salisbury, Carlisle and the rest of the Council agreed to this and Northumberland was recalled and told that his terms were accepted. Later, in private, Richard was heard to swear that if Bolingbroke was to come into his hands he would put him to death in such a terrible way that it should long be recounted – even in Turkey.

Richard and his party were subsequently ambushed at Llanddulas which is about 4 miles from Abegele. In a glen flanked by limestone rocks, they suddenly found themselves surrounded by a large troop of armed men and Northumberland stepped forward to seize the bridle of Richard's horse.

He pretended that the troops were for Richard's safety, but Richard was not fooled and told the Earl, "It is contrary to your oath, for you had promised to have but six in your company. I will return to Conwy." Northumberland was then virtually forced to arrest him and Richard was taken first to Rhuddlan Castle and then to Flint Castle.

Henry Bolingbroke saw Richard the following morning, on Tuesday 19 September, and told him that he was to be taken to the Tower of London. Richard reluctantly submitted to Henry and accompanied him as a prisoner first to Chester, where he was lodged in the donjon over the great gateway of the walled town. They then travelled on to London, where he was placed in the Tower, from which five months earlier he had embarked on his expedition to Ireland.

Adam of Usk was present in the Tower on 21 September 1399, where King Richard was imprisoned:

> I was present while he dined and I marked his mood and bearing, having been taken thither for that very purpose by Sir William Beauchamp. And there the then king discoursed sorrowfully in these words: 'My God!, a wonderful land is this, and a fickle; which hath exiled, slain, destroyed, or ruined so many kings, rulers, and great men, and is ever tainted and toileth with strife and variance and envy;' and then he recounted the histories and names of sufferers from the earliest habitation of the kingdom. Perceiving then the trouble of his mind and how that none of his own men, nor such as were wont to serve him, but strangers who were but spies upon him, were appointed to his service, and musing on his ancient and wanted glory and on the fickle fortune of the world, I departed thence much moved at heart.

Richard II and Henry Bolingbroke arriving in London

Parliament was summoned in the king's name to meet at Westminster on 30 September. The day before, a formal renunciation of the crown was obtained from the king, so that when Parliament assembled the following day the throne was vacant. Richard had signed a document which stated that he absolved all his subjects, lay and ecclesiastical, from homage and obedience. He renounced his kingship and everything that went with it and declared that he had been "noughtt worth to govern, being useless and insufficient." However, Richard maintained that he resigned his rights to the crown to God, rather than Bolingbroke. Bolingbroke then replied that he claimed it by descent from Henry II, "and through the right which God had given him by conquest when the realm was nearly undone for want of good government."

King Richard's renunciation of the throne was read out to the assembly by Richard Scrope, the Archbishop of York, and this was followed by a vote of acceptance of Richard's abdication, which was carried unanimously.

Henry Bolingbroke, the Duke of Lancaster, then rose to his feet and spoke in English to the assembly. "In the name of the Son, and the Holy Ghost, I, Henry of Lancaster, challenge this realm of England with all the members and appurtances thereto, I that am descended by the right line of the blood coming from the good Henry III, and through that right that God of His Grace hath sent me, with the help of my kin and of my friends, to recover it; the which realm was in point to be undone for default of governance and undoing of the good laws."

Shouts of "Aye" echoed around the chamber and the Archbishop, Thomas Arundel, who had been banished by Richard and had returned with Bolingbroke, took him by the right hand and led him to the throne.

A short sermon was then preached by Arundel and then Bolingbroke stood up and spoke again.

"Sirs, I thank God and you spirituals and temporals and all the estates of the land, and I do you to wit that it is naught my will that no man think that by way of conquest I would disinherit any man of his heritage, franchise or other rights that he ought to have, nor put him out of that he hath, and hath by the good laws and customs of this realm, except them that hath been against the good purpose and the common profit of the realm."

Meanwhile, young Prince Henry had been brought back from Ireland by a certain Henry Dryhurst to join his father in London.

On Sunday 12 October, King Henry IV announced forty-five new knights in preparation for his coronation the following day. Topping the list was his son young Henry of Monmouth and the fact that he had already been knighted by King Richard was ignored.

Coronation of Henry IV, 13 October 1399

So on Monday 13 October (St Edward's Day), Henry was solemnly crowned in Westminster Abbey. He had the sword 'Curtana' which he wore on landing at Ravenspur borne naked and erect before him by the Earl of Northumberland and he confirmed the Isle of Man, which had belonged to Sir William Scrope, the Earl of Wiltshire, on the earl, in fee 'for himself and his heirs, for the service of carrying this sword at the present and all future coronations.' His son Henry was present as a representative of the House of Lancaster and wearing the pointless sword – Curona – the emblem of Justice and Mercy.

Adam of Usk was watching the ceremony from the Sanctuary and he noted the sequence of misfortunes which befell the King: 'First, in the procession he lost one of his coronation shoes... secondly, one of the golden spurs fell off... thirdly at the banquet a sudden gust of wind carried away the crown from his head.' It was also commented by Adam that after the annointing with oil, 'there ensued such a growth of lice, especially upon his head, that he neither grew hair, nor could he have his head uncovered for many months.'

King Henry then proceeded to honour his son with a series of titles. On October 15 he was created Prince of Wales and Earl of Chester. The same Parliament on 23 October declared him Duke of Aquitaine, and on 10 November he was further made Duke of Cornwall.

During the sitting of the House of Lords on 23 October, it was decided that Richard should be imprisoned for the term of his natural life. After signing his abdication in London, Richard was taken from the tower on 28 October to Gravesend and removed from there, in the disguise of a forester, to Leeds Castle in Kent and from there he was taken from castle to castle, until he was brought to Pontefract, which at that time was the most important castle in the north of England. He was placed under the care of a staunch Lancastrian official, Thomas Waterton, but six months later, at the age of 33, he was dead.

Pontefract Castle, where Richard II spent his last days

It is uncertain how Richard died. Perhaps he was starved to death, but it is more likely that Henry IV had him murdered at Pontefract Castle where he certainly spent his final days. One account suggests that he fought with his assasins and received a fatal dagger wound in the head or alternatively that he was hit on the head with an axe. However in 1871, Richard's body in Westminster Abbey was exhumed and the skull was examined by a certain Edward King, who found no evidence of any 'marks of a blow, or wound upon it, as could at all warrant the commonly received history of this wretched king's unhappy end.'

On February 17, 1400, £80 was paid from the Exchequer to cover the cost of bringing Richard's corpse from Pontefract to London so that the people could see that their late king was indeed dead. The body was conveyed with considerable funeral pomp in a carriage drawn by two horses, one placed before the other. The carriage was covered with black cloth, having four banners emblazoned with the arms of St George and St Edward. It was attended by one hundred men all clad in black, and was met on its approach to the city by thirty Londoners dressed in white and bearing torches. King Henry himself walked in procession, bearing a corner of the pall.

Richard's emaciated body was encased in lead with just his face visible and he lay in state for two days in St. Paul's Cathedral. King Henry himself attended the service for the dead, and gave twenty shillings in offerings to the poor. The body was later taken to the Friars Preachers at Langley, Hertfordshire, and a thousand masses were arranged to be said in various churches. He was laid in a marble tomb that had been ordered by Richard himself long before his death. Displayed on it were copper effigies of Richard and Queen Anne. Richard lay there with his face uncovered for all to see, and twenty thousand citizens filed past, to pay respects to their king.

Adam of Usk comments:

> The body of Lord Richard, late King of England, was brought to the church of St Paul in London, the face not covered but shown openly to all; and the rites being there celebrated on that night and a mass on the morrow, he was buried at Langley among the Dominican friars. My God! how many thousand marks he spent on burial-places of vain-glory for himself and his wives, among the Kings at Westminster! But fortune ordered it otherwise.

There were many, particularly in Wales, who firmly believed that Richard had escaped and was living in Scotland, and would, just like King Arthur, one day return. Rumours that Richard II was still alive and planning to lead the Scots in war were so prevalent that Henry found it necessary to make a public proclamation, stating that Richard was indeed *mortus sepultus*.

The council of Henry had placed on record a minute to the effect:

> It seemeth expedient to the Council to speak to the King, that in case Richard, lately King, be still alive, to be put in safe keeping, in conformity with the advice of the lords; but if he be departed this life, that then he be shown openly to the people, that they might have knowledge of it.

But the public exposition was regarded by many as a mock funeral and the belief remained strong that Richard was still alive, perhaps at liberty, and that the corpse was that of some other person, probably the priest Maudelin.

Accounts of Richard's death have been given by several contemporary writers. Walsingham asserts that Richard died in Pontefract Castle on 14th February from voluntary starvation, having fallen into a state of deep depression. Thomas of Otterburn confirms this account, except that he adds that Richard, being persuaded at length to take food by his keepers, found the orifice of his stomach closed from long abstinence and perished in consequence. The Chronicle of Kenilworth, the Chronicle of Peter de Ockham in the Harleian Collection, and Hardyng assert that he was starved to death by his keepers.

The story of Richard's assassination by Sir Piers Exton and his eight ruffians is found in a French manuscript held in the Royal Library at Paris and is repeated by Fabyon, Hall, and Haywood. All accounts agree that the murder of Richard in some form occurred in Pontefract Castle.

A false Richard appeared in Scotland, having, it was said, escaped from Pontefract. He was positively declared by the former jester of King Richard to be that king, and also by the sister-in-law of the Lord of the Isles, who declared she had seen him in Ireland. This supposed Richard is declared by Wyntain "to have seemed half-mad or wild, from the manner in which he conducted himself," and therefore it was supposed that he had lost his understanding through his misfortunes. Though we are told Lord Percy and other noblemen came to him, we are also informed that he would not see them. Yet for seventeen years at least, this mysterious person was maintained at the court of Scotland as the veritable King Richard. He was however identified by some as one Thomas Ward, a man of *weak intellect.*

As far as the Welsh were concerned, if Richard was still alive then Henry Bolingbroke could not be the lawful sovereign. This also meant that Henry, his eldest son, being the offspring of a usurper, could not be accepted as Prince of Wales, and the obvious alternative was Owain Glyndŵr.

Repeated proclamations had to be made by King Henry against the rumour concerning Richard. He also found it necessary to execute Sir Roger Clarendon, the natural son of the Black Prince, along with nine Franciscan friars and several other persons, for spreading false information.

King Henry IV

Following Richard's abdication and brief imprisonment, his young wife Isabella was confined by Henry IV at Sonning, and, in July 1401, she was allowed to return to France. In 1406 she married her cousin Charles, Duke of Orleans and died three years later on 13 September 1409 whilst giving birth to her first child, the future Duchess of Alencon. Isabella was buried in the Abbey of St. Saumer, Blois, but was transferred to the Celestines, Paris, in 1624.

It was King Henry V who later had Richard's remains brought to Westminster Abbey. His short life was from 1367-1399.

Two

Sycharth to Llangollen

Few strangers but an occasional antiquary ever see the well-defined and flat-topped tumulus on which the manor house of the most famous of all Welshmen stood.

A.G. Bradley

I decided that my starting point for research into the life of Owain Glyndŵr should be the site of his home at Sycharth in the ancient commote of Cynllaith, which was once a part of the old Welsh kingdom of Powys. It was lunch time when I arrived in the village of Llansilin, which is situated about half-a-mile from the English border. Inside the Wynnstay Arms I enjoyed a satisfying bar snack, and then consulted the writings of George Borrow, who had also dined in this pub when he came here in 1854 on his famous walking tour. I opened *Wild Wales* at the appropriate page and read his description of Sycharth.

Owen Glendower's hill or mount at Sycharth, unlike the one bearing his name on the banks of the Dee, is not an artificial hill, but the work of nature, save except that to a certain extent it has been modified by the hand of man. It is somewhat conical and consists of two steps or graduations where two fosses scooped out of the hill go round it, one above the other, the lower one embracing considerably the moat space. Both these fosses are about six feet deep, and at one time doubtless were bricked, as stout large, red bricks are yet to be seen, here and there, in their sides. The top of the mount is just twenty-five feet across. When I visited it, it was covered with grass, but had once been subjected to the plough as certain furrows indicated. The monticle stands not far from the western extremity of the valley, nearly midway between two hills which confront each other north and south, the one to the south being the hill which I had descended, and the other a beautiful wooded height which is called in the parlance of the country Llwyn Sycharth or the grove of Sycharth, from which comes the little gush of water which I had crossed, and which now turns the wheel of the factory and once turned Owen Glendower's mill and filled his two moats, part of the water by some mechanical means, having been forced up the eminence. On the top of this hill or monticle in a timber house dwelt the great Welshman Owen Glendower, with his wife, a comely kindly woman, and his progeny, consisting of stout boys and blooming girls, and there, though wonderfully cramped for want of room he feasted bards who requited his hospitality with alliterative odes very difficult to compose, and which at the present day only a few bookworms understand. There he dwelt for many years, the virtual if not the nominal king of North Wales, at times no doubt looking down with self-compliance from the top of his fastness on the parks and fish ponds of which he had several; his mill, his pigeon tower, his ploughed lands and the cottages of a thousand retainers, huddled round the lower part of the hill, or strewn about the valley; and there he might have lived and died had not events caused him to draw his sword and engage in a war, at the termination of which Sycharth was a fire-scattered ruin, and himself a broken-hearted old man in anchorite's weeds...

In a short time I reached Brynderi Farm, which stands close to the site of Sycharth, and quickly realised that this was certainly a well chosen site for a manor house. The name Sycharth means 'dry hill' or dry enclosure, for 'arth' from garth can have either meaning and it occurs as early as 1300 in a grant to the Bishop of St Asaph.

The moated mound at Sycharth 7 miles east of Oswestry is where Owain Glyndŵr once had an impressive fortified home, where he lived with his wife Margaret and their large family. Excavations in 1962-3 revealed the site of two timber halls on the summit of the flat-topped mound. One of them was an impressive building about 43ft (13m) long and evidence of charred wood confirmed that it had been destroyed by fire, as claimed by Prince Henry in a letter to his father in May 1403. Public access to the site has been negotiated by Cadw and an information board can be seen at the entrance gate.

A letter contained in the Mechain and Crosswood MSS in the National Library at Aberystwyth was written by John Evans of Llwyn y Groes to Sir Watkin Williams Wynn. He described his visit to examine Sycharth on 17 May, 1786 and recorded his observations as follows:

> We rode on to Sycharth, where the Fuller's house and mill make a picturesque appearance... We then visited the house which stands pleasantly upon a rounded green knoll and corresponds exactly with the site of Owain Glyndŵr's habitation as described in a poem of a British Bard at that time called Iolo Goch, previous to his high advancement in life and residence at Glynwrdy. The name of this place was Sycharth and had a park on high ground adjoining; that is exactly the case, and what still confirms the opinion is an high keep castellet just above the house, surrounded by a deep ditch, and high mound similar to that at his subsequent place of residence. The Court for the manor of Cynlleth Owen... was kept in the parlour of this house within these few years. The roof is now in ruins, and the spars and timbers exposed to the weather.

I did a circuit of the mound, immersing myself in the atmosphere and gained an impression of its dimensions. The mound is about 8 metres high and 12 metres in diameter on its summit. It is surrounded by shallow ditches and gives no real impression of the one-time grandeur of Owain's estate. Fortunately, a detailed description of Sycharth has been provided by Iolo Goch, who was Owain Glyndŵr's domestic bard:

> Encircled with a moat, filled with water, the entrance into this Baron's palace, this mansion of generosity, the magnificent habitation of the chief Lord of Powys, is by a costly gate; Gothic arches adorned with mouldings, every arch alike; a tower of St. Patrick in the elegant antique order, like the cloisture of Westminster; every angle united together with girders, a compact noble golden chancel, concatenated in linked orders like an arched vault, all conjoined in harmony. A Neapolitan building of eighteen apartments; a fair timber structure on the surmount of a green hill reared towards heaven on four admirable pilasters; on the top of each of these firm wooden supporters is fixed a timber floor of curious architecture, and there four pleasant and elegant floors connected together, and divided into eight chamber lofts, every part, and stately front covered with shingles and chimneys to convey away the smoke; nine halls of similar construction and a wardrobe over every one; neat clean and commodious well-furnished warehouses, like shops in London; a quadrangular church, well built and whitewashed chapels, well glazed, plenty on every side, every part of the house a palace - an orchard and vineyard well fenced; yonder below are seen herds of stags feeding in the park; the rabbit warren of the chief Lord of the Nation; implements, mettlesome steeds, and fair meadows of grass and hay; well ordered corn fields; a good corn mill on a clear stream, and a stone-turret for a pigeon-house; a deep and spacious fish pond; pikes, mearlings, and other

fish in plenty; three tables well furnished with the best breed of peacocks and cranes; all necessary tools and instruments for every sort of work, the best Salopian ale, choice wassail and braggets, wines, all kinds of liquors and manchets; and the cook, with his fire in the noble kitchen.

I am blest with her politeness; with wine and meads; a charming female of a noble extraction, liberal and of an honourable family. His children come in pairs, a beautiful nest of chieftains. A lock or latchet is seldom seen within his mansion, or a doorkeeper or a porter. Refreshments are never wanting, hunger, thirst, want or reproach are never known in Sycharth. The proprietor of this domain is hardy and valiant, the best of Britons; a tall handsome accomplished gentleman owns this most delightful palace.

Iolo Goch (Red Iolo) was the Lord of Llechryd in the upper Clwyd Mountains and his home was at Coed Panton in the village of Llannefydd, but he no doubt preferred to live at Sycharth with Owain Glyndŵr where he wrote many poems for the benefit of his patron. Twenty-one of them have been preserved in the Myvyrian Manuscripts held in the British Museum and seven relate to Owain.

The southward-facing slope to the north-west of the mound must have been the site of Owain's vineyard and at the bottom of the valley was the fish pond which supplied his table

In the third poem we are provided with details of the pedigree of Owain Glyndŵr, while the fourth is an ode to a comet which appeared in March 1402. Iolo relates how a star appeared in the east to announce the birth of Christ and that a similar star was the signal for the coming of Arthur. He claimed that the new comet heralded the rising of Owain Glyndŵr.

He also wrote an ode to Sir Howell y Fwyall, a noted soldier who had been in the retinue of the Black Prince at the battle of Potiers, 1356. The story was that Sir Howell with one blow of his battle-axe beheaded the King of France's horse and that he was ever afterwards authorised to quarter the battle-axe upon his coat-of-arms.

Iolo was also a competent harpist and no doubt, during Glyndŵr's rebellion, he was encouraged to compose warlike songs to rouse his countrymen against the English. Iolo's bardic teacher was Llewelyn Goch ap Meurig Hen, who was the family bard at Nannau, near Dolgellau, the house of Hywel Sele, who was Owain's cousin.

The earliest of Iolo's poems relating to Owain Glyndŵr deals with the return of Owain from the wars in Scotland and welcomes him back to Sycharth. In the second poem Iolo provides a remarkable description of Owain's grand house, his family, his household and way of life.

The fifth ode is in praise of Owain and was probably written just after his coronation at Machynlleth. In the sixth poem, Owain has fallen, having fought his last battle and, like Arthur of old, he has disappeared.

Iolo was composing poetry before Dafydd ap Gwilym (the famous medieval poet) was born, yet his own life was of such length that he was still around to compose an ode on the death of Owain Glyndŵr:

> One thousand four hundred, no less and no more,
> Was the date of the rising of Owain Glyndŵr;
> When fifteen were added still Owain bold,
> Some years he lived longer, though broken and old.

There is no record of the date of Owain's marriage, but if he had married at 21 then it would have taken place in about 1370. His wife Marged (Margaret), is described by Iolo as 'honourable, generous and noble,' and her children, he calls 'a beautiful nest of chieftains.' She was the daughter of Sir David Hanmer and her brothers were Griffith, Philip and John. (John Hanmer joined up with Owain and even visited France on a mission to gain support for the Welsh cause).

The Hanmers lived at Bettisfield Park in Maelor Saesneg (English Maelor) – a detached part of Flintshire to the south of Wrexham. They were a border family of Anglo-Saxon extraction and settled in this area initially as administrators to Edward I, but later having lived in Wales for many years had become Welsh both in their speech and outlook. Owain's father-in-law had been one of Edward III's top judges and his own father had served as steward to the Earl of Arundel at Oswestry. At the time of the wedding of Owain and Margaret, Sir David Hanmer was a distinguished Judge of the King's Bench, appointed by Richard II in 1383 and knighted by him in 1387.

35

Owain Glyndŵr at his estate of Sycharth

He is portrayed by Shakespeare as follows:

"In faith he was a wealthy gentleman,
Exceedingly well read, and profited
In strange concealment; valiant as a lion,
And wondrous affable, and as bountiful
As mines of India."

Eleven children were born to Owain and Margaret. They had six promising sons: Gruffydd, Madoc, Maredydd, Tomos, Sion and Dewi, who all became captains in Owain's army during the uprising. We are told that Gruffydd and Maredydd fought bravely with Owain, but Madoc, Tomos and Sion are given little mention in the records of those eventful years.

Hanmer Church is situated in the furthest corner of Maelor Saesneg, a detached part of old Flintshire to the south of Wrexham. Hanmer takes its name from the mere (lake) called Hanmer Mere on the road between Overton and Whitchurch.This parish church is dedicated to St Chad, who was known as the Saint of the Midlands and became Bishop of the Kingdom of Mercia. It was in an earlier church on this site that, Owain Glyndŵr married Margaret, the daughter of Sir Richard Hanmer of Betisfield Park. The ceremony would have taken place in an earlier church on this site. During the Wars of the Roses, Hanmer Church was burnt down and then rebuilt in about 1500, but the tower was not completed until 1570. A fire in 1889 destroyed the Tudor interior, leaving only a shell. It was rebuilt in the old style and re-opened in 1892, but the chancel was not reconstructed until 1936. It was rebuilt in the time of Henry VII but in 1889 it was largely destroyed by another fire and reconstructed.

Owain's five daughters all married into wealthy families. Isabel the eldest married the Welshman Adda ab Iorwerth Ddu. Alicia married Sir John Scudamore who held lands in Ewyas, Kentchurch and Holme Lacy. He was the deputy squire of Henry IV's Lordship of Brecon. Janet married John Croft of Croft's Castle, also in Herefordshire, whilst Margaret married Roger Monnington, also of that county. Katherine, the youngest daughter, married Sir Edmund Mortimer after he became her father's ally.

She certainly set the poets scribbling and was known as 'Gwenllian of the Golden Locks' and 'Gwenllian of the house of drifted snow' by the bard Lewis of Glyncothi.

Glyndŵr also fathered several other children. These were mainly daughters who married sons of respectable Welsh families. Thomas Pennant looked into this matter and tells us:

> A daughter married into the house of Gwernau; another named Myfanwy to Llewelyn ap Adda ap Trefor and Gwenllian to Philip ap Rhys of St Harmon in Radnorshire.

Sycharth was excavated in 1962-3 and the site of a timber framed hall was revealed on the summit of the mound. Evidence of charred oak confirmed that it had been destroyed by fire (the work of Prince Henry in 1403). It may be safely assumed that this was indeed Owain Glyndŵr's hall, described by Iolo Goch. A large piece of timber found in the ditch surrounding the motte in the 1890s was used for many years as a name board in Llansilin Parish Hall. The motte is most likely the site of an earlier castle and it is interesting that the Domesday Book provides evidence that the commote of Cynllaith was one of the first of the border areas to come under Norman influence and it is thus reasonable to suppose that the motte was constructed at the end of the eleventh century.

From the mound I looked north into the beautiful Vale of Ceiriog, through which Owain must have ridden so often when travelling to his other home at Glyndyfrdwy, near Corwen. It was time for me to move on, so, with reluctance I descended from Sycharth and returned to my car. After a short distance I stopped at the village of Llansilin, which was once the ecclesiastical centre of Cynllaith and is named after Silin or Sulien, a Dark Age missionary from Cornwall.

The Lord of Cynllaith, Einion Efell, was a first cousin of Prince Madoc ap Gruffydd, the great-grandfather of Owain Glyndŵr and founder of Valle Crucis Abbey, near Llangollen in 1199. Llansilin Church was probably built at this time but later largely destroyed during the Glyndŵr rebellion. It is likely that Prince Henry of Monmouth burned Llansilin church when he destroyed Sycharth. It was rebuilt in its present rectangular form from 1450-1500 and the enlarged Norman aisle was dedicated to St Sulien. In 1534 it contained a statue of the saint, but this was destroyed during the Civil War when Parliamentary forces took possession of the church. But part of the church would have been there in Glyndŵr's day and no doubt he and his family must have often sat within its walls.

Following the B4500 I made for Glyn Ceiriog and then drove east to Chirk, where I joined the A5 and the tourist traffic heading towards Snowdonia.

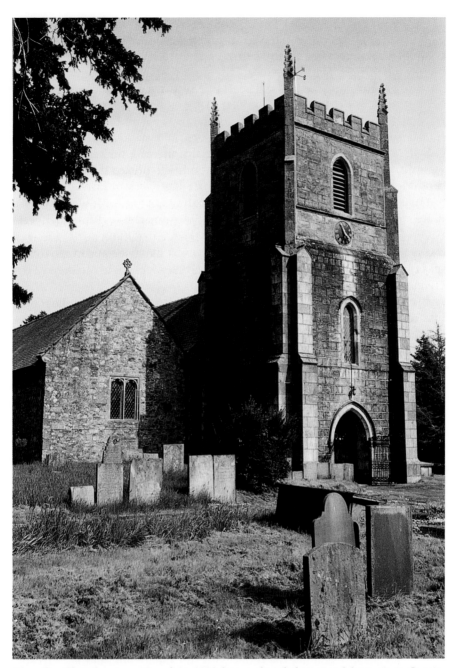

Llansilin Church was restored in 1890 but a church has stood here since Owain Glyndŵr's time and he and his family would have worshipped here.

On arriving in Llangollen, I decided that it was time to stretch my legs by walking to the summit of the conical hill crowned by the jagged ruins of Castell Dinas Brân. Built on the site of an ancient British hill-fort, this once important fortress held the key to the Valley of the Dee, which can be regarded as the gateway into the heart of North Wales.

Situated at an altitude of about 250 metres there is a tradition that this medieval castle is named after the legendary hero Brân, a name which translates as 'crow' and not surprisingly it is sometimes referred to as 'Crow Castle.' The ruins cover most of the summit of this hill, which rises steeply, except at one point, where a deep fosse was dug to protect the approach on that side.

Castell Dinas Brân has a long and fascinating history, for it was once the home of the Princes of Powys Fadog – the middle kingdom between Gwynedd in the north and Deheubarth in the south. Of interest to me was the fact that this castle was once held by Owain Glyndŵr's ancestors, for he was descended from the Princes of Powys through the line of Bleddyn ap Cynfyn.

Bleddyn ap Cynfyn had a son named Maredydd who died in 1129 and his son Madog ap Maredydd died in prison in Winchester in 1160. He was buried in the family burial ground at Meifod, near Welshpool. His successor was his son Gruffydd ap Madog who see-sawed between alliance with the English and loyalty to his own people, and it was he who replaced the wooden fort at Dinas Brân with a stone castle. His son, also named Gruffydd, served under King John in two Welsh expeditions and he married Angharad, the daughter of Owain Gwynedd. They had four sons and three daughters. The eldest son was named Madoc, and when he died in 1190, he was buried at St Teilo's, Meifod, the premier church of Powys. Following his death, Powys was split into two portions; Powys Wenwynwyn in the south and Powys Fadog in the north, where Dinas Brân was the main fortress. Madoc, who succeeded his father to become Prince of Powys, married Gwladys, the daughter of Ithel ab Rhys ab Morgan of Ewyas.

In 1200 Madog ap Gruffydd, who was the great-great-grandfather of Owain Glyndŵr, founded the beautiful abbey of Valle Crucis. In order to secure his Deeside estates he shrewdly shifted his allegiance accordingly. At first he sided with Llewelyn, then transferred his support to King John in 1209. But when John's campaign in Wales failed, Madog returned to his ancient allegiance. He died in 1236 and was buried alongside his father at Valle Crucis. The poets lamented his death and one of them was Einion Wan, who asked, "Will not the tribes weep for the loss of Madog." His son and successor later threw in with the English side, and the castle of Dinas Brân was besieged but found impregnable.

A view of Castell Dinas Brân from the grounds of Plas Newydd, Llangollen

Castell Dinas Brân is built on the site of an ancient British fort and it was an important fortress guarding the Dee Valley. For many years it was held by the Princes of Powys, who were the ancestors of Owain Glyndŵr.

Madog Fychan became the new owner of Dinas Brân in 1277 but he was killed when Powys was taken by Edward I. Dinas Brân then, for the first time, became an English castle and it was occupied by Roger le Strange.

The Edwardian conquest of Wales led to the three ancient kingdoms of Gwynedd, Powys and Deheubarth losing their importance and Edward I organised Wales into five divisions. These were represented by the counties of Anglesey, Caernarfon, Merioneth, Cardigan and Carmarthen, which constituted the Principality of Wales and was governed directly by the Crown. The rest of Wales was a mosaic of Marcher-Lordships, governed by the Anglo-Norman baronial families who had won them at the point of the sword in earlier times, or been granted them for military service. Welshmen in many places now fought under the English flag and even the garrisons of the numerous castles, originally English, were now largely Welsh.

In 1282 the castle was attacked and captured by the Welsh who repaired it and occupied it for about a year, when it was retaken by the English. Powys ceased to be a principality and Dinas Brân passed into the hands of the Trevor family and during the time of Richard II it was owned by the Earl of Arundel. Living there at this time, with her father, was the lovely Myfanwy Fechan, a maiden renowned for her beauty and charm. She captivated the heart of the poet Howel ap Einion Llygliw who wrote the following lines:

> Though hard the steep to gain
> Thy smiles are harder to obtain.

But to Howel's disappointment Myfanwy ignored his attentions and married someone else. She and her family must have been the last occupants of this hilltop eyrie and she was buried at Valle Crucis Abbey. Welsh poetry is certainly full of tributes to her beauty for later poets such as Ceiriog dreamed:

> Would that I were a gust of wind blowing through the garden of Dinas Brân, whispering mine secret in thine ear, making ringlets of thine hair.

I sat beside the jagged ruins and admired the view. It was quite breathtaking. To the west the Dee could be seen following its winding course to Corwen, while to the north towered the limestone terraces of the Eglwyseg Rocks. South west rose the Berwyn Hills and to the east the Vale of Llangollen led to the broad plain of Shropshire. By the time of Henry VIII this proud fortress was a deserted ruin and when his antiquary, Leland, came here he commented:

> The castelle of Dinas Brân was never a bygge thing, but sette all for strength in a place half inaccessible for enemies.

Leland went on to tell of eagles nesting in the rocks and claimed that every year someone was lowered in a basket to take the young. The man had to wear another basket over his head to protect himself from the parent birds!

I descended from Dinas Brân and then drove up to Valle Crucis Abbey which is situated in a green valley about two miles from Llangollen. In its time this was the largest religious house in Wales and it was founded in 1200 by Madoc, son of Gruffydd Maelor; Lord of Bromfield and Dinas Brân. Its construction was financed from the booty that he had amassed in his endeavour to assist Llywelyn the Great in his struggle against King John for the independence of Wales. According to Cistercian records, a colony of 13 monks from Strata Marcella, near Welshpool, arrived at Valle Crucis on 28 January, 1201, and erected temporary buildings on the site.

Madoc ap Gruffydd's lands stretched from the Tanat beyond the Berwyns to the outskirts of Chester. He lived for thirty-six years after founding the beautiful abbey church and when he died his broad lands were divided among his four sons.

Owain Glyndŵr was fifth in descent from Madoc ap Gruffydd, Prince of Powys and Lord of Dinas Brân. In the *Myvrian Archaiology* the following verse tells of the burial of Madoc beneath the stately Gothic aisles of this once great abbey in 1236.

> Will not the tribes weep for the loss of Madoc?
> Hawk of battles, a proud and mighty chief.
> Cold and unseemly in his bed
> A man who is made like Gwair the son of Gwestli
> The hero of men in the ground of Llangwestli.

Madoc's name is preserved in the hamlet of Pont Fadog in the Glyn Ceiriog Valley. His son Gruffydd ap Madoc was also buried at Valle Crucis in 1269.

I entered the ruins by a fine doorway at the west end of the church, where three fine windows pierce the wall above, and high in the gable of the west front is a rose window. Upstairs in the monks' dormitory are several mutilated sepulchral slabs, which were used as coffin lids, laid out in a row. Counting them from the north, I found the first, fourth, fifth and twelfth stones of particular interest.

The first stone is a mutilated fragment of a slab similar to the carved lid of Princess Joan's coffin which can be seen in Beaumaris Church, Anglesey. It is thought that this fragment at Valle Crucis is part of the tomb of Madog ap Gruffydd Maelor, who founded Valle Crucis Abbey and died in 1236.

Valle Crucis Abbey was founded in 1200 by Madog ap Gruffydd, who was the great-great-great grandfather of Owain Glyndŵr. Madoc and his son Gruffydd were both buried within the walls of this noble Cistercian abbey. Owain Glyndŵr's bard, Iolo Goch, was also laid to rest here, but his tombstone was unfortunately destroyed at the Dissolution.

Many years ago the complete tombstone was discovered somewhere within these ruins, but, unfortunately, it disappeared. However, the Latin inscription was written down and translated as follows:-

> Madoc a penitent erected this monastery to the honour of the blessed and holy virgin and appropriated for this work and for the better maintenance there of an hundred monks which he freely settled on them.

The fourth stone was once believed to commemorate Myfanwy Fychan – the beautiful Princess of Dinas Brân, who was descended from the House of Tudor Trefor. However, it is more likely to be that of the wife of a certain Adam ap Trefor who was interred here beside her.

The fifth stone has decayed badly, but it bears the names Owinus and Madoci, suggesting that it may be the memorial stone of Owain ap Madoc ap Maredydd – otherwise called Owain Brogyntyn, who was living in 1213. Stone number six commemorates Gweirca, daughter of this Owain, and it is inscribed 'May God have mercy on her soul AD 1290.'

The twelfth stone was found in front of the high altar in the church. It is said to be the finest surviving example of its period in North Wales. The inscription reads: 'Here lies Madog son of Gruffydd, called Fychan.' He died in 1306 and was the great-grandson of the founder and a cousin of Gweirca mentioned above. Of particular interest to me was the fact that he was the great-grandfather of Owain Glyndŵr.

Somewhere within the walls of this abbey, Owain Glyndŵr's bard Iolo Goch lies buried, but unfortunately his tombstone was destroyed at the Dissolution. Iolo lived to a ripe old age even describing himself as decrepit when writing about the 1402 comet, nevertheless he outlived Owain Glyndŵr by a few years.

Valle Crucis was the first monastery in Wales to be suppressed by King Henry VIII in 1535 and its revenues at that time were estimated at £188.8s per annum.

The surviving remains consist of the Church and the east range of the cloister buildings. In Llangollen parish church, the roof, richly carved with beasts, birds, flowers, trumpeters and angels, is said to have come from Valle Crucis Abbey.

Initially, Valle Crucis was built as a Benedictine Abbey, until the Cistercians came and built the church. It has been suggested that it took the name Valle Crucis (Valley of the Cross) because the abbey once possessed a piece of the true cross which was given to Edward I, and he in turn granted several immunities to the abbey.

However, there are many places, including Canterbury Cathedral, which are supposed to have obtained pieces of the 'true' cross, which was said to have been discovered in the Holy Land in 327. It would seem that during the Reformation there were in existence sufficient claimed pieces of the 'true' cross to build a galleon!

A more likely explanation for the name of the abbey is the fact that nearby stands an ancient sepulchral cross known as the Pillar of Eliseg. It stands on a tumulus and was erected by Cyngen ab Cadell , last of the Kings of Powys, in memory of his great grandfather Eliseg, Lord of Dinas Brân, who fell at the battle of Chester in 613, when the Angles, under Aethelfrith, defeated the Britons. On the death of Cyngen, the kingdom of Powys passed to the kings of Gwynedd.

 The pillar, which stands about 2 metres high, is about five hundred years older than the abbey to which it gave its name. The cross, which once surmounted the pillar was destroyed during the Civil War. When the mound was dug in 1779 to re-erect the pillar, a skeleton was found which was assumed to be that of Eliseg.

The Pillar of Eliseg can be seen near Valle Crucis Abbey. It was erected by Cyngen ab Cadell Deyrnllwg, last of the kings of Powys, in memory of his great grandfather, Eliseg, Lord of Dinas Brân, who fell at the battle of Chester in 613.

The valley became known as the Valley of the Cross – 'Valle Crucis' – and the field where the ancient cross stands used to be called Llwyn y Groes, 'The Grove of the Cross'. Long before the Cistercian Abbey was founded, the first church here was called Llan Egwestli after its founder Egwest who lived here at the end of the 5th century.

It is possible that the pillar was originally a Roman column which Cyngen re-used as a memorial stone. There is a long Latin inscription inscribed on this pillar but it has weathered so badly that it is now impossible to read. Fortunately, it was written down in 1696 by the antiquary Edward Llwyd and it shows that Eliseg traced his ancestry to both Vortigern and Magnus Maximus. The inscription is in 31 horizontal lines (only 7 can be seen now), divided into paragraphs, each introduced by a cross. Translated into English it reads as follows:-

+ Concenn son of Cadell, Cadell son of Brochmail's son
  of Eliseg, Eliseg son of Guaillauc

+ And so Concenn, great grandson of Eliseg, erected this stone
  for his great-grandfather Eliseg

+ This is that Eliseg, who joined together the inheritance of Powys...
  out of the power of the Angles with his sword of fire

+ whosoever repeats this writing, let him give a blessing on the soul of
  Eliseg

+ This is that Concenn who captured with his hand eleven hundred acres
  which used to belong to his kingdom of Powys

(The next two paragraphs were illegible)

Maximus of Britain

Concenn, Pascent... Maun, Annan

+ Britu, morever (was) the son of Guorthigirn (Vortigern)
  Who Germanus blessed and whom
  Sevira bore to him, daughter of Maximus the king, who
  killed the king of the Romans

+ Conmarch painted this writing at the request of King Concenn

+ The blessing of the Lord upon Concenn and upon his entire
  household and upon all the region of Powys until the day of doom.
  Amen.

Before leaving the Llangollen area I drove up the Eglwyseg valley towards the aptly named craggy heights of World's End. My destination was a Tudor black and white half-timbered house known as Plas Eglwyseg or Plas Cadwgan. It was once the hunting lodge of Owain ap Cadwgan ap Bleddyn, who is best remembered for his abduction of Nest, the beautiful wife of Gerald – the keeper of Pembroke Castle. Previously she had been the mistress of Henry I. Owain brought the lovely Nest to his hunting lodge and no doubt believed that they would be hidden from pursuers, here at the 'end of the world.' But when King Henry located him and sent soldiers to this lonely place, Owain ap Cadwgan was forced to flee to Ireland.

An inscription over the doorway records that this ancient manor house was inherited by the Princes of Powys from Bleddyn ap Cynfyn, King of North Wales, who was killed in 1073. He was the most important of Owain Glyndŵr's noble ancestors.

The lonely manor house of Plas Eglwyseg situated in the hills above Llangollen was once a possession of Bleddyn ap Cynfyn, King of North Wales and one of Owain Glyndŵr's noble ancestors

Sign outside the village hall in Glyndyfrdwy

Three
Glyndyfrdwy to Corwen

The celebrated Welsh Chieftain, generally known as Owain Glyndwr, was surnamed after this valley, the whole of which belonged to him, and in which he had two or three places of strength...

George Borrow

The A5 led me on into Glyndyfrdwy, a small village in the Dee Valley from which Owain Glyndŵr (Glyndyfrdwy) took his name. Through this narrow valley the limpid waters of the Afon Dyfrdwy, better known as the Dee, flow between densely wooded banks and above this scattered community rises the heather-clad slopes of the Berwyn Mountains.

Dyrdwy means 'sacred river' and it flows from Llyn Tegid (Bala Lake) through the ancient commote of Glyndyfrdwy which stretches along both banks of the Dee from just above Berwyn to Corwen. Through this valley the Dee flows down a deep wooded ravine from Dyffryn Edeyrnion to the plain of Maelor. It is significant that in mountain country such as this, history evolves along the course of the rivers.

From Nant-y-Pandy to Moel Ferna is a farm lane which after two miles becomes a quarry track and then a miners' path. For centuries it has been known as Owain Glyndŵr's Way (a name given to it long before the official Owain Glyndŵr's Way) and it is said to be traceable from Sycharth in the Severn Valley to Glyndŵr's second home at Glyndyfrdwy in the Dee Valley.

Driving along the A5 towards Corwen, I saw ahead of me a high and circular mound crowned by fir trees, marking the site of Owain's second home. This was an outpost of his territory and to the north lay the estates of Reginald de Grey, the notorious Lord of Ruthin. Before leaving the car to explore this site, I dipped once again into *Wild Wales* and read George Borrow's description of Glendower's Mount.

> The mount of Owen Glendower stands close upon the southern bank of the Dee, and it is crowned with trees of various kinds. It is about thirty feet high from the plain, and about the same diameter at the top. A deep black pool of the river which here runs far beneath the surface of the field, purls and twists under the northern side, which is very steep, though several large oaks spring out of it. The hill is evidently the work of art, and appeared to be of some burial place of old.

'Owain Glyndŵr's Mount' at Glyndyfrdwy in the Dee Valley, is where his uprising began on 16 September, 1400, when his relations and followers met to swear their allegiance to him and make plans to march on Ruthin

Most people find *Wild Wales*, a tedious read, but when you just consult the book to read George Borrow's comments on particular locations it becomes quite fascinating. Not only was he a friendly talker who sought every opportunity to practice his self-taught Welsh, but he was also a powerful walker. His normal speed was six miles an hour and he could quite easily put a spurt on if he was late or in need of a drink of cwrw – good Welsh ale.

On this memorable ramble through Wales he walked about two hundred miles on a pair of boots which were re-soled during the journey. Apart from crossing Plynlimmon, most of his route followed roads, so in today's terms it could hardly be called wild. However, Wales in those times was undoubtedly a wild place where few natives spoke English and a solitary walking tour from pub to pub was something very new.

Glyndŵr's hall of residence (Llys Glyndyfrdwy) must have been situated below the mound on the level field. It would have been set in the 'fine park' mentioned by Prince Henry in a letter to his father, written after he came here to destroy the home of Glyndŵr (see page 95). At one time traces of the foundations were visible under the turf. It was his main property and the estate stretched from Corwen to Llangollen. An old farm beyond here, named Pen-y-bont, is said to contain some of the stone of Glyndŵr's farm buildings and an adjoining field is known as the 'Field of Council'.

Sitting on top of the mound, which is probably of prehistoric origin, I surveyed the scene and considered how a watch tower sited here would have provided a fine vantage point, commanding this valley. It would have been an excellent defensive position with Castell Dinas Brân six miles away as the crow flies, which is perhaps an appropriate statement. The summit of the mound has a diameter of 13 metres and it may have been used as a signal station in ancient times. I tried to picture the occasion when a large number of men gathered here on 16 September 1400 to swear their allegiance to Owain and hear his plans of war.

Those present included Owain Glyndŵr, Tudur (his brother), Gruffydd (his eldest son), Robert Puleston (his sister's husband), Gruffydd and Phillip Hanmer (his wife's brothers), Hywel ap Madoc Kyffin (Dean of St. Asaph), Ieuan Fychan of Moeliwrch, Gruffydd ab Ieuan of Lloran Uchaf, Madog ab Ieuan ap Madog of Eyton, John Astwick and Crach Ffinnant (their seer or 'prophet').

The object of the meeting was to discuss plans for an uprising and to proclaim Owain Prince of Wales – a title already bestowed upon young Prince Henry (of Monmouth), at an investiture held in Westminster Palace the previous year. Little did those present at this gathering realise that it was to be the beginning of a struggle which would be furiously fought for seven years and then simmer for another eight years. It would last through the entire reign of Henry IV and cause him so much strain and anguish that it probably shortened his life.

Below the mound, I scratched around in the loose soil, optimistically hoping for a lucky find, a Glyndŵr souvenir. The field surrounding the mound is known as Parliament Field, probably in memory of the meeting that was once held here prior to the uprising. The mound itself is variously known as Y Pigyn, Pen-y-Pigyn and Owain Glyndŵr's Mound. It was originally one of a series of prehistoric burial mounds spread along the Dee Valley, but in this instance it was developed into a defensive position. Glyndŵr's house here was not as large as his home at Sycharth, but it was in an important location, a veritable mountain eyrie, set in the heart of the hills, providing a rallying place in times of war.

Back on the A5 once more, a sign pointing to Carrog reminded me that there was once a building of interest across the river at Llansantffraed. It was a fourteenth-century stone cottage known as 'Cachardy Owain' (Owain's Prison). Unfortunately, it was demolished many years ago by the local council and some houses built in its place. It is very sad when historic buildings are unnecessarily destroyed in the name of progress or slum clearance and such actions are generally much regretted in later years.

Owain Glyndŵr's prison house (Cachardy Owain) was not far from his home in the parish of Llansantfraed Gyndwrdwy. It consisted of a room thirteen feet square and 10ft 6in high.

In 1893, large pieces of oak timber mortised with wooden pegs, evidently sections of a roof, were discovered in the River Dee near Carrog Bridge. The timbers were too large to pass through the arches of the bridge and it was believed from their shape and length that these beams were fragments of the roof of an ancient church, which traditionally existed about 500 yards higher up the river, on a site just above Glyndŵr's Prison.

Corwen was my next stop. It is one of those places which most people briefly take in with no more than a glance as they pass through on their way to the mountains of Snowdonia. However, travellers who are more familiar with Corwen will know it as a grey but pleasant market town nestling below the north side of the Berwyn Mountains. There is much more to the place than most people realise and historically it is really quite fascinating, with several curiosities to visit. In the centre of Corwen, a metal statue to Owain Glyndŵr has been erected on a paved area near some parking bays at the junction of the A5 and Green Lane. To my mind it is a very unsatisfactory representation of Owain Glyndŵr and a poor return for its cost of £7,000. I understand there are plans for it to be replaced.

George Borrow stopped in Corwen at "about two o'clock, and feeling rather thirsty I went to an inn very appropriately called the Owen Glendower, being the principal inn in the principal town of what was once the domain of the great Owain". He spent an hour inside quenching his thirst so I decided that I would do the same and have lunch as well.

The Owain Glyndŵr Hotel, Corwen, is built on the site of an ancient monastery and parts of the present building are said to date from 1329.

I paused at the entrance to the Owain Glyndŵr Hotel in order to read a plate near the front door:

Owain Glyndŵr Hotel
Formerly the New Inn
* Corwen *
The first Eisteddfod to which the
public were admitted was held
in this Hotel on 12th May 1789.

It is interesting that the 1789 Corwen Eisteddfod became the forerunner of the Welsh National Eisteddfod which is now held in a different area every year. It was the first one to which the public were admitted, for previously only the competitors and judges were allowed to attend. A monastery used to stand on this site and parts of the present building are said to date back to at least 1329.

Inside, I chose the public bar hoping to find some atmosphere and perhaps a few interesting local characters. As I ordered my beer I asked the barman if he knew any stories about Owain Glyndŵr. "I'm not from round here," he replied in an English accent, and turned his back on me to fill a whisky glass.

So I turned to three men who were propping up the bar and looked like possible locals. They had certainly heard of my friend Owain and one of them told me the story of how when Owain Glyndŵr once threw his dagger from the top of Pen y Pegwyn, it struck a stone in the churchyard, leaving its mark, which can still be seen to this day. The other two men nodded their heads in agreement. The bearded one obviously wanted to impress me with his knowledge of the matter and spoke with an air of authority. "He fought most of his battles against the Romans on the Dinas opposite." I nodded my head, not wishing to put him down in front of his friends. I refrained from informing him that the Romans had left this island nearly a thousand years before Glyndŵr ever came to Corwen.

Leaving the hotel, I next visited Corwen Church which was originally established in the sixth century by St Mael and St. Sulien, who were two Celtic missionaries from Brittany. The present church was built in the early seventeenth century, for the previous one on this site, where Owain Glyndŵr himself had probably worshipped, was swept away by the Dee in flood.

It has been suggested that Owain is buried near the priest's door but Corwen is just one of many places that make such a claim. The stone, forming a lintel above the porch is reputed to bear the mark of Owain's dagger (measuring twenty-two inches), which as the man in the hotel had told me, Owain hurled in a fit of temper from Pen y Pegwn, a conical hill behind the church.

Corwen Church is one of many places where Owain Glyndŵr is said to be buried

Pen y Pegwyn is a crag that looms above Corwen Church. Crowned with fir trees and a cairn, out of which rises a flagstaff, it is a spur of the Berwyn mountains. Local people refer to the summit of the crag as Glyndŵr's Seat.

This stone which forms a lintel over a doorway at Corwen Church is said to bear the mark of Owain Glyndŵr's dagger.

Turning up beside the Midland Bank, I passed through a metal gate and followed a narrow path leading up through the woods. The route was rocky in places and tumbling streams flowed noisily down to join the Dee in the valley below. At last I reached the summit of the crag where a flagpole rises out of a conical stone cairn, bearing a plaque which commemorates the marriage of the *Prince of Wales with the Princess Alexandra of Denmark* on March 16, 1863.

The view from this point, which is known as *Glyndŵr's Seat*, is certainly impressive and I looked towards the hill fort of Caer Derwyn, then up the valley to Carrog and, immediately below me, it was but a 'dagger throw' to the Church. Corwen nestled snugly in the valley below while the Dee, pursuing its serpentine course, glinted in the sunlight. The white limestone of the Eglwyseg Rocks above Llangollen also shone brightly in the afternoon sun.

Whilst I was taking photographs, an elderly gentleman accompanied by a little white dog arrived. I greeted him with a friendly "Hello", which he appeared to ignore. Then, partly to be polite and make conversation, but also perhaps to air my knowledge, I stated in the form of a question, "This is the spot from which Owain Glyndŵr is supposed to have thrown his dagger, isn't it?"

He looked at me with obvious disinterest. "Is it? I don't know anything about that."

"Are you a local?" I asked.

"Yes," he said. "I've lived in Corwen all my life."

He then turned on his heel and, with the little dog close behind him,walked up the slope behind the cairn to disappear into the trees. I was left feeling disappointed that the people of Corwen I had met during my brief visit, knew so little about their local hero, and apparently did not wish to improve their knowledge either.

Caer Derwyn Fort, on the other side of the valley, is an immense Iron Age fortress with a rampart of stones encircling the crest of Mynydd y Gaer. Unfortunately, over the years thousands of the stones have been carried away for the construction of farm buildings and mountain enclosures.

The impressive remains of a rampart, five to seven metres across and about 800 metres in circumference, however, can still be seen. The wall was well faced on both sides and in some respects it is similar to Carn Goch in Carmarthenshire. Measuring roughly 248 metres from its western side to its north eastern gateway and 195 metres across the widest part (north to south), it is as wide as Garn Coch but longer by 418 metres.

Caer Derwyn Fort on the summit of Mynydd y Gaer

Caer Derwyn was the old fortress of Edeyrn Edeyrnion who made use of it in the 6th century and it was next used by Owain Gwynedd in 1165 while Henry II lay encamped in the Berwyn hills on the other side of the valley.

According to Pennant, Owain Glyndŵr also 'made use of this fortress, in his occasional retreats'. It is more likely, however, to have been Owain Gwynedd who made it his headquarters. He was King of North Wales when Henry II was attempting, with all the vigour of his fierce and tenacious nature, to conquer Wales. Against his powerful army, Owain Gwynedd gathered his force at Corwen and for once the various Welsh princes banded together in a common cause. With Owain was his brother Cadwaladr, Owain Cyfeilog, the Prince of Powys, and Lord Rhys ap Gruffydd, who was then the most powerful ruler in southern Wales.

Between Glyndyfrdwy and Ruthin and near the villages of Nantclwyd and Gwyddelwern used to be a strip of moorland known as Croesau. It had always been part of the Glyndyfrdwy lands, although the Lords of Ruthin made claim to it. The dispute went to law during the reign of Richard II and a decision was given in favour of Glyndŵr. His peasant tenants lived on this land in humble contentment until Lord Grey of Ruthin suddenly descended upon them to drive them away from their holdings and claim the common as his own.

Owain demanded the return of his land and laid his case before Parliament which Henry summoned in the spring of 1400, six months after he had seized the throne. But Owain's suit was not even accorded the courtesy of a hearing and was dismissed with contempt. Henry was a close friend of Reginald de Grey and supported him, by stating that Glyndŵr had no right to the land. He not only confirmed Lord Grey's title to the property he had seized, but also ordered Glyndŵr to grant him further concessions. The Bishop of St Asaph, John Trefor, tried to mediate between Glyndŵr and Lord Grey but failed.

An account of Glyndŵr's appeal to Parliament is given in a monastic chronicle known as *The Eulogium*.

Owen de Glendour, a Welshman who had been esquire of the Earl of Arundel, came to Parliament complaining that Lord de Grey Ruthin had usurped certain lands of his in Wales, but no argument helped against Lord de Grey. The Bishop of St Asaph gave counsel in Parliament that they should not entirely despise Owen, as the Welsh might revolt. But those in Parliament said they cared nothing for the bare-footed clowns.

This painting of Owain Glyndŵr riding into battle was painted by Arthur Michael of London, who exhibited eleven works at the Royal Academy between 1905 and 1909. The painting appeared in a Welsh gift book entitled *Land of my Fathers*, published to support the 1915 national fund for Welsh troops. Unfortunately the original painting has disappeared.

𝔉our
𝕿he 𝕌prising

They saw in the valiant figure of Owain of Glyndyfrdwy the fulfilment of the ancient prophecies that a Welsh prince should once again wear the crown of Britain.

A.G. Bradley

Formerly known as Rhudd-din, Ruthin is situated on the banks of the River Clywedog near the centre of the Vale of Clwyd. The name is pronounced 'Rithin' and it lies in the heart of territory once owned by Owain Glyndŵr's unfriendly neighbour, Reginald de Grey. He was probably the most fierce and unscrupulous landowner in Wales since William de Braose, the twelfth century Lord of Abergavenny.

Founded by Edward I, Ruthin Castle was completed by Reginald de Grey, the first Lord de Grey, who also raised the town walls in about 1284. The King had granted him the Cantref of Dyffryn Clwyd, which from that time onwards was known as the Lordship of Ruthin.

A descendant of the first Lord Grey, also named Reginald, became Lord of Ruthin in 1388. It was a hereditary title with estates granted at the time of Edward I and he was undoubtedly a very important landowner. Not only did he hold the Lordship of Ruthin, but he also possessed considerable land on the borders of Wales and in the east of England. He was a member of the English Parliament, and for a time had been Governor of Ireland. Being a close friend of Henry Bolingbroke, he attended his coronation feast and became a member of the Council which gave the king advice.

Henry IV at this time was preparing to make an attack on Scotland and in Reginald de Grey's capacity as Chief Marcher of North Wales it was his personal duty to summon the nobility and gentry in his district to serve with the royal forces. Realising that here was an opportunity to put Owain Glyndŵr out of favour with the king, Lord Grey deliberately delayed summoning the Welshman until it was much too late for him to appear in person or to send an explanation for his non-attendance. Everything went as De Grey had planned, with the result that Henry IV declared Owain Glyndŵr a traitor. The king well remembered how Owain had faithfully served his old enemy Richard, so he sent orders to Lord Grey to deal with him.

Parliament had debated the matter and John Trefor, Bishop of St Asaph, not only exonerated Owain Glyndŵr from blame, but warmly remonstrated against the policy of provoking a man of his character and influence with the Welsh people. The majority of the English nobles answered the eloquent prelate with the contemptuous assertion that they were not afraid of these 'barefooted scrubs' and Reginald de Grey was consequently authorised to seize Owain's whole estate under the pretext of forfeiture for high treason.

A Valle Crucis Chronicle (in the Mostyn Manuscript No. 131) records that at Henry IV's command, Lord Grey sent an invitation to Owain inviting him to dine with him and talk matters over with a view to reconciliation. Owain consented to meet him on the condition that De Grey came with no more than thirty unarmed followers. Lord Grey accepted his terms, but ordered a large force to approach and surround the house while he was inside. Fortunately, Owain had positioned his bard Iolo Goch to look out for treachery. The bard saw the approach of De Grey's men and, entering the dining hall, struck his harp and sang in Welsh a verse which Lord Grey could not comprehend, alerting Owain that a large number of soldiers were waiting outside. Owain understood the bard's warning and quickly made his escape. Revolt was now the only course open to him.

Owain and his small force marched from Glyndyfrdwy across the hills to the north and then concealed themselves in Coed-Marchon, a wood behind Ruthin Castle to wait for dawn to break. It was the eve of St Matthews Fair Day (21 September) in 1400, and when the gates were opened early that morning the band of two hundred and fifty men entered the walled town disguised as peasants. They were led by Owain and his brother Tudur and came mainly from Ederynion, Glyndyfrdwy and Penllyn.

Ruthin was full of goats, cattle, sheep, and thronged with people. Suddenly, Owain's men went berserk, looting and setting fire to the town, but not surprisingly, they failed to storm the strongly fortified castle where Lord Ruthin, who was absent at this time, normally resided. Damage in the town, however, was later estimated at £12,000, which was then a large sum of money. When they departed, only three buildings were untouched. These were No.2 Well Street, Nantclwyd House and Ruthin Castle. Fourteen of Owain's band were taken prisoner by Lord Grey's soldiers and no doubt put to death.

Today there is little to be seen of the original castle for it has largely been re-constructed and is now an elegant hotel, standing in thirty acres of parkland and offering medieval style banquets. In De Grey's time it comprised an inner and outer ballium and was defended by moats and earthworks. A deep fosse separated the inner ward from the outer ballium and in the western wall was a strong doorway protected by a portcullis. The inner ballium or court, was constructed in the form of a pentagon and four of its angles were defended by massive round towers. The entrance at the fifth angle was guarded by two towers.

The Market Place in old Ruthin

Ruthin Castle was once the home of Reginald de Grey the Lord of Ruthin, who became Owain Glyndŵr's enemy. Now largely reconstructed it is an elegant hotel where medieval banquets are held.

De Greys were at Ruthin Castle for more than two hundred years, from 1282 to 1508, when the last to hold the title, Lord of Ruthin, was Richard de Grey, 3rd Earl of Kent. He sold the lordship to Henry VII when the family became impoverished. They were no doubt still suffering from the massive ransom paid to Owain Glyndŵr for the release of Reginald de Grey in 1402.

From Ruthin, Glyndŵr's band marched on to sack Denbigh and during the next three days they attacked Rhuddlan, Flint and Hawarden, but failed to take the castles. Reaching Welshpool, which was then the most important town in Wales, they met stiff resistance led by Hugh Burnell, a Shropshire landowner and professional soldier. All the men of Staffordshire and Worcestershire had heard that the Welsh were raiding England from their mountain land and they joined up to form a great army. The two forces met on the banks of the Vyrnwy, just north of Welshpool, on Friday September 24, and Glyndŵr's small army was scattered. They fled into the woods and mountains for safety and the rebellion which had lasted for just one week, appeared to be over.

King Henry was in the north of England when he heard about Glyndŵr's uprising and he lost no time in heading south to gather together an impressive force. By September he was passing through Shrewsbury and then riding towards Wales at the head of a large army. His apparently formidable progress, however, was actually nothing more than an idle and futile procession through the valleys, for not a single Welsh soldier was encountered.

The only incident of note was when Henry had to fight a brief battle against a group of men led by Owain's cousins William and Rhys Tudur at Rhos Fawr near Beaumaris, and the king had to take refuge for a while inside the castle. For the sake of appearances, Henry then sacked the Franciscan monastery at Llanfaes, (just north of Beaumaris in Anglesey) which had been built by Llywelyn the Great over the tomb of his wife Joan.

As King Henry marched back via Caernarfon and Mawddwy to Shrewsbury, the weather broke. Thunder shook the valleys, the skies opened their windows to swell normally placid rivers into raging torrents that surged over the banks and washed away tracks and roads. Baggage was lost; horses floundered into marshes and were swallowed up. Wind, rain and snow harried the miserable column for every mile of its progress. Provisions ran short. Hunger, cold and sickness devastated the ranks, while all the time the Welsh army sheltered in the mountains and consolidated their strength.

There were many who firmly believed that Glyndŵr possessed magical powers which he used to control the elements to aid him in his campaign. It was claimed that he was a sorcerer who was in league with the powers of the air and could himself ride upon the wings of the wind.

Rhuddlan Castle was attacked by Owain Glyndŵr in 1400

Glyndŵr also tried to take Flint Castle in 1400

On reaching Shrewsbury, Henry declared Owain Glyndŵr an outlaw and sent letters to his sheriffs:

> ...the king is informed that Owen Glendourdy and other rebels of Wales in no small number have risen in insurrection against his majesty, inflicting great grievances and destruction upon his faithful subjects there, who took no heed to consent to their malicious designs, and ceasing not daily to do so, in so much that great part of the men of those parts have submitted to the said rebels, and the residue of the men of Wales and the marches are like to submit if the king resist not their malice.

No doubt wishing to make an example of a Welshman of noble blood, Henry then ordered the execution of Gronw ap Tudur, a magnate of some standing who was accused of sympathising with Owain Glyndŵr. The body of the unfortunate man was then drawn and quartered and the pieces put on public display at Chester, Hereford, Ludlow and Bristol. He was the ancestor of the Tudors of Ynys Mon (Anglesey) and ultimately the Tudor monarchs of England.

His first attempt to subdue Owain Glyndŵr having failed, Henry IV then returned to London where he found that he had other enemies. Treason dogged his steps into his very bed chamber and he came near to losing his life on a sharp instrument with three long points which was concealed in his bed. Fortunately for Henry, he discovered the device just in time.

Henry ordered the estates of Owain Glyndŵr and the Hanmers to be confiscated. He gave Owain's lands to John Beaufort, his half-brother and the eldest son of John of Gaunt and Katherine Swynford. But it would be many years before Beaufort would be able to occupy his new estates. In 1443 John Beaufort succeeded to the earldom of Somerset and was afterwards created Duke of Somerset.

Owain Glyndŵr had apparently disappeared into thin air and it was not surprising that King Henry had failed to make contact with him, for following the failure of his initial rising, Owain had headed south to the seclusion of Pen Pumlumon Fawr (Plynlimon). Here he established a new base that was well concealed in the mountains and suitably placed for mounting expeditions into both North and South Wales. His camp was situated on the western slopes of Pumlumon where entrenchments, spear heads and assorted weapons have been found there over the years. Unfortunately, further exploration of the location is no longer possible for it now lies beneath the Nant-y-Moch Reservoir.

It was here, beneath Pumlumon, in the Hyddgen Valley, that the first real battle of the war was fought. Owain's opponents consisted of a large force of English soldiers accompanied by Flemish mercenaries from south

Pembrokeshire. They were descendants of the immigrants whom Henry I had settled in Wales in 1108, to boost the woollen trade, to help subjugate the Welsh of that area and to help establish a bridgehead for his conquest of Ireland. These people had been driven from their own country by an innundation of the sea. It was hoped by Henry I that they would assist in quelling the turbulent Welsh and pacify the country. But for a long time they were compelled to defend their lives and their homes with the sword. For centuries the Flemings lived among the Welsh a race apart, differing from the natives in costume, in habits, in customs and in language.

Now accompanied by men from south Ceredigion they marched on the Hyddgen Valley, where Owain had established a base to the north of Pumlumon. At this time he had only 500 men and this opposing force was 1,500 strong. Obviously the Flemings expected to intimidate Owain's band by their superiority of numbers. However, despite the overwhelming odds, Owain's men won the day after a fierce fight. Two hundred of his followers perished in the battle, but the remainder managed to put the Flemings to flight after killing a large number of them. It was a short but decisive battle which enhanced Owain's reputation and boosted the morale of his followers.

The only reference to this battle is found in *The Annals of Owen Glyn Dŵr,* written by Gruffydd Hiraethog between 1556-1564 and based on an early fifteenth century source:

> The following summer Owen arose with 120 reckless men and robbers and he brought them in warlike fashion to the uplands of Ceredigion and 1,500 men of the lowlands of Ceredigion and Rhos and Penfro assembled there and came to the mountain with the intent to seize Owen. The encounter was on Hyddgant Mountain and no sooner did the English troops turn their backs in flight than 200 of them were slain. Owen now won great fame, and a great number of youths and fighting men from every part of Wales rose and joined him, until he had a great host at his back.

The battle probably took place in the middle of the valley on a level area called Esgair Ffordd (Ridgeway). A cairn on Esgair y Ffordd adjoining Hyddgen may have been erected by Glyndŵr to commemorate this battle and similarly it is feasible that Carn Owen on Cerrig yr Hafen may have been erected after the battle. There is a local tradition that the hoofprints of Owain's horse Llwyd-y-Basie can be seen on top of nearby Craig y March.

Not far from the mountain road to Nant y Moch Reservoir on the west bank of the Hyddgen can be seen two large lumps of white quartz, known as Cerrig Cyfamod Owain Glyndŵr (Owain Glyndŵr's Covenant Stones). Aligned north and south, they mark the site of the battle. The tradition is that on this spot Owain 'held parly and made his covenant.'

This plaque commemorating the battle of Hyddgen has been installed in a cairn at the eastern end of the Nant-y-moch dam. It was unveiled on 16th July, 1976 by Gwynfor Evans and reads:

'This cairn was built to commemorate Owain Glyndŵr, who raised his standard on the River Hyddgen in May 1401. The ensuing battle resulted in a victory for the Welsh against the crown forces of Henry IV.'

Two large lumps of white quartz known as Cerrig Cyfamod Owain Glyndŵr (Owain Glyndŵr's Covenant Stones) are said to mark the spot where Owain held parley and made covenant with the Flemish force. Only one block of stone is now visible, but it is believed that they were placed here to mark this historic event.

Some years ago the blade of a two-edged British spear was found near the summit of Pumlumon and it is supposed to have been dropped by one of Glyndŵr's men. Today, the battle of Hyddgen is commemorated by a plaque fastened to a stone cairn on the eastern end of the Nant y Moch dam. The slaughtered were buried at several sites in this area including Bryn y Beddau (Hill of Graves) near Nant y Moch and Mynydd Bychan, which is above an impressive waterfall.

This was an important victory for Owain which enhanced his reputation and did much to boost the morale of his followers. News of his success quickly spread through Wales and many men came to join him. Since the days of Llywelyn the Great, the people of Wales had waited for a strong leader to emerge and an ancient prophecy had even foretold that the name of such a man would be Owain. The Welsh were eager to grasp an opportunity to shake off the English rule that they hated so much. Here at last they had an opportunity to make Wales free, with Owain as their sovereign. From all parts of the Principality, Welshmen rushed to join him and fight for this heir of Prince Llywelyn. Owain raised the old standard of Llywelyn – the ancient dragon of Wales upon a white background – and to his followers this was the symbol of the fulfilment of the bards' ancient prophesies that a Welsh prince would again wear the crown and wave the sceptre of Britain. The gold dragon standard was a deliberate reminder of the freedom that had been lost with the coming of the Saxons, for it was inspired by the standard of the old hero Uther Pendragon.

Owain's call to arms brought a massive and immediate response. Welsh students at Oxford sold their books and travelled north to join him. Welsh labourers working in Herefordshire and Shropshire left their employment and returned to Wales to assist in the struggle for independence.

Gwilym and Rhys ap Tudur, who were Owain's Anglesey cousins, decided to further the cause by capturing Conwy Castle, which was held by John de Mascey with a garrison of fifteen-men-at-arms and sixty archers. Choosing a Sunday, when the garrison was attending church in the town, the two brothers only had to deal with two soldiers who had been left to guard the castle. These two men were tricked into opening up the castle gate to a man pretending to be a carpenter.

On gaining entry, he then let in a band of men led by the Tudur brothers, while the remainder of their force set the town on fire and demolished the town bridge.

Hotspur, the Chief Justice of North Wales, was at Denbigh when he received news of the events that had taken place at Conwy and quite naturally he was most disturbed. He immediately led a small army of one hundred and twenty men and three hundred archers to Conwy, but was unable to regain the castle from the Tudur brothers.

Conwy Castle was started in 1283 by Edward I on the site of an earlier fortress as one of the chain that would help him subjugate the Welsh. It is an impressive fortress, oblong in shape and built on a steep rock, with two sides being defended by deep water, the remaining two facing the town and having the protection of a moat crossed by a drawbridge. The walls of considerable thickness are flanked by eight circular embattled towers, four of which are surmounted by slender watch towers. Two of the towers are known as the King's and Queen's, after Edward and his consort Eleanor. The town walls of Conwy form a triangle, each side being nearly three-quarters of a mile long.

The parish church of St Gredifael at Penmynydd, contains the effigy of Gronw Fychan and his wife Myfanwy. In 1232 Ednyfed Fychan,, the ancestor of Gron was a steward of Llywelyn Fawr, Prince of North Wales. Gronw's half-brother, Meredydd, was the great-grandfather of Henry VII. With his four brothers, Meredydd, Gwilym, Rhys and Ednyfed, Gronw lived at nearby Plas Penmynydd.

Gronw's nephew was Owen ap Meredydd, commonly called Owen Tudor, who became a Welsh squire and was to later marry Katherine de Valois, widow of Henry V. She had three sons by Owen, two of them, Edmund and Jasper, became Earls of Richmond and the third a monk. Edmund, Earl of Richmond, married Lady Margaret Beaufort, daughter of the Duke of Somerset, and a claimant to the throne. Their son Henry, was chosen by the Red Rose party as their candidate for the throne. At the second attempt he was successful, becoming Henry VII. He was the first of five Tudor sovereigns, a dynasty which had its beginnings in the village of Penmynydd.

The tomb of Gronw and Myfanwy was originally placed in the Franciscan monastery of Llanfaes, near Beaumaris. At the time of the dissolution of the monasteries it was removed to Penmynydd Church to escape destruction.

It is interesting that Owain Glyndŵr was a cousin of the Tudor family of Penmynydd from which Henry Tudor (Henry VII) was descended. The family line can be traced back through Rhodri Mawr, King of all Wales (d.878) and Cadwaldr (d.664).

On May 4, Hotspur wrote a letter to the Privy Council stating that all North Wales was quiet and submissive with the exception of Conwy Castle and the followers of the Tudur brothers, who were hiding in the mountains. He was no doubt very embarrassed about the situation. However, some weeks later, after a siege lasting three months, negotiations for the surrender of the castle were completed on 24 June (Midsummer Day). The Welsh garrison were required to pay a fine of 1000 marks, as an indemnity for themselves and their dependents. They were also required to hand over nine hostages, who were promptly executed to appease Henry IV. The garrison was then allowed to march out of the castle unmolested. Prince Henry, who was also present at this time, then returned to London and his governor, Sir Hugh Despenser, took over from Hotspur and entered the castle.

Subsequently, Hotspur, tired of the whole business, resigned his position and returned to Scotland. Henry IV later accused him of making a secret treaty with Owain Glyndŵr. The Earl of Rutland was made Lieutenant of North Wales, while Thomas Percy, Earl of Worcester, was entrusted with the less difficult task of looking after South Wales.

Near Dolgellau, a country mansion known as Nannau stands about 800 feet above sea level on the north side of the Wnion Valley. A much earlier house on this site was once the residence of Owain Glyndŵr's illustrious ancestor Cadwgan ap Bleddyn, Prince of Powys. In Glyndŵr's time the house was occupied by his cousin Hywel Sele, who, although of Welsh blood, was unfriendly to Owain's cause and refused to join the Dragon Standard.

As a supporter of Henry IV, Hywel Sele invited Hotspur to visit Dolgellau and he came in June of that year with a large force. Glyndŵr seized the opportunity to attack and a brief conflict took place below the heights of Cadair Idris, but without success on either side, although Owain himself narrowly escaped being captured.

When Hotspur departed from the area, Owain, now convinced that Hywel Sele was a dangerous adversary, besieged Nannau and took him prisoner. However, on the way back to Dolgellau he was ambushed by Gruffydd ap Gwyn, son-in-law of Sele, with two hundred men. It is said that a fierce fight took place on the bridge, but Owain cut his way through with his prisoner, leaving many wounded and nearly a hundred men dead.

The Abbot of Cymmer, who sympathised with Owain, tried to effect a reconciliation, and at length Hywel Sele was set free upon agreeing to separate himself from the House of Lancaster. Shortly after, Owain visited Nannau to discuss the situation. When their meeting was over, Hywel offered to entertain his guest with a deer hunt in the nearby forest.

The original house at Nannau was built by Cadwgan ap Bleddyn, Prince of Powys and the later building on this site takes its name from Hugh Nannau (d.1623) who is credited with its construction.

The two men strolled in the parkland around Nannau and suddenly a buck dashed out of the trees in front of them. Hywel immediately put an arrow to his bow and took aim, but suddenly wheeled around and fired it at Owain's chest.

Fortunately, Owain had come prepared for treachery and he was wearing a light and flexible vest of chain mail, fashioned by skilled hands, beneath his tunic. The arrow struck the finely tempered steel and fell harmlessly at his feet. Hywel Sele turned and fled, but Owain pursued and killed him with his dagger.

Owain lifted the dead Lord of Nannau and dropped his lifeless body into the hollow trunk of an ancient oak tree. He then set Nannau on fire and departed. Forty years later the oak was struck by lightning in a storm and it split open to reveal the skeleton of a man clutching a rusty sword.

In later years the tree became known as 'Ceubren yr Ellyll' or the Hobgoblin's Hollow Tree and it was still standing in 1813 when Sir Richard Colt Hoare visited the Vaughans at Nannau.

He made a drawing of the tree and recorded that it was 27 feet in circumference and was in the last stages of decay. That very night on 13 July, the tree, untouched by wind or lightning, finally collapsed from old age.

The 'Hobgoblin's Hollow Tree' (Derwen Ceubren yr Ellyll) at Nannau was drawn by Sir Richard Colt Hoare in 1813. There is a tradition that it once concealed the body of Hywel Sele after he was killed by Owain Glyndŵr.

During the summer of 1401, Owain ravaged Mid Wales. In particular he took revenge on the monks of Abbey Cwmhir who are said to have informed the English of his movements. The scanty remains of Abbey Cwmhir are situated on the banks of the River Clywedog and it is sad to think that this could have been the greatest abbey in Wales. If it had been completed, it would have boasted the largest nave in Wales. Measuring 224 feet long it was only surpassed by the English cathedrals of Winchester, York and Durham.

Abbey Cwmhir was founded on the banks of the Clywedog in 1143 by Cadwallon ap Madoc on behalf of the Cistercian monks of Whitland. The name translates as the abbey in the long valley or dingle. Llywelyn the Great began rebuilding the Abbey Church in about 1228 and its fourteen bay nave must have been very impressive, being 242ft (74.5m) long by 72ft (22.4m) wide and at least 60ft (18.5m) high. Work ceased in 1231 as a result of the war between Henry II and Prince Llywelyn ap Iorwerth. Although never completed this was once the largest abbey in Wales, with a nave even longer than those of Canterbury and Salisbury Cathedrals and twice as long as the one at St David's.

Originally the Abbey was endowed for sixty monks of the Cistercian order, but when the establishment was broken up by Henry VIII, it contained no more than three and had an annual revenue of just £24 19s 4d. After the dissolution the property passed to the Fowler family and it remained with them until the direct line died out in 1771, and it was finally destroyed by Roundheads during the English Civil War.

This slate memorial, near the site of the altar in the great nave, marks the supposed burial place of Llywelyn ap Gruffydd, the last native Prince of Wales. There is a tradition that after he was murdered at Cilmeri, near Builth Wells, on Friday 11 December 1182, he was refused a Christian burial by the Archbishop of Canterbury, so his faithful followers carried the headless body over the hills to this remote abbey and buried it here. The burial was obviously a well kept secret and no gravestone has evere been found.

Owain's paternal grandmother was a L'Estrange of Knockin in Shropshire, granddaughter of the Baron L'Estrange whose troops killed Llywelyn ap Gruffydd at Cilmeri. It is a strange irony of fate that Owain's great grand-grandsire should have slain the last true Prince of Wales.

First founded by Cadwallon ap Madoc in 1143 on behalf of the Cistercian monks of Whitland, Abbey Cwmhir was only intended for sixty monks which is a surprisingly small number considering its size. Cadwallon was succeed by his son Maelgan who died in 1198, and his son died in 1234, having been killed, along with his brothers, by the Mortimers. By the middle of the 13th century the Abbey was under the patronage of the Mortimer family. This is of particular significance, for when Owain Glyndŵr partially burned the abbey in 1401, his anger was directed against the Mortimers.

Most of the monks residing there were English and Owain had decided that they were Henry IV's informers. One would really have expected Glyndŵr to have had more respect for this abbey, considering that his ancestor Llywelyn ap Gruffydd, Prince of Wales, lies buried within its walls. The tradition is that after Prince Llywelyn was murdered at Cilmery, near Builth Wells, he was refused Christian burial by the Archbishop of Canterbury, so his faithful followers carried the headless body over the hills to this remote abbey, and in the darkness, buried it here. No doubt his burial was a well kept secret and no gravestone has ever been found, but it is generally believed that Llywelyn's bones lie near the site of the altar in the great nave. Abbey Cwmhir never really recovered from Owain Glyndŵr's raid and when it was dissolved in 1536, only three monks were found to be in residence.

Owain took several castles in Mid Wales, including New Radnor, where sixty of the defenders were beheaded and their bodies hung from the ramparts to discourage the remaining garrison. The *Illustrated London News* in 1845 describes how, when the old church at New Radnor was demolished and a new one built, 'proofs of the sad story of the garrison were found in a mass of human bones in one spot; in another, of a corresponding collection of skulls only.'

New Radnor Castle, originally called Trefaesfed was founded by Harold Godwin. It was rebuilt by Philip de Breos at the end of the eleventh century as a fortress of considerable strength. When the Mortimers became a great power in the Marches it came into their possession. The mound on which the keep once stood still dominates the village, but since the castle's destruction by Owain Glyndŵr in 1401 all the stonework has been removed. Owain Gylyndŵr stormed the castle in 1401 and beheaded and hanged the bodies of sixty of the defenders from the curtain walls to discourage the remaining garrison. By 1405 Henry IV had re-possessed the castle and garrisoned it with 30 men-at-arms and 150 archers under the command of Richard, Lord Grey.

Montgomery was then attacked, but the well defended castle held out against Glyndŵr's force. This Norman fortress was at that time as important as its neighbours of Chirk and Powys. It owes its origin to Baldwin, who was William the Conqueror's Lieutenant of the Marches, and it was accordingly known by the Welsh as Tre Faldwyn. Then along came Roger de Montgomery, whom William had made Earl of Shrewsbury, and he built a new and much larger castle on this site which was named after him. Roger was related to both the Conqueror and also to Ralph Mortimer and William Fitz-Osbern. It is significant that he was so great a lord that he had been able to contribute sixty ships for the invasion of England in 1066.

It was to Montgomery that Henry II and Llywelyn, Prince of Wales, came in 1267, to sign a treaty of peace which recognised Llywelyn as lawful Prince of Wales. They were entertained by the almost princely Roger Mortimer who was then in possession of the castle.

In September 1401, King Henry arrived at Worcester with his son the Prince of Wales. They continued to Shrewsbury, Chester, Leominster and Hereford, and assembled a mighty army of one hundred thousand men. This massive force then advanced with King Henry marching from Shrewsbury with the main body. There were two flanking columns supporting him – one from Chester and the other from Hereford – commanded by Prince Henry.

Montgomery Castle held out against Owain Glyndŵr when he attacked it in 1402. He sacked the walled town which remained in ruins for the next 200 years. The town walls were never rebuilt.

On reaching Llandovery in Mid Wales, King Henry was approached by Llywelyn ap Gruffydd Fychan, a wealthy landowner from Caeo, who offered to lead his army to a cavern where he claimed Owain Glyndŵr was hiding. Henry believed his story and told Llywelyn to proceed.

After leading them for five long and weary days on a circuitous route through steep mountain valleys, which tired the English until they were exhausted, Llywelyn then made the mistake of boasting that his two sons were fighting with Glyndŵr. It at last dawned upon the English that their guide was leading them on a wild goose chase. He paid for his trickery with his life and was savagely hung, beheaded and quartered in Llandovery market place. Adam of Usk described Llywelyn ap Gruffydd as 'a man of gentle birth and bountiful, who yearly used sixteen tuns of wine in his household.'

Henry IV then descended on Strata Florida Abbey and allowed his soldiers to plunder the buildings and stable their horses at the high altar. The monks were turned out of their home and accused of supporting the cause of Glyndŵr.

Adam of Usk describes how:

> ...the English invading these parts and ravaging them with fire, hunger and sword, left them a desert, not even sparing children or churches, nor the Monastery of Strata Florida, wherein the King himself was a guest, the church of which and its choir, even up to the high altar, they used as a stable and pillaged even the patens.

Strata Florida Abbey was once regarded as the Westminster of Wales for no less than eleven Welsh princes of the House of Dinefwr were buried there in the twelfth and thirteenth centuries. Funeral processions bearing these men of royal and noble birth used to travel great distances to reach this remote abbey. Pilgrims also used to come here to see the abbey's greatest treasure - a wooden bowl, thought to be the Holy Grail.

An earlier abbey was founded by monks from Alba Landa as a daughter-abbey of Whitland. It was built at Ystrad Fflur on the banks of the Fflur which is about two miles south-west of the ruins of the second abbey. The spot is still known as Yr Hen Monachlog (The Old Monastery) and the building stood on a tongue of land lying between the rivers Glassffrwd and Teifi. This site has now been cut in two by the river Fflur which over the years has changed its course. Measurements taken of the foundations indicate that the building was about 402 metres long and 14 metres wide and there is a tradition that it was destroyed by fire.

The new abbey was founded in 1164 by Rhys ap Gruffydd and the name Ystrad Fflur was Latinised to Strata Florida which means 'the flowery vale'. Its patron Rhys ap Gruffydd was the grandson of Rhys ap Tudor who had been patron of the original abbey. During this period other Welsh princes were also founding great Cistercian establishments such as Strata Marcella, Cwmhir, and Valle Crucis.

There is a tradition that the sandstone used to form the pillars, arches and various decorative work was brought here all the way from Somerset. It was conveyed by ship to the small port of Aberarth and local legend claims that from there every stone was passed from hand to hand by a human chain covering a distance of about twenty miles! It was two decades before the abbey was completed and over the years it came to own most of the upper Teifi Valley and also the mountain land directly above the building.

I arrived at Strata Florida Abbey on a misty afternoon in early November and, wandering alone around the ancient ruins, I found myself caught up in its very special atmosphere. As I pondered on the remarkable history of this lonely place, I pictured a small chamber within the abbey, where monks once laboured day and night over a period of one hundred and thirty years, writing the *Brut y Tywysogion* – the Chronicle of the Princes, which recorded the great events that took place in Wales during the Middle Ages. It certainly makes fascinating reading.

In 1175 Cadell (son of Gruffydd ap Rhys and brother to Rhys ap Gruffydd, the founder) was buried here. He was followed in 1190 by Owen ap Rhys, the son of the founder. In 1197, the founder himself, Rhys ap Gruffydd died and was buried in his fine abbey.

Four years later he was followed by his son and immediate successor, Gruffydd ap Rhys. The *Brut y Tywysogion* speaks of him as follows:

> This Gruffydd was a valiant and discreet prince and one that appeared likely to bring all South Wales into good order and obedience, for in all things he trod in his father's footsteps and made it his business to succeed him, as well as in his valour and virtuous endowments, as in his government; but the vast hopes conceived of him soon proved abortive; for on St James Day 1202 he died, to the great grief and loss of the country and shortly after he was buried at Ystrad Fflur, with great pomp and solemnity.

In 1204, Howel ap Rhys, a blind son of the founder, was slain by some of the followers of his brother Maelgan and was buried near his brother Gruffydd. Young Rhys, son of Gruffydd ap Rhys was buried here in 1221, followed in 1230 by Maelgwyn the son of Prince Rhys. Five years later in 1235, Owen, another son of Gruffydd ap Rhys, was brought here to be buried by the side of his brother Rhys.

Strata Florida Abbey was once regarded as the Westminster of Wales, for no less than eleven princes of the House of Dinefwr were buried there. The abbey was plundered by King Henry IV in 1401, when he used it as a base during his campaign against Owain Glyndŵr.

The west doorway, with its very fine Norman arch is the most impressive surviving feature of Strata Florida Abbey. Within the ruins one can trace the foundations of the long nave, the choir, presbytery, transepts and aisles; chapter house, library and other smaller buildings.

Near the eastern wall of the south transept is the monks' cemetery, where about a dozen graves are decorated with interlaced ropework-carvings of Celtic design. These were revealed when this area was cleared and they represent the graves of early abbots and possibly some of the many princes buried here.

The large tree in the adjoining churchyard is said to mark the grave of Dafydd ap Gwilym, the greatest of all the medieval Welsh poets. He was born in about 1340 at Llanbadarn, near Aberystwyth, and died in 1400, which was the year that Owain Glyndwr began his uprising. A memorial slab has been erected on the north wall of the north transept by the Honourable Society of Cymmrodorian and it is inscribed in Latin and Welsh, which were the two languages spoken by Dafydd ap Gwilym. The claim for his burial here is based on a poem by Gruffudd Grug which suggests that his remains lie beneath a yew tree. But it is also claimed that the poet lies at Talley Abbey near Llandeilo in Carmarthenshire where a memorial stone to him was erected in September 1984.

In 1238 Llywelyn the Great came here to conduct a solemn function to which he had summoned all the chiefs and lords of Wales, to swear fealty to his son Dafydd from his marriage to an English princess (Joan the daughter of King John). This was Llywelyn's last council and he asked those present to swear allegiance to Dafydd as his successor. They all swore the oath but for many of them their sympathies no doubt lay with Dafydd's brother Gruffydd who sought a hostile independence of England. Prince Llywelyn then retired to the Cistercian monastery that he had founded at Aberconwy where he died on 11 April, 1240.

In 1249 the abbots of Strata Florida and Aberconwy obtained 'through pressing solicitation' the body of Prince Llywelyn and brought it with them from London to Aberconwy for burial.

In 1254 a great bell was brought to Strata Florida to be raised into place and consecrated by the Bishop of Bangor. At this time there were one hundred and nine monks residing in the abbey. (There is a tradition that when the abbey was dissolved in the reign of Henry VIII, this great bell was taken to St. Paul's Cathedral in London.)

The Chronicle of St.Werburgh records that in 1284:

> A great misfortune struck the belfry and burned the whole of it, with the bells, without the flames being seen; and then (the fire) devoured the whole church, which was completely covered with lead, as far as the walls, except the presbytery which was seen to be miraculously preserved in as much as the body of our Lord was kept there on the great altar (as elsewhere is the case, according to the universal custom). Whatever was there, except the walls of the church was burned in that fire, including the choral books and bells.

It is of interest that some people have claimed to come here at night on Christmas Eve and seen candles burning amongst the ruins and a phantom monk trying to rebuild the altar!

Disaster struck again in 1295 when the abbey was partially destroyed by fire during the wars of King Edward I and the Welsh. In the King's charter dated 30 March 1300, he gave the monks permission to rebuild, together with a grant of £78 upon condition that they cut down the woods and repaired the roads in the vicinity under the direction of his Justiciary of West Wales. From that time until its dissolution in the reign of Henry VIII all records perished.

Near the eastern wall of the south transept is the monks' cemetery, where about a dozen graves are decorated with interlaced ropework-carvings of Celtic design. These were revealed when this area was cleared and they represent the graves of early abbots and possibly the princes buried here.

In the adjoining churchyard, I walked over to a large yew tree beneath which is said to be the grave of Dafydd ap Gwilym who was the greatest of all the medieval Welsh poets. He was born in about 1340 at Llanbadarn Fawr, near Aberystwyth, and died in 1400, which was the year that Owain Glyndŵr began his uprising. A memorial slab has been erected on the north wall of the north transept by the Honourable Society of Cymmrodorian and is inscribed in Latin and Welsh, which were the two languages spoken by Dafydd ap Gwilym.

Two years after the burial of Dafydd ap Gwilym, this abbey was desecrated by Henry IV. He even plundered the sacred vessels and it was to be another six months before services were once more held here, when the king placed the Abbey in the charge of Thomas Percy, Earl of Worcester.

Before leaving Strata Florida, Henry dispatched troops into the surrounding countryside to search for the ever elusive Glyndŵr who had apparently gone into hiding. No doubt he had decided against risking a battle against such a large army and had retired to his secret base below Pumlumon Fawr, leaving the Welsh weather to do his work for him.

The king decided that it was now time to return to England, but he was faced with yet another horrendous journey. It rained in torrents and even snowed, despite the fact that it was still summer. The thunder roared and the lightning flashed from peak to peak. Drenched to the skin the long line of half starved soldiers pressed on, desperate to escape from Wales. Exhausted by famine and fatigue and weakened by sickness, this huge army had accomplished nothing more than the destruction of a once grand and noble abbey.

In November, Owain attacked Caernarfon Castle, which at that time was held by twenty men-at-arms and eighty archers, but suffered a terrible defeat, losing three hundred men. Following this disaster, he tried to make peace with Henry and asked only that his property should be returned and his life spared, but Lord Grey advised the king to crush the rebellion and make no compromises. The king was of the opinion that he might use the peace talks as a possible way of taking Owain prisoner, but such a plan was opposed by Henry Percy, who was an honourable man.

King Henry then made a grant of all Glyndŵr's possessions in Wales to John de Beaufort, Earl of Somerset, on the plea of forfeiture by treason. At the end of the month Henry proclaimed a free pardon to all Welshmen(with the exception of Owain Glyndŵr and his close followers such as Gwilym and Rhys ap Tudur) who chose to appear at Chester before the next session of Parliament.

Owain made an unsuccessful attack on Harlech Castle in December, but reinforcements from Chester caused the Welsh force to make a hasty withdrawal.

Glyndŵr then opened diplomatic relations with Robert II, King of Scotland, offering an alliance against their common enemy. However, Owain's emissary was captured before reaching Scotland and beheaded. Adam of Usk tells us that:

> ...a certain knight called Sir David ap Jevan Goz, of the County of Cardigan, who for full twenty years had fought against the Saracens with the King of Cyprus and other Christians, being sent by the King of France to the King of Scotland on Owen's behalf, was taken captive by English sailors and imprisoned in the Tower of London.

Parliament was called in January 1402 and they discussed hard and long 'what to do about Wales'. The outcome was a series of many harsh laws concerning Wales and the Welsh people. Henceforth:

> No Welshman is permitted to purchase any land in England. He is not allowed to hold any corporate office, nor to bear arms within any city, borough or market town.

> No Welshman, unless he was a bishop or a temporal lord, can possess a castle or defend his house.

> No Welshman can hold important public office in Wales.

> All castles and walled towns are to be garrisoned by Englishmen.

> An Englishman married to a Welsh woman loses his right to hold any public office in Wales and the Marches.

> No Englishman is to be convicted at the suit of any Welshman.

> No provisions or arms are to be received in Wales without special permission from the king or his council.

> No Welshman is allowed to have the charge of any castle, fortress or place of defence even though he might be the owner of it, nor to fulfil the offices of Lieutenant, Justice, Chancellor, Treasurer, Chamberlain, Sheriff, Steward, Coroner or any office of trust, not withstanding any patent or license to the contrary.

> No Welsh child is to be brought up as a scholar, nor permitted to be apprenticed to any trade in any town in the kingdom.

> A Welshman marrying an Englishwoman is subjected to severe penalties; and all Englishmen marrying Welshwomen are disfranchised in the boroughs.

No Englishman can marry with any of the family of Owain Glyndŵr. Also it is ordained and established that no Englishman married to any Welsh in friendship or alliance with Owain Glyndŵr, traitor to our lord the king, or to another Welshwoman since the rebellion of the said Owain, or who in time to come shall make himself to be married to any Welsh woman, shall be put in any office in Wales or the said March.

The bards were not to travel the country. Welshmen were not to assemble for any purpose or carry arms or wear armour in town, market, church or on the highway. Nor were they allowed to put any place in a state of defence. The old custom of Cymmartha – i.e. meeting together to assist each other in harvest or other agricultural work – was strictly forbidden and the assembling of bards and minstrels was declared illegal.

It is not surprising that the Welsh were goaded to desperation and when such a leader as Owain Glyndŵr came forward he was hailed as the saviour of Wales.

"Owain, uniting in his veins the Princely blood of Powys and North Wales was not merely a redoubtable warrior, but throughout England he was regarded as a magician, who could summon the tempest at will and call sprits from the vasty deep."

A.G. Bradley 1920

This statue of Owain Glyndŵr, carved in 1916 by Alfred Turner, can be seen in the City Hall, Cardiff. The contemporay citation read as follows:

"The statue represents the great Welsh patriot as the soldier statesman – the enthusiast with lofty ideals and noble aims – not a mere ambitious rebel as wrongfully depicted in English histories, but a man who fought with splendid courage for the independence of Wales and the advancement of the people. Spiritual aspirations rather than desire for material success is depicted in the figure."

Five
The Year of the Comet

This year was ushered in with a comet, or a blazing star; which the bards interpreted as an omen favourable to the cause of Glyndwr.

Thomas Pennant

In February, 1402, a comet appeared in the sky and the prophets all agreed that this was a good sign for Owain Glyndŵr. It was visible throughout the months of February and March and was believed to signify deliverance for the men of Gwynedd as it passed high over Anglesey in the northern sky. When the comet disappeared it was followed by violent thunderstorms. Such happenings were all good material for the bards of the time – for had not Christ been born beneath 'a blazing starre' and had not a mighty comet blazed across the heavens to herald the coming of Arthur?

Iolo Goch in particular took the comet very seriously, seeing it as a good omen for his patron and he wrote a poem entitled *Cwydd y Deren* to celebrate the event.

There were many bards who believed that the ancient prophecies of Taliesin of Arthurian times had come true and that the saviour of Wales had at last returned. Owain Glyndŵr was the 'mab dragon' (the Son of Promise) who would free Wales from the English. There is no doubt that his gold dragon standard was inspired by the one said to have been used by Uther Pendragon.

Adam of Usk managed to observe two comets, but he was always inclined to exaggerate! Today, we know this blazing star as Halley's Comet and it comes about every seventy years. For example it made an appearance in 1066 and is portrayed in the Bayeux tapestry.

Events certainly started to go right for Owain after the sighting of the comet. His first real stroke of good fortune was to capture Lord Grey in a battle near Ruthin on the last day of January. An ambush was laid on Bryn Saith Marchog ('The hill of the Seven Knights'), halfway between Ruthin and Corwen and Lord Grey was captured with seven of his men. There is a local tradition that Owain created an impression that his force was much larger than it actually was by driving stakes into the ground and putting helmets and cloaks on them, so that they appeared to be a company of armed men camping amid the thick bare undergrowth which covered the knoll.

He then positioned his men a short distance away in a wood and there they waited in ambush. When the enemy approached, they saw a shining row of helmets on the knoll and, presuming them to be Owain's force, they stopped to assess the situation. Glyndŵr's men then rushed upon Lord Grey's soldiers from all sides and as they attempted to flee they were all struck down and killed.

The Lord of Ruthin was at last in Owain's hands. He was put in chains and taken to Llywelyn the Last's old fortress at Dolbadarn, a lonely tower overlooking Llyn Peris in the heart of Snowdonia. A ransom of ten thousand marks (£6,666) was demanded, which was an enormous sum of money for those times. Six thousand marks had to be paid within four weeks, and hostages, in the person of his eldest son and others, were to be delivered to Owain as guarantee for the remaining four thousand marks. Lord Grey was also required to swear a humiliating oath that he would never take arms against Glyndŵr again.

The King gave way, authorising Sir William de Roos, Sir Richard de Grey, Sir William de Willoughby, Sir William de Zouche, Sir Hugh Huls, John Harvey, William Vans, John Lee, John Longford, Thomas Payne and John Elnestow to treat with Owain. He then told the Council 'to conclude in what way they should conceive most expedient and necessary to be done for his (Lord Grey's) redemption' They consented to give the sum demanded by Glyndŵr, and the king gave license to Robert Braybroke, Bishop of London, Sir Gerrard Braybroke the father and Sir Gerrard the son, to sell the Manor of Hertelegh in the County of Kent towards the raising of the ransom. Lord Grey was released at the end of the summer of 1402 and from that time onward there is no record of any further hostilities between the two men, but financially, Lord Grey was left a ruined man for the rest of his life.

Owain then burned St Asaph Cathedral and marched on Harlech Castle, but he found that a force of one hundred men-at-arms and four hundred archers had arrived there from Chester to assist in its defence. So he wisely decided to leave this prize for another day. He then marched to Radnorshire to seek further support from the inhabitants of that area.

On 22 June (St Alban's Day), a strong detachment of Owain's army under the command of his loyal Lieutenant Rhys Gethin (the Fierce) from Cwm Llanerch in Conwy, encountered an army of Herefordshire men and Welsh archers, who under the command of Edmund Mortimer had marched from Ludlow Castle to intercept Glyndŵr's army. Mortimer was acting in his role as defender of the Marches and as a representative of the King. The two forces met at a place called Pilleth in the narrow valley of the Lugg. This valley runs from the Malienydd hills right down to Wigmore and was therefore the easiest route for Owain's force to follow, in order to strike at the heart of the Mortimer territories.

Dolbadarn Castle overlooking Llyn Peris in Snowdonia where Lord Grey was kept prisoner by Owain Glyndŵr for a year and released on the payment of a ransom of ten thousand marks. A castle has stood on this rock since the sixth century and it was at one time the home of Maelgwyn Gwynedd. But it was the ancestors of Llywelyn the Great who built a stone fortress here in the 12th century – replacing an earlier wooden castle. In the same century the great round keep was constructed. It became a fortress of considerable importance, commanding a good view down the valley. Situated in the heart of the Snowdonia mountains this medieval fortress has certainly witnessed a great deal of history.

The Welsh army positioned themselves on top of Bryn Glas hill and waited for the English force to charge up the slope. Rhys Gethin ordered his archers to fire and they showered their shafts on the heads of the advancing army. Mortimer's Welsh archers, who mainly came from Radnorshire and in their hearts sympathised with Glyndŵr's cause, decided to change sides and fired arrows at the backs of the English.

It was a very bloody battle and the English were cut to pieces. Edmund Mortimer was taken prisoner and a large number of soldiers, including many knights and nobles, were left dead and dying on the battlefield.

According to Adam of Usk, eight thousand men were slain, but this was probably a very exaggerated figure and in other accounts, it ranges from two hundred to eleven hundred. It is reputed that after the battle was over, the female supporters of the Welsh came to Bryn Glas Hill and 'dismembered' the corpses of the English soldiers. Shakespeare refers to this act of mutilation in his play *Henry IV, Part One.*

The English knights killed included Robert Whitney (whose castle at Whitney-on-Wye was soon afterwards destroyed), Kinard de la Bere, Kinard of Kinnersley (Sheriff of Herefordshire in 1387, 1396 and 1401); Walter Devereux of Frome and Weobley (Sheriff of the Shire in 1401).

It was a bright sunny afternoon when I drove through the Lugg Valley along the B4356 to reach Pilleth. I parked the car just below Pilleth Court and walked up through a field to reach Pilleth Church, known by the Welsh as Eglwys y Forwyn Fair. I noted that the old building obviously had a subsidence problem for it is propped up with massive timbers at the back.

The foundations of the earlier tower, burned by Glyndŵr's men can be seen on the north side of the present one. The building was restored some time after the battle of Pilleth but in 1894 it was gutted by fire and it remained a burnt out shell until it was again restored in 1905 at a cost of £400.

To the north of the tower is a Holy Well which was much frequented in the Middle Ages being well known for curing eye diseases. People also visited it to see a statue of the Virgin Mary - known as "Our Lady of Pilleth', which once stood near the well.

On the south side of the building a plain rectangular curbstone marks the grave of some of the soldiers who died in the battle. Their bones were buried here by Sir Richard Green-Price.

I had expected the door to be locked, but when I gave it a firm push, it creaked loudly and swung open. Stepping inside, I was immediately aware of a sudden drop in temperature. As I took in the simple, austere interior, I looked up at the lime washed timbers in the roof and then chuckled as I noticed that after painting the walls, there had been enough lime left over to paint the font as well.

Fastened to the wall was a single edged mortuary sword. The guard was embossed with a flowing decoration and it was obviously once a good fighting sword, but, dating from about 1650, it was unfortunately not a relic of the battle of Pilleth.

Leaving the cool silence of the church, I returned into the welcome warmth of the afternoon sun and followed a path leading down steps to a gate. From there I followed a green lane around the side of Bryn Glas hill. For a moment I stood and gazed up at the tall trees which mark the place where the English soldiers were buried.

Four Wellingtonias on Bryn Glas Hill at Pilleth in Shropshire mark the burial site of soldiers killed in the battle of Pilleth, when, in 1402, a Welsh force led by Glyndŵyr's loyal lieutenant, Rhys Gethin, defeated an English army commanded by Sir Edmund Mortimer.

Pilleth Church is dedicated to St. Mary and it is of special interest that this church was here at the time of the battle and there were no other buildings at this location at that time. The only remaining part of the original church is the belfry. However the font is 14th century and is probably older than any part of the church.

The burial site was confirmed just over a hundred years ago when a local farmer unearthed a heaped pile of bones there with his plough. At the end of the nineteenth century the burial site was marked with some young trees planted by Sir Richard Green Price in a small enclosure about one hundred metres square. Over the passing years these matured to form a conspicuous grove of Wellingtonias which represents a memorial to the battle of Pilleth.

I tried to imagine the dreadful action that took place here in 1402 but found it difficult, for although this green valley conveys an atmosphere of history, there is no feeling of violence or death but just an air of sleepy tranquility. The present road (B4356) was not in existence at that time and Mortimer's army had probably marched along the track on which I was standing.

Near the river Lugg can be seen a Norman motte and bailey castle known as Castell Foel Allt which was built at the end of the eleventh century but it was no longer in use by 1402.

It has been suggested that other mounds in the river meadows below the road mark the graves of soldiers killed in this battle, but this would have been marshy ground in the fifteeth century. It is more likely that the dead were buried where they fell, on the slopes of Bryn Glas Hill.

My thoughts turned to King Henry who was resting at his Berkhamstead palace when a messenger brought him news from Wales of Edmund Mortimer's defeat and capture.

Henry had made strenuous efforts to secure the release of his friend Lord Grey of Ruthin, but on this occasion Henry did nothing to assist Edmund Mortimer. This was no doubt because he was very much aware of the fact that the Mortimers had more right to the throne than himself. He probably considered them already too powerful and was perhaps even relieved that Edmund had been *taken care of* by Owain Glyndŵr.

After the battle, Edmund Mortimer was taken to Leominster where he was imprisoned in the old gaol, while Owain's men plundered the priory of its rich ornaments and damaged other property in the area before returning to Wales with their prisoner.

Later, after the battle of Pilleth, Henry IV ordered the Lords Marcher to equip their castles with 'men, stores, arms, artillery, and all things necessary and suitable for defence.' Among the castles mentioned were Stapleton, Huntingdon, Richard's Castle and Lyonshall. Despite the King's precautions and warnings, Glyndŵr finally succeeded in capturing Stapleton Castle, whose situation, just a mile over the border from Presteigne, made it of strategic importance.

Leaving Pilleth, I drove down the road to Monaughty Grange, a large Elizabethan mansion which was once known as Mynachdy (Monastery) and was originally a grange of Abbey Cwmhir.

When Owain destroyed Abbey Cwmhir, he allowed the Lord Abbot to end his days here, and it is also said that Rhys Gethin spent a night here prior to the battle of Pilleth. However, a similar claim is made for Monaughty Poeth in Llanfair Waterdine. Both places have been described as granges belonging to Abbey Cwmhir.

Consulting the map, I realised that I was just twelve miles from Wigmore Castle, the ancestral home of Edmund Mortimer. So I decided that this should be my next destination. Within half an hour I was parking near Wigmore Church.

Built by the Mortimers, this church is impressive on the outside, but the interior I found rather disappointing, having been much restored by the Victorians in 1864. The only items of interest to me were some ancient stalls which once belonged to Wigmore Abbey.

Outside, I stood under the shadow of the north wall of the church and to the north-west I saw a prominent hill crowned with the remains of Wigmore Castle. Ethelfleda, the eldest daughter of King Alfred, established the first fortress here and it was rebuilt in 1067 by Fitzosbern, the Earl of Hereford. Subsequently, it was awarded to William the Conqueror's kinsman, Ralph de Mortimer, as a reward for subduing Eric the Saxon. He was granted the town and castle of Wigmore.

In 1089 William Rufus was a visitor to the castle. The next royal visitor was Henry III, who on escaping from his imprisonment in Hereford Castle, was brought here for safety, under the protection of Roger, the sixth Lord of Wigmore.

Before the Conquest this location was known as Wiggen yn Mere, which comes from the Saxon words 'wigge,' signifying warrior, and 'mere' – a pool or great water. Presumably this water is below ground for it used to be said by local people that the fields below Wigmore Castle are undrainable. Alternatively, it has been suggested that the name is derived from a Danish camp which stood here and signifies 'The Moor of the Sons of War.' It is mentioned in the Domesday Book and in its time has been a place of considerable importance.

I approached the castle along a lane, which soon narrowed into a footpath providing a pleasant walk through an attractive valley. Sooner than I expected the castle rose up in front of me, with its ruined towers crowning an impressive knoll that provided a natural defensive position.

It certainly made a change to visit a Norman Castle where there is no entrance fee, no interpretation, no commercialisation and no 'Do Not' notices. Here I was, alone with my thoughts, enjoying a fascinating ruined castle and a seemingly endless supply of mouth-watering juicy blackberries.

Wigmore Church was constructed by the Mortimer family

I passed the impressive walls of the great gateway, once reached by a drawbridge, and set into a curtain wall protected by square and round bastions. On gaining the summit of the mound where the square Norman keep once stood, I looked down on the neglected collection of ancient walls that surrounded me and imagined Edmund Mortimer standing here gazing disdainfully on the peasants working in the fields below. This is the heart of Mortimer Country and Wigmore Castle was strengthened and developed by that family over the passing centuries to make it one of the most powerful fortresses in the Marches of Wales. At one time it was the largest castle on the Welsh border and was one of a chain of strongholds of which Clun, Hopton, Brampton Bryan lay due north; Lingen and Lyonshall were to the south, whilst to the east stood Croft Castle and Richard's Castle. Also, within striking distance were the more important castles of Ludlow and Shrewsbury.

After the time of Glyndŵr, Wigmore castle remained a possession of the Crown from the days of Edward IV to the reign of Elizabeth I, who granted it away. In 1601 it was purchased by Thomas Harley and in 1643 it was said to be the strongest castle in England. However, it was then dismantled by its owner Sir Robert Harley who, during the Civil War, was not able to defend it as well as his other castle at Brampton Bryan. In later years, part of the castle was used as a prison and it ended up as a quarry for building stone.

The Mortimers were a fierce and cruel family, who, for generations, played off the Welsh and the Crown against one another to their own advantage. After first acquiring land in Wales, they intermarried with princely families, Sir Ralph de Mortimer marrying Gwladys the daughter of Llywelyn the Last. Her first husband had been Sir Reginald de Braose, Lord of Caerphilly Castle. So on the death of Dafydd in 1245, a Ralph Mortimer was a candidate for the Welsh crown. Later Mortimers seem to have inherited the qualities and defects of both races, blending the cool cunning of the Norman with the wild passion and fiery imagination of the Celt.

When their son Roger Mortimer died in 1282, he was buried at Wigmore Abbey. His eldest surviving son Edmund succeeded, and is famous for his attack on the Welsh at Builth, and for conveying Prince Llywelyn's head to the King. After this event, he was kept busy quelling outbreaks of Welsh resistance and, in putting one down at Builth in 1303, he received a mortal wound. Roger, the first Earl of March, was hanged, drawn and quartered at The Elms, now the Marble Arch, Hyde Park, London, on 29 November, 1330. His remains were taken to Wigmore Castle and then deposited in the family vault in Wigmore Priory. He left four sons and seven daughters, who all married into the families of England's aristocracy. His eldest son Roger became the second Earl of March.

Wigmore Castle was the ancestral home of the Mortimers and was once one of the most powerful fortresses in the Marches of Wales. As late as 1643 it was described as the strongest castle in England but was dismantled during the Civil War.

He married Philippa, daughter of William de Montacute, the first Earl of Salisbury, and the Countess of Salisbury. Their son Edmund was born at Llangynwyd Castle, near Margam in Glamorgan, on 1 February, 1351. He, in 1370, married Philippa, daughter of Lionel, Duke of Clarence, the second surviving son of Edward III and Lady de Burgh, daughter of the Earl of Ulster, Ireland. Philippa Clarence was the grand-daughter of Edward III and accordingly their children stood next-in-line to the crown after Richard II, the son of the Black Prince.

Their daughter, Lady Elizabeth, was born at Usk Castle, Monmouthshire, on 12 February, 1371. She married Henry Percy (Hotspur). Edmund and Philippa also had a son, named Roger (4th Earl of March) who was born at Usk Castle on 11 April, 1374. The following Sunday he was christened by Roger Craddock, Bishop of Llandaff who, with the Abbot of Gloucester and the Prioress of Usk, acted as his sponsors, and were supported by Adam of Usk.

Roger Mortimer married a niece of Richard II, fought at Crecy and was one of the founders of the Order of the Garter. He was declared by Parliament to be the heir presumptive to the throne when Richard died, provided Richard had no children. Roger was made Lieutenant of Ireland and during his service in that country, he was slain at Kells, by a band of men from Leinster in 1398. It was Roger's brother, Edmund and Philippa's second son (also named Edmund), who was the Mortimer taken prisoner by Rhys Gethin at Pilleth. Roger de Mortimer, who was killed in Ireland, left two sons – Edmund and Roger – and daughters – Anne and Eleanor. The two boys were imprisoned in Windsor Castle by Henry IV after he had deposed Richard II.

Edmund, the older boy, became the fifth Earl of March when he was just seven years of age, just one year before Richard II was murdered by Henry Bolingbroke, but his interests were jealously guarded by his uncle Edmund (who was captured at Pilleth). Young Edmund Mortimer, Earl of March, was a direct descendant of Edward III and was accordingly King Richard II's rightful heir. Sir Edmund Mortimer, his uncle, was his nominal guardian and representative. The youngster spent his childhood with the young Prince Henry, son of Henry IV. The two brothers were kept in captivity throughout the reign of Henry IV and not released until Henry V came to the throne. Edmund outlived Henry V, the victor of Agincourt, and was later sent by Henry VI to govern Ireland where he died of the plague, childless. He represented the last direct line of the Mortimer family and was buried at Wigmore Abbey.

Between 1282 and 1398 five Roger Mortimers were laid to rest at Wigmore Abbey and a total of eleven Mortimers were buried there. Unfortunately, not one of their elaborate tombs has survived.

The half-timbered gatehouse to Wigmore Grange

In Much Marcle Church, Herefordshire, can be seen the tomb and effigy of Blanche Mortimer, a daughter of Roger Mortimer, first Earl of March and widow of Sir Peter de Grandison. Above the tomb is a canopy of five arches with panels above them containing the arms of Grandison hanging from a head. The second and fourth panels contain Mortimer arms. At the head of the canopy is a moulded cornice with a flower design and painted shields of Mortimer and Grandison. The tomb of Blanche's husband is in the Lady Chapel of Hereford Cathedral. On her marriage to Sir Peter Grandison, Blanche was granted a portion of the Manor of Much Marcle by her father. Sir Peter died in 1350 and, there being no children of the marriage, the estate reverted to the Mortimer family. On the accession of Edward IV it became part of the Royal Estates.

The Mortimers of Wigmore were one of the most powerful families in the kingdom for over three centuries and their blood still runs through the veins of the British royal family

It is also of interest that Gwladys, the daughter of Llywelyn the Great, and Princess Joan (daughter of King John and sister to Henry III), became the bride of a Mortimer, and in later years Edmund Mortimer married one of Owain Glyndŵr's daughters. It is an interesting thought that if Owain Glyndŵr's uprising had been successful, then Wigmore Castle may well have become a royal residence, for this ancestral fortress of the Mortimers was once one of the most powerful in the Marches of England and Wales.

Returning to my car at Wigmore Church, I then drove on to the site of Wigmore Abbey, but as it is private property, I had to be content with viewing the surviving buildings from the road. All that is left now is a large farmhouse, known as Wigmore Grange, and the remains of a half-timbered gatehouse to the Abbot's Court.

Wigmore Grange was built by Ralph Mortimer's grandson Hugh Mortimer, who died in 1185. It was his chief steward, Oliver de Merlymond, who founded a community of Augustinian canons here. The foundation stone of the Abbey was laid by Lord Wigmore, who graciously finished the building at his own expense. In 1282 the Abbey was invaded by the Welsh who carried off all its valuables and burnt everything except the church. After being rebuilt by Edmund Mortimer in about 1370 it continued as one of the chief monastic houses of the border country until Abbot Skypp and his ten monks surrendered their fine abbey to the King's Commissioners in 1538.

This magnificent abbey once ranked in size and wealth with Gloucester, Dore, Wenlock, Buildwas and Shrewsbury. It was surrendered to Henry VIII's Commissioners on 18 November, 1538. Its endowments were confiscated and the church plate and jewels sold. The abbey was then destroyed and today only a few fragments of its walls remain.

In 1574, Dr Dee found the records of the abbey lying in a heap inside Wigmore Castle. He commented that they were found, 'rotting, spyled and tossed in an old decayed chapell, not committed to any man's special charge, but three quarters of them I understand to have been taken by diverse (eyther taylors or others) in tymes past.' Dr Dee requested Lord Burghley to send a letter to Mr Harley, the keeper of Wigmore Castle, giving him authority to examine and collect these records, but nothing further was heard of them, and they were no doubt destroyed.

Returning along the A4110, I soon reached the crossroads known as 'Mortimer's Cross'. Here stands the inn of that name, displaying a colourful sign which commemorates a terrible battle that was fought on 2 February, 1461, during the Wars of the Roses.

IN·THIS·ABBEY· LIE· THE · REMAINS · OF · THE
NOBLE · FAMILY · OF · MORTIMER
WHO·FOUNDED · IT · IN · 1179. · AND · WHO
RULED·THE·MARCHES·OF·WALES·FOR · 400 YEARS.

RALPH·1140. · HUGH · 1185. · ROGER · 1215.
HUGH · 1227. · RALPH · 1248. · ROGER · 1282.
EDMUND · 1318. · ROGER · 1330. · EDMUND · 1331.
ROGER ·1360. · EDMUND · 1381. · ROGER, EDMUND.

THE·ABBEY·COVERING·SEVERAL·ACRES·WAS·DESTROYED
BY· THE ·WELSH · 1221· REBUILT· BY· EDMUND· ABOUT ·1370,
WAS ·FINALLY· DESTROYED· BY· KING· HENRY · VIII · 1538.

The gatehouse of Wigmore Grange used to have a plaque on the front wall which named thirteen members of the Mortimer family, in the male succession, who were buried at Wigmore Abbey. The line ended when the last one died unmarried.

Buck's 1732 engraving of Wigmore Castle from the south

This battle was of course after the time of Owain Glyndŵr but it was particularly relevant to the future of the Mortimer family, for on that day the nineteen-year-old Edward Mortimer won the Crown of England.

Edward, the young Duke of York, had ridden out of Wigmore Castle, that cold February morning, to lead his army against a mighty force commanded by Owain Tudor on behalf of Henry VI. It was Candlemas day and this battle was to become the first step towards the restoration of the elder branch of Plantagenet to the throne, and the accession of a king descended from the Herefordshire family of Mortimer.

That morning, Edward was rewarded with a good sign when three suns appeared in the sky. This strange illusion was caused by the very cold weather bringing a freak refraction of light and ice particles. It is a phenomenon known scientifically as porhelion.

The battle lasted all day and it was a violent and bloody affair in which four thousand men lost their lives. A mile down the road is the Monument Inn, where a large inscribed stone mounted on a square block commemorates the events that occurred on the day when three suns appeared in the morning sky.

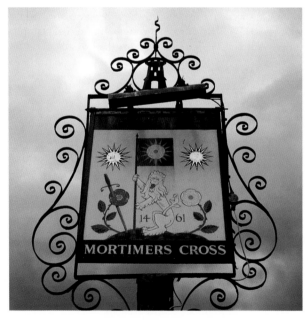

Inn sign at Mortimer's Cross.

Nearby, is Mortimer's Cross Mill, which houses a small museum set up to tell the story of the battle. A video of a re-enactment of the battle is shown here and among the relics is the original inscribed stone which used to stand outside the Monument Inn. It deteriorated over the years and had to be replaced, but the original one has now been restored. Maps of the battle in its various stages and a fine model of Edward, Earl of March, dressed in his Maltese style suit of armour can also be seen here. He was an impressive young man being 6 feet 3 inches tall, and he used his knowledge of the local area to the best advantage whilst fighting the battle. His father had been slain at the battle of Wakefield on 30 December, 1460. Edward reigned for twenty-two years and died after catching a cold in 1483. I found it very worthwhile to come to this museum and spend time watching the video to gain a realistic impression of a fifteenth century battle. The story is well told and the gruesome battle is re-enacted on the site where it actually took place.

Edward Mortimer, Earl of March

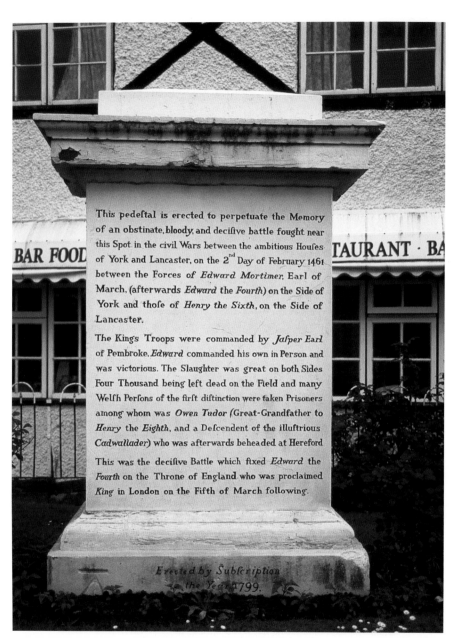

This pedeftal is erected to perpetuate the Memory of an obstinate, bloody, and decifive battle fought near this Spot in the civil Wars between the ambitious Houfes of York and Lancaster, on the 2nd Day of February 1461 between the Forces of *Edward Mortimer*, Earl of March, (afterwards *Edward* the *Fourth*) on the Side of York and thofe of *Henry the Sixth*, on the Side of Lancafter.

The Kings Troops were commanded by *Jafper Earl* of Pembroke, *Edward* commanded his own in Perfon and was victorious. The Slaughter was great on both Sides Four Thousand being left dead on the Field and many Welfh Perfons of the firft diftinction were taken Prisoners among whom was *Owen Tudor* (Great-Grandfather to *Henry* the *Eighth*, and a Defcendent of the illuftrious *Cadwallader*) who was afterwards beheaded at Hereford

This was the decifive Battle which fixed *Edward* the *Fourth* on the Throne of England who was proclaimed *King* in London on the Fifth of March following.

Erected by Subfcription the Year 1799.

This inscribed stone stands outside the Monument Inn and a long inscription gives an account of the battle of Mortimer's Cross, which was fought in 1461 and resulted in Edward Mortimer, Earl of March, gaining accession to the throne, to become Edward IV.

Ludlow Castle, in Shropshire was held by the Mortimers for five generations and it was a more important centre of power for them than their ancestral castle at Wigmore, being a much larger and stronger fortress.

In one of the stained glass windows of Ludlow Church can be seen figures and coats of arms of the main Lords Marcher connected with this town. They include Roger of Montgomery, Roger of March, Edmund of March and Arthur Prince of Wales (son of Henry VII).

In July 1402, the people of Hereford, concerned about the defeat and capture of Edmund Mortimer, wrote to the king sending him a solemn warning that unless he came to deal with Owain Glyndŵr in person then all would be lost. As a result of this request, Henry IV arrived in Hereford in September and stayed for four or five days.

But, in the meantime, Owain and his army had burst into Brecknock and Gwent and it was not long before the castles of Crickhowell and Abergavenny fell, with assistance from local people, whose spirit had been aroused by the cruel laws which Parliament had made against the people of Wales.

At the start of the uprising Gwent had been solidly behind Henry IV, but after Rhys Gethin captured Sir Edmund Mortimer at Pilleth and in consequence of his going over to Glyndwr's side, the Lordships of Caerleon and Trellech, which were all Mortimer possessions, became sympathetic to the Welsh cause. The castles of Monmouth, Skenfrith, Whitecastle and Grosmont, on the other hand, were part of the Duchy of Lancaster and were held by the king.

Owain spent the remainder of this year in South Wales in order to capture and destroy numerous castles and to win the native Welsh over to his cause. The castles of Usk, Caerleon and Newport were all taken and he then moved on to Cardiff, where he sacked the castle and set fire to the castellated mansion of the Bishop of Llandaff. Despite the fact that he had destroyed the cathedrals of North Wales, Owain spared the fine cathedral of Llandaff, for the clergy there were not antagonistic to the House of York which he supported. The Franciscans or Grey Friars was the only section of the church that was partial to his cause and the houses of this religious order throughout Wales were the only ones to escape damage from the hands of his men. When the Cardiff Friars Minors begged him to return their books and chalices, which they had placed in the castle, he replied:

"Wherefore did you place your goods in the castle? If you had kept them in your convent they would have been safe." The Franciscans were strong supporters of Richard II, and therefore were warm friends of Glyndŵr; hence the survival of their property.

Hearing of Owain's march into Glamorgan, a large number of Bristol men under the leadership of James Clifford and William Rye set sail from that port with a fleet of armed vessels. Their intention was to share in the spoils of the Welshman's ravages. They pillaged the church at Llandaff, but were prevented from carrying off any loot by the local people who drove them away.

Caerffili, Dunraven and many other Glamorgan castles soon fell into Owain's hands and within a short time the whole of Glamorgan was in his possession.

Today, all that remains of the castellated Bishop's Palace at Llandaff, Cardiff, are the remains of a 14th century gatehouse. After Glyndŵr's destruction of his home, Bishop Peveral decided to move the official palace to east Monmouthshire. Twenty-one bishops in succession had lived at Llandaff, so this was a very big step. The Church already owned a house and land at Mathern, near Chepstow, and this became the site of the new palace for the Bishops of Llandaff.

In early September 1402, King Henry marched towards Wales again, with three armies. These were led by himself, Prince Henry, and the Earls of Warwick, Arundel and Stafford (jointly). But once again they were beaten back by terrible weather. It was firmly believed that the mighty magician Owain Glyndŵr was using his supernatural powers to overcome his enemies yet again!

The autumn skies were swept by black low-lying clouds which deluged the advancing host with torrents of water. The rivers Severn, Wye, Usk and Dee were all in flood, roaring over their banks and spreading themselves into the lowlands. Powerful winds uprooted trees and cast them across the muddy roads, little better than water-courses, hindering the advance of horses or engines of war. The tent of the king himself was blown down in the night and had he not been sleeping in his armour he would have been flattened by the heavy central pole and killed. Their wagons of food were washed down the rivers and their changes of clothing were sodden before they put them on. For two weeks the gallant army struggled against the elements, needing no other foe to wrestle with and seeing none. By the end of that time those who had not drowned or starved, or been cut off by roving bands, were across the border once again. The king had made his third attempt against Wales and for the third time had been ignominiously beaten by the Welsh weather.

An entry in *Annales Henrici Quarti*, the English recording of the times, reads that Glyndŵr, 'Almost destroyed the King and his armies, by magic as it was thought, for from the time they entered Wales to the time they left, never did a gentle air breathe on them, but throughout whole days and nights, rain mixed with snow and hail afflicted them with cold beyond endurance.'

Meanwhile, in Northumberland, the Earl of Northumberland was fighting for the English king against the restless Scots, who were led by Archibald Douglas, the fourth Earl of Douglas, and grandson of James 'the Good'. His son, Henry Hotspur, joined him there and on September 14 they fought a decisive battle at Homildon Hill. The Scottish knights charged the English archers, but were defeated by a lethal shower of arrows; a total of eighty noblemen (including thirty Frenchmen) were captured by the two Percys.

The Percys refused to hand over their captive, the Earl of Douglas, to King Henry, and claimed the ransom money for themselves, on the grounds that Henry was already much in their debt. Hotspur in particular complained that Henry IV had failed to repay the money spent by his family in fighting this campaign. As a result of this quarrel with the king, Hotspur, his father and uncle then rose in rebellion and denounced Henry Bolingbroke as a usurper.

Negotiations were completed in November for the release of Lord Grey with the sum of six thousand marks being paid to Glyndŵr on 11 November and a further four thousand pledged by Grey's son.

Sir Edmund Mortimer was released from captivity during this month and soon afterwards he married Catrin Glyndŵr. It was a good alliance, for both families could claim descent from Llywelyn the Great. Edmund was twenty-six and a member of one of the most powerful and influential families in the Marches. He and Catrin were to have six years together during which four children were born.

In December, Edmund Mortimer wrote from Malienydd to his tenants in Herefordshire informing them of the alliance and seeking their support to bring down King Henry. He wrote the following letter to his estate manager:

> My very dear and well-beloved John Greyndor, Howel Vaughan, and all the gentles of Radnor and Prestremde (Presteign), I greet you very much and make known to you that Oweyn Glyndŵr has raised a quarrel of which the object is, if King Richard be alive, to restore him to his crown; and if not that, my honoured nephew, who is the right heir to the said crown shall be king of England, and that the said Oweyn will assert his right in Wales. And I, seeing and considering that the said quarrel is good and reasonable, have consented to join in it, and to aid and maintain it, and by the grace of God to a good end, Amen. I ardently hope and from my heart that you will support and enable me to bring this struggle of mine to a successful issue.
>
> Written at Melenynth the 13th day of December

In December, Henry IV married Joanna, the daughter of Charles of Navarre and widow of John Montfort, Duke of Brittany, and for a while he was occupied with various festivities which, with wars in three lands, helped to drain his exchequer, which never seemed to contain sufficient for his needs. Constantly in debt, Henry borrowed from rich merchants such as Richard Whittington, who had been Mayor of London for the first time in 1397. He had made his fortune by supplying the court with expensive garments and fabrics.

Since the king owed his crown chiefly to his election by the national assembly, Parliament was able to keep a strict check on the royal expenditure. It insisted on having the accounts audited, and placed on record the claim to have the sole right to suggest any new taxation.

Six
Henry of Monmouth
Prince of Wales

It was Owain's misfortune that he was to face the greatest soldier of his day. This was Harry of Monmouth, who was Prince of Wales and Henry IV's Lieutenant for the Welsh territories.

John Miles 1969

In Agincourt Square, Monmouth, I gazed up at the deformed looking effigy of Henry V, which looks down on the passing shoppers from an arched recess on the front of Shire Hall. This statue was made by Charles Peart, a local man, and installed in its niche in 1792 and, perhaps in compensation for making poor Henry look hunchbacked, it is more than lifesize being no less than 7 feet 2 inches tall.

Charles G. Harper, who wrote a guidebook to this area in 1894, was so irritated by the effigy that he observed: 'It should be destroyed forthwith and so relieve the town of Monmouth from the reproach of caricaturing its hero.'

Originally called Market Square, the location was renamed Agincourt Square in 1842 and nearby Inch Lane became Agincourt Street. Greyndor Street, originally named after an English commander who fought the Welsh, was renamed Glendower Street.

There only appears to be one surviving portrait of Harry of Monmouth and that does not portray him very favourably either, but in his day he was described as having 'an oval handsome face with a broad open forehead and a straight nose, ruddy cheeks and lips, a deeply indented chin and small well formed ears and his bright hazel eyes, gentle as doves, when at rest, could gleam like a lion when aroused to wrath. In stature he was above the average, and his frame, with its comely, well-knit limbs, was that of a man accustomed to active pursuits.'

Leaving Agincourt Square, I crossed the road and walked up Castle Hill to seek the scanty ruins of Monmouth Castle which are tucked away out of sight at the back of the town.

The first castle at Monmouth was built in 1067 by William Fitz-Osbern of Breteuil, Normandy. Later it was replaced by a stone building and, under the protection of this Norman fortress, Monmouth gradually developed into a town of reasonable size.

In the fourteenth century the castle came into the possession of the House of Lancaster through the marriage of John of Gaunt (Henry V's grandfather) to Blanche, who was heiress to the estate. John made many additions to the building, including the construction of the Great Hall which was later used as a Court Room. The castle became one of the favourite residences of both John and his son, Henry Bolingbroke, who later became Henry IV.

Prince Henry was born in 1387 in a room in the Queen's Chamber, a part of the castle which, with the castle gatehouse had been restored by John of Gaunt in 1370. The 16 September, 1387 is the birth date favoured by today's historians, but visitors to Monmouth will observe that the date below the statue in Agincourt Square is 9 August, 1387.

Prince Henry of Monmouth.

Statue of Henry V on the front of the Shire Hall, Monmouth

Monmouth, at the time of the birth of Prince Henry, was recovering from the effects of the Black Death – a terrible plague which killed half of the population; carried by rats and fleas, it affected the whole of Britain.

In my imagination, I visualised Henry Bolingbroke, the eighteen year old Earl of Derby, returning from a meeting at Windsor and hurrying home to Monmouth Castle, where any day his young wife, Lady Mary, was due to give birth to their first child.

Near the end of his long ride, he spent the night at Ross-on-Wye and then continued the next morning shortly to reach the Wye, crossing near Goodrich Castle, where a ferry operated. To his delight, the friendly boatman, who was up to date with all the news, congratulated him on the birth of a son.

Old Ferry on the River Wye, below Goodrich Castle

Feeling in a generous mood, the young Earl of Derby, acted the proud father and gave the ferry and all its profits to the boatman and his descendants – a right that continued for several generations, until the ferry was made redundant by the construction of Kerne Bridge. According to Charles Heath, the deed granting the ferry to the ferryman, with the seal of Henry IV, was to be seen at Hill Court in 1799.

Mary was a young lass of sixteen years. She was the younger daughter and co-heiress of Humphrey de Bohun, who as the last male descendant of the de Bohuns, inherited the dignitaries and estates of the Earls of Hereford, Northampton and Essex. He had lived in splendour in Brecon Castle,which he enlarged and re-fortified in grand fashion. At his death in 1377 he was mourned by the local people as a true friend. His other daughter, Elinor, was married to Thomas Woodstock, younger son of Edward III and uncle of Henry Bolingbroke.

Mary had been married at the age of ten and this was in fact her second child, for she had previously given birth, at the age of twelve, to a son, but he did not survive very long. The proud parents decided that the new baby should be called Henry after his father.

Humphrey de Bohun is depicted in a stained glass window in Brecon Cathedral. He lived in splendour at Brecon Castle, which he enlarged and re-fitted in grand fashion.

He lived there for eleven years and is described as wise and generous, living at peace with his neighbours, granting charters to the town and bestowing alms and oblations on the church.

At his death in 1377, he was mourned as a true friend by the local people. His second daughter Mary had married Henry, Earl of Derby, who now became Lord of Brecknock and later Henry IV of England.

Monmouth Castle was the birthplace of Prince Henry, the son of Henry Bolingbroke. He was born in the castle gatehouse on 16 September, 1387.The castle was originally a timber fortress established by William Fitz-Osbern in 1067. It was later rebuilt in stone and in the fourteenth century came into the possession of the House of Lancaster through the marriage of John of Gaunt to Blanche, who was heiress to the estate. Monmouth Castle became a favourite residence of John of Gaunt who made many additions, including the Great Hall which in later times was used as a Court Room.

It was believed at that time by some people that young Henry would prove to fulfil an ancient prophecy. It foretold that a prince called Henry 'through the nobility of his character and the splendid greatness of his achievements will illumine the whole world with the rays of his glory.' King Richard II was fond of mentioning this prophecy to young Henry, for he firmly believed that he was indeed that prince.

The chamber in Monmouth Castle where, Prince Hal, was born was part of an upper storey in the Great Tower, 58 feet long by 24 feet wide and it was decorated with ornamented Gothic windows. Some of the remains of the Great Tower were still standing when Archdeacon Coxe came here in 1799 and described the ruins of the room where Prince Henry was born. He mentioned that about fifty years previously a considerable portion of the upper wall had fallen down with a loud crash, which alarmed the whole town.

Nearby stands the Great Castle House which was built in 1673 by the second Marquis of Worcester (who later became the 1st Duke of Beaufort) on the site of a thirteenth century round tower. He was so keen for his grandson to be born near the same spot as Henry V that he utilised the stone from the ruins of the great tower in which the birth took place. This impressive stone mansion has mullioned windows and inside are beautiful plaster ceilings decorated with foliage, flowers and fruit in three-dimensional relief. It is said that Cromwell's face can be seen in the patterns. However, it takes a vivid imagination to see it! In 1875 the house became the headquarters of the Royal Monmouthshire Engineers' Militia, the oldest non-regular unit in the British Army.

Castle House, Monmouth, was built in 1693 by the second Marquis of Worcester, on the site of a 13th century round tower. It was constructed of stone taken from the ruins of the building in which Prince Henry was born. In 1875 the house became the headquarters of the Royal Monmouthshire Engineers' Militia, the oldest non-regular unit in the British Army.

Mary, the young prince's mother, died at Peterborough Castle on July 4, 1394, at the age of 24, having given birth to three more sons and two daughters. These were: (1) Thomas, Duke of Clarence, born 1389, killed at Bauge in Anjou, March 22, 1421; (2) John, Duke of Bedford, born 1391, died at Rouen, September 14, 1435; (3) Humphrey, born 1391, died, it was supposed, by foul means, early in 1447; (4) Blanche, married to Louis, son of Rupert, King of the Romans; (5) Philippa, married to Eric, the thirteenth King of Denmark.

The infant Prince Henry was taken to Courtfield, just outside Monmouth, to be brought up by Lady Margaret, the wife of Sir John de Montacute and lady-in-waiting at Monmouth Castle. Her manor at Welsh Bicknor, six miles away was called Greenfield but was renamed Courtfield on account of Prince Henry spending his childhood here up to the age of about seven. His nurse was Joanna Waring, the daughter of the ferryman near Goodrich. She was rewarded for her work when the Prince became king, with an annual payment of £20.

Some historians have mistakenly referred to Lady Margaret as the Countess of Salisbury. She was in fact the daughter-in-law of the Earl of Salisbury and mother of the future Earl John de Montague, who was beheaded at Cirencester in 1400. Lady Margaret was also related to Prince Henry for they were both descended from Edward I.

An effigy of Lady Margaret can be seen in Welsh Bicknor Church. The Manor of Welsh Bicknor was retained by the descendants of Sir John and Lady Montacute and eventually descended to Margaret, daughter of George Plantagenet, brother of King Edward IV, and wife of Sir Richard Pole. Sir Richard and his lady were both beheaded in 1541.

Troy House on the south-east side of Monmouth, for five centuries kept in storage the sword that Henry used at Agincourt and also his supposed cradle – which is now in Windsor Castle, although its authenticity is somewhat dubious.

The household book of John of Gaunt provides some interesting glimpses of Prince Henry's education. An entry for February 1396 states that '4s. for seven books of grammar bought at London for the young Lord Henry,' and in the following years, '8d by the hand of Adam Gastron for harp-strings for the harp of the young Lord Henry.' In 1397, '12d was paid for a new scabbard and 1s 6d for three-quarters of an ounce of tissue of black silk for the sword of the young Lord Henry' – which showed that he took an interest in weapons at a very early age. The continued weakness of his health may be seen in the payment of a courier, who was once sent to inform his father that the prince was ill.

This monumental effigy can be seen inside Welsh Bicknor Church.

It is a sculpture of a lady dressed in a long gown and a fourteenth century headdress. There are angels at her pillow and a dog at her feet. This effigy represents Margaret Montacute, the wife of Sir John Montacute, whose father, by arresting Mortimer the usurper, helped to place the boy king Edward III on the throne. Lady Margaret, a lady-in-waiting at the court in Monmouth, brought up Prince Henry, following the death of his mother in 1394. It is not known how long Prince Henry was at Courtfield, but Lady Margaret died in 1395 so probably he would have left there when he was seven or eight. His nurse at Courtfield was Joanna Waring to whom he later left an annuity of £20.

This drawing shows the little fourteenth-century carved oak cradle in which the baby Prince Henry is said to have reposed whilst in the care of Lady Montague, the grand-daughter of Edward I at Courtfield. Constructed in oak it was slung between short strong posts surmounted by carved wood Falcon finials. The cradle is now in the museum at Kensington Palace, London.

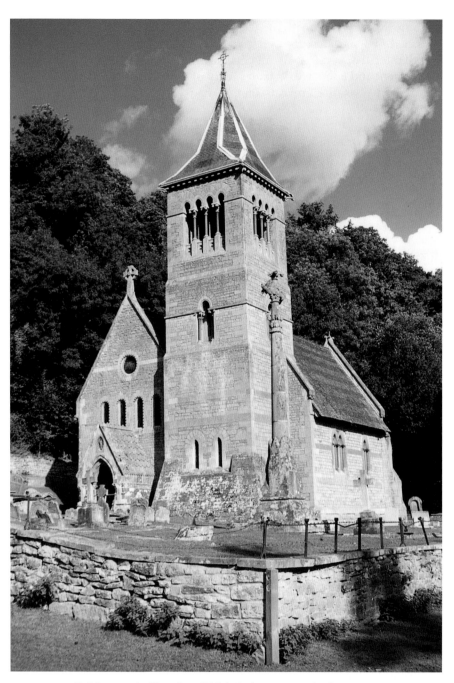

St Margaret's Church at Welsh Bicknor was rebuilt in 1858

Young Henry had just entered his twelfth year when his father was banished. He remained in England, probably under the care of his grandfather. But John of Gaunt died in the February following his son's banishment and a few weeks later Henry of Lancaster's estates were seized by the crown on the grounds that he had slandered the king, and was consorting with his enemies abroad.

Prince Henry accompanied King Richard to Ireland, and was sent to the castle of Trim in Meath, the ancient meeting-place of the Irish Parliament. He seems to have been kindly treated and received the honour of knighthood from the king's hands. He was then left behind in Ireland in company with his cousin, the young Duke of Gloucester, when Richard returned to England in July.

On August 18, Richard was made a prisoner and Prince Henry was immediately sent for, and brought to England in a ship provided by a citizen of Chester. Arriving at Chester, Henry met his father, whom he accompanied to London. On September 29, Richard, who was now in the Tower, signed a deed of abdication. Parliament met on the following day, and declared him to be deposed; on the same day the Duke of Lancaster was seated on the throne by the Archbishops of Canterbury and York.

Henry is said to have been created Prince of Wales by his father on the day of his coronation. An eye witness at the ceremony was Creton, a French chronicler, whose wise words proved to be correct:

> The King conferred on him the whole of the land of Wales; but I think he must confer it, if he will have it, for, in my opinion, the Welsh will on no account allow him to be their lord, for the sorrow, evil and disgrace which the English, together with his father, had brought upon King Richard.

The king subsequently granted to his 'most dear eldest son Henry, Prince of Wales, Duke of Cornwall, and Earl of Chester, the custody and rights of all the lands of heirs under age in the principality of Wales and the counties of Chester and Flynt', and also ordered him to be put in possession of the revenues of the duchy of Cornwall.

Henry was the fourth English Prince of Wales and he was heir to the vast possessions of John of Gaunt. He was also invested with the titles of Duke of Cornwall, Aquitaine, Lancaster, and Earl of Chester. At the time he was just twelve years and two months old, but two years later he would be fighting for his king and country in the battle of Shrewsbury.

Before long, negotiations were entered upon for his marriage and towards the end of the year a mission was sent to the king of France, proposing in general terms alliances between the two royal families. The proposal was rejected contemptuously.

The King of France knew of no King of England but his son-in-law Richard. Before many weeks were past, Richard was dead, leaving a virgin widow, Isabella of Valais. She was the eldest of the five daughters of Charles VI of France and was then in her thirteenth year. Henry lost no time in asking her hand for his eldest son. However, the demand was not welcome either to the French court, which was not disposed to recognise Henry's title, or to the young lady herself, who cherished a fond recollection of her husband. King Henry was later to win for himself, by a very rough wooing, a bride of the same house, the younger of Isabella's sisters.

Henry of Monmouth, Prince of Wales, 1399

A contemporary described Prince Henry as follows:

His head was round in shape, indicating wealth of judgement as well as wisdom, which is borne out further by the width of his forehead. He had a mass of smooth brown hair. His nose was straight and his face strikingly open. He had a florid complexion and an expression of great charm. His eyes were brown and shone as gently as a dove's when he was in a good humour, but flashed like a lion's when aroused. He had snow white teeth, conspicuously regular. His ears were well shaped and small. He had a dimple on his chin.

Ancient gateway of Queen's College, Oxford

There is a tradition that Prince Henry studied for a time at Queen's College, Oxford, under the care of his uncle, Henry Beaufort, whom we know to have been Chancellor of the University during the period 1397-8. Queen's College had been founded in 1341 by Robert Eglesfield under the auspices of Philippa, Queen of Edward III, and might therefore be considered a particularly appropriate residence for princes of the Plantagenet line. A room in the college over the gateway that fronts St. Edmund's Hall was long shown as having been occupied by Prince Henry. A Latin inscription over the gateway used to read:–

> Imperator Britanniae
> Triumpator Galliae
> Hostium rector et sui
> Henricus Quintus, hajus Collegii
> Olim magnus incola.

Translated:–

> 'Henry the fifth, all Britain's Lord
> Who conquered France beneath his sword,
> mastering his foes and his own soul,
> was entered on this college-roll,
> and here a little room had spun
> enough to house the mighty man'

His portrait was to be seen painted on the glass of the window, while a Latin inscription, which disappeared with the gateway in the 18th century, recorded the fact that 'Henry V, conqueror of his enemies and of himself, was once the great inhabitant of this little chamber.' The glass was eventually moved to the upper library.

In November 1401, half-way through his sixteenth year, Prince Henry was appointed to the civil and military command of the most disturbed part of the king's dominion. About six weeks later the men of Shropshire wrote to the Council complaining of the ravages of the Welsh rebels and requested that soldiers be sent to deal with the problems. At the age of sixteen, Prince Henry was in command of an army marching through Wales and his father, the kin, had issued a brief to the Lieutenants of Gloucestershire, Shropshire, Worcestershire and Herefordshire, directing them to put themselves at the command of his son, Henry, Prince of Wales.

Two days after the battle of Shrewsbury the king expressed his trust in the loyalty and prudence of his son, Henry, and gave him full power to amnesty, at his discretion, such persons concerned in the Glyndŵr rebellion as he might think fit, in the county of Chester and other places named.

With boyish enthusiasm, Prince Henry tackled the task of dealing with the Glyndŵr uprising. As far as he was concerned, he was the appointed Prince of Wales, and this struggle for power involving Prince Henry and Owain Glyndŵr lasted for about twelve years.

In April 1406, the Privy Council held a meeting at which the succession of the Prince of Wales to the throne was considered, as was also the subject of his lieutenancy in Wales, and of his power to amnesty rebels who were prepared to give their submission. Also at this time, the House of Commons asked the king to thank the prince for his diligence in the government of Wales, to which he had been appointed three years before. On April 5, the king renewed the appointment of the Prince as Lieutenant of Wales until November 11 of that year. Special authority was also confirmed upon him to admit rebels to grace on such terms as might be acceptable to the Prince and his counsellors.

The House of Commons, on June 7, voted an address of thanks to the Prince, which was to be forwarded to him in Wales. At the same time Parliament passed an Act declaring that the succession to the throne was in the Prince of Wales and the heirs-male of his body lawfully begotten, and, failing these, to the other sons of the king and their heirs in succession. Six months later this was amended by another Act, which abolished the restrictions to heirs-male.

In a brief session of Parliament during the same year (October 20 – November 21), the Prince again received public thanks. Later in the year, the king re-appointed Henry his Lieutenant in Wales for the fourth time. The appointment was twice more renewed – on December 27, 1407, and again on January 19, 1409.

Seven
The Battle of Shrewsbury

I am the Prince of Wales, and think not Percy
To share with me in glory any more.

William Shakespeare, Henry IV, Part One

rince Henry was now aged 16 and an ordnance of the king in Council at Westminster dated 7 March, 1403 confirms his appointment as Lieutenant of Wales and the Marches:

> The King to all whom it may concern, greeting.
> Know that, wishing to provide for the good government of the region of Wales, and of the Marches and parts adjacent thereto, and for resistance to the rebels who have contrary to their allegiance treasonably risen against us, and having full confidence in the fidelity and energy of our dearly beloved eldest son, Henry, Prince of Wales, we constitute the said Prince our Lieutenant in the said region of Wales.

Six weeks later the men of Shropshire wrote to the Council complaining of the ravages of the Welsh rebels, and asking that some men-at-arms and archers should be sent to protect them until the prince himself could come. They obviously had faith in the teenage Prince who had so recently been appointed to the civil and military command of the most disturbed part of the King's dominions.

In the Spring of that year, Prince Henry marched back into Wales with an army. They made their way to Owain's Sycharth estate and left it a heap of blackened, smouldering debris. The garden was devastated, orchards uprooted, walls thrown down and even the cluster of huts and houses, where the estate workers lived beneath the security of Sycharth's walls, were swept away. Henry then marched his men on to Glyndyfrdwy, which was also reduced to a battered pile, but failed to find Owain himself, who was now regarded by all his people as Lord of Wales. These two estates were now of course owned by John Beaufort, Earl of Somerset, having been awarded them by King Henry soon after Glyndŵr's uprising. No doubt he was not at all happy when he received news of the Prince's devastating actions.

On 15 May, Prince Henry wrote to his father from Shrewsbury:–

> We were lately informed that Oweyn de Glendourdy caused to assemble his force of rebels and other of his adherents, a great number, purposing to override and also to fight, if the English people should resist his purpose, and thus he boasted to his people; whereupon we took our people and went to a place of the said Oweyn, well built, which was his principal mansion called Saghern (Sycharth), where we supposed that we should have found him if he had been willing to have fought in the manner as he said; but upon our arrival there we found no one; hence we caused the whole place and many other houses of his tenants in the neighbourhood to be burnt, and then went directly to his other place of Glyndourdy to seek for him there. We caused a fine lodge in his park to be burnt, and all the country thereabout, and we lodged there at rest all that night ... and then we went into the commote of Dedirnyon (Edeirnion) in the county of Merioneth, and there we caused a fine well inhabited country to be burnt; and then we went into Powis, and in want of food for the horses we made our people carry oats with them...

However, the young Prince had his own problems for his men had not been paid and he was without money. His soldiers wanted to know when they would be paid; unless he had some money sent he could not remain where he was and he had already pawned his jewels.

From Shrewsbury on 30 May, he wrote to his father again:–

> ...And because that our soldiers desired to know if they will be paid for the third month of the present quarter, and tell us that they will not wait here unless they are soon paid their wages according to their indentures, we pray you very dearly that you will order our payment for the said month, or otherwise let us know, and to take order promptly for the safety of these marches, for the rebels hear every day if we are paid, and they know well that without payment we cannot continue; and they strive to raise all the forces of north Wales and of south Wales to over-ride and destroy the march and the counties adjoining thereto; and there is no resistance here, so they well can accomplish their malice; and when our men have retreated from us, it is necessary that we should by all means retreat into England, there to be disgraced for ever... And at present we have very great expenses and have made all the pawning we are able of our little jewels to destroy them, for two of our castles, Hardelagh (Harlech) and Lampadern (Aberystwyth) are besieged and have been for a long time, and we must rescue the march around us with the third body against the entry of the rebels.

The Prince added a postscript to emphasise the urgency of the matter:–

> And be pleased to be well advised that we have well and fully shown you the peril which may happen whatsoever thing may come hereafter if remedy be not sent in time.

Shrewsbury Castle was founded by Roger of Montgomery, but only the castle gateway dates back to his time. This fortress was often used as a base by Henry IV and his son Henry, Prince of Wales, during their campaigns against Owain Glyndŵr. It was first built by Roger of Montgomery, the Conqueror's Earl of Shrewsbury. He was the Conqueror's kinsman and adviser, who supplied part of the fleet which brought the Normans to England. He was given Shrewsbury and much of Shropshire as his reward. He also founded the abbey outside the city walls, where he lies in an unknown grave beneath the noble church.

On June 10, Richard Kingeston, the Archdeacon of Hereford and Dean of Windsor, wrote to the King from Hereford :–

> The Welsh rebels in great numbers have entered Archenfield, and there they have killed the inhabitants, and ravaged the country to the great dishonour of our King and the unsupportable damage of the country. We implore you to consider this very perilous and pitiable case and to pray to our sovereign Lord that he will come in his royal person or perhaps send some person with sufficient power to rescue us from the invasion of the rebels. Otherwise we will be utterly destroyed, which God forbid: whoever comes will as we are led to believe have to engage in battle, or will have a very severe struggle with the rebels. And for God's sake remember that honourable and valiant man, the Lord of Abergavenny, who is on the very point of destruction if he is not rescued.

The King was now facing a challenge from a new front, for the Percys had turned against him and gone over to the side of Owain Glyndŵr. They had also been joined by the band of Scots under Earl Douglas, whom they had taken prisoner at the battle of Homildon Hill.

The Earls of Northumberland and Worcester had renounced their allegiance to King Henry, charging him with perjury, because he had stated on his return from exile that he had come to claim, not the throne, but his own inheritance. Instead, he had imprisoned and murdered King Richard and had himself crowned. Also he had failed to carry out his promise that he would not to tax the clergy or people without the consent of Parliament. In addition he had not permitted free Parliamentary election and he had refused to pay the ransom requested by Owain Glyndŵr for Edmund Mortimer.

Sir Henry Percy (Hotspur), the eldest son of the Earl of Northumberland, had been a trusty lieutenant of Henry IV. He had served in Wales against Glyndwr and had been employed both in negotiations against the Scots and in military action against them. He felt himself to have been unjustly treated and to avenge his wrongs he formed an alliance with Owain Glyndŵr and with the Earl of Douglas on behalf of the King of Scotland.

Henry IV was actually on his way northwards to support the Percys against the Scots when the astounding news that the Percys of Northumberland had risen in revolt against him, was received on his arrival in Burton-on-Trent. He must have been astonished, for not only were the Percys his most faithful supporters, but they were also the most powerful of his friends, who had practically placed him on the throne. It would appear that the Percys were now marching towards the Welsh border, where by all accounts Glyndŵr and his army were to join them.

Owain's negotiations with the Percys had resulted in a plan that the Percys should make their way down from the north and join forces with Edmund Mortimer and himself for a march on London. But the hot-headed Hotspur, on reaching Chester, where he was joined by large numbers of men from that area, decided that he would take on King Henry single-handed, and accordingly ignored the agreed plan of campaign. His new plan was to capture the Prince of Wales at Shrewsbury, hold him hostage in the castle, and await the arrival of his father the Earl of Northumberland, who was raising an army in the north. The Welsh forces of Glyndŵr and Mortimer would also march to join them and they would then deal with the King once and for all.

On Saturday 21 July, Hotspur sent a message to Henry IV:–

> We do intend to prove with our own hands personally against thee, Henry,
> Duke of Lancaster, unjustly presuming and named King of England, without
> right of title, but only of thy guile.

Hotspur's bold plan failed because Henry IV heard of the revolt and immediately marched on Shrewsbury with 25,000 men and reached the town (and his son), just a few hours before Hotspur on July 29. The house of William Betton provided accommodation for Hotspur, while his 15,000 men set up camp at a spot about five miles to the north-west of Shrewsbury. Thomas Prestbury, the Abbot of Shrewsbury, was sent by the king to offer terms to Hotspur. But he refused to listen and instead sent the Earl of Worcester to offer insults to Henry.

Much to his dismay, Hotspur discovered that he had left his favourite sword behind at Berwick, and being very superstitious, he took this loss as a bad omen and exclaimed, "I perceive that my plough is drawing its last furrow, for a wizard told me in Northumberland that I should perish at Berwick, which I vainly interpreted as that town in the north."

This sword had been used by Hotspur to trace the outline of his hand on an oak panel in the old house at Berwick near the River Severn and the owners cherished this panel for centuries afterwards. A local prophecy maintained that if they lost this piece of wood then they would also lose their estate. In time the prophecy was fulfiled.

The royal army marched out of Shrewsbury in three divisions. Leading the van was the young Earl of Stafford and the two rival forces met at a flat fertile tableland known as Haytleyfield (later called Battlefield). There was a stretch of growing peas between them and a gentle slope behind, giving Hotspur's army some slight advantage. The two armies numbered 40,000 in all and were full of the highest and noblest blood in England. Both sides were equipped with long bows. Hotspur had recruited his archers in Cheshire, which was a renowned area for bowmen.

Large numbers of Welshmen, believing that Richard II was still alive, had flocked to the standard of Lord Archibald Douglas, whom Hotspur had previously captured at Homildon, and was now ready to fight alongside his captor. The Welshmen wore Richard's badge – the white hart – upon their shields and tunics.

The Abbot of Shrewsbury, Thomas de Prestbury, supported by John Prophete, dean of St Chad's and clerk of the Privy Seal, rode out of the royal army towards the forces of Percy and offered on behalf of the King, redress of grievances, pardon and peace. Hotspur it is said was inclined to accept, but his uncle, the Earl of Worcester scornfully rejected the peace offer.

The Battle of Shrewsbury

At mid-day King Henry threw his mace into the air as a signal and the battle commenced. Hotspur's side opened the action with a flight of deadly arrows from their Cheshire archers. They hissed through the air to descend like a rain of hail upon the king's troops, who according to Walsingham, 'fell like leaves in autumn, every one struck a mortal man.' Hotspur's horse and spearmen then charged, the Royal Standard was overthrown and the Earl of Stafford, Constable of England, fell dead beside the fallen standard and its bearer – Sir Walter Blout.

Henry Bolingbroke rode backwards and forwards through his frightened army, to show that he was still unhurt and rallied his troops to a fresh resistance and they made a spirited advance – with their superior numbers.

An arrow whistled across the cheek of Prince Henry, and, although bleeding profusely, he bravely refused to withdraw from the field, fearing that his men might lose heart. This was the young Prince's first battle and he would rather die than stain his reputation as a soldier by taking flight.

Douglas sought all over the field for the King and three times he slew figures wearing the royal armour, but no sooner had he killed one, than another met his astonished gaze.

Knowing that his life would be eagerly sought, the King had cunningly clad several of his knights in the same distinctive dress. So on five occasions, Hotspur's men thought with triumph that King Henry had been vanquished. At the head of a band of specially picked horsemen, Hotspur rode into the thickest of the fighting again and again, endeavouring to cleave a passage to the king's own person. Nearly suffocating in his armour from his exertions, Hotspur for an instant raised his visor for air. At that moment a bowman marked his plume and crest and sent his arrow flying to strike him in the face and pass through his brain. He fell dead, surrounded by the enemy and in sight of the King, just as the summer sun sank beneath the ridge of hills to the west and it must have seemed as though with his death the light of day itself faded.

According to Shakespeare, it was Prince Hal who struck down Hotspur, but this was probably theatrical thinking for it is not known who in fact killed him as no one actually saw him fall.

Hotspur's men had fought gallantly despite being overwhelmed by sheer weight of numbers. When the news of his death was known the wearied ranks turned and fled. Like sheep without a shepherd they were scattered – each seeking safety in flight. Many fell from exhaustion and wounds or were cut to pieces by the pursuing soldiers before they could reach a place of safety. Large numbers fled in the direction of Wem in the north while others ran to the wooded ridge of Houghmond in the east.

Haytleyfield, where the battle of Shrewsbury was fought, is a short distance from Shrewsbury and the site is now known as Battlefield.

The King's army with their superior numbers were now winning the day. But the slaughter continued until sunset. Men lay down in mixed heaps, weary, beaten and bleeding. It was the bloodiest battle that England had ever known, with 4,600 of the king's men killed and wounded. Of Hotspur's men, five thousand were slain and this figure included two hundred knights and gentlemen of Cheshire, thirty-six of whom, it is said, were slain by King Henry with his own hand.

The face of the rising moon was veiled by a blackness which lasted about an hour, a great shadow being cast upon it – which frightened many of the English men-at-arms and they ceased pursuing the foe and gathered together to watch the portent and asking, "What could it mean ?" It was, of course, an eclipse of the moon.

The battle had lasted three hours, and it had been fought with a fierceness and a slaughter hitherto unequalled. An area three miles in length, extending from near Great Berwick to Houghmond Hill was covered with the bodies of the slain.

A large number of Hotspur's followers were taken prisoner. Amongst them was Earl Douglas, who was pardoned, and the Earl of Worcester, Sir Richard Venables and Sir Richard Vernon, who were beheaded at Shrewsbury two days later. Worcester's head was sent to London Bridge, but his body was buried in the Church of St Chad's at Shrewsbury.

Douglas, wounded and weary, endeavoured to escape from the battlefield but was captured on the wooded slopes of Houghmond Hill. He was later unconditionally released. Thomas Percy was tried for treason and executed with many other knights suffering the same fate. A great pit was dug 126 feet wide and 65 feet long and the multitude of dead were buried inside it.

It is said that when Henry looked on the corpse of Hotspur, he wept, but within a day or so he had overcome his grief. Hotspur's body was first buried by his nephew, Thomas Neville, Lord Furnival, at Whitchurch, with honours, but, following many wild rumours floating around that Harry Hotspur had escaped from the battle, Henry had his body exhumed and taken to Shrewsbury.

Here it was rubbed with salt and then exhibited between two millstones near the pillory in the market place, with two armed men standing guard over it. Later the head was chopped off and sent to York to decorate the gate to the north – which led to Percy's own country. The body was quartered and the pieces sent to London, Bristol, Newcastle-on-Tyne, and Chester. There they remained until November, when the king ordered that the head and quarters should be given up to Hotspur's widow, Lady Elizabeth Percy, who finally interred her husband's remains in York Minster, at the right side of the altar.

This stone cross on Pride Hill. Shrewsbury, was erected to replace a wooden one installed there in July 1903 to celebrate the 500th anniversary of the battle of Shrewsbury.

The Earl of Worcester, Sir Richard Venables and Sir Richard Vernon were beheaded on 23 July at Shrewsbury. Worcester's body was interred in the Abbey Church, whilst his head was sent to London Bridge.

After the battle, King Henry rode north to treat with Northumberland, Hotspur's father, who had delayed his start and never joined the battle. He begged the King for his pardon, which was granted. Henry then returned with satisfaction to London, but young Prince Hal remained in Shrewsbury, for his wound was troublesome and he had a fierce fever.

Shrewsbury is built in a loop of the Severn, which gives it an island-like situation. It is a fascinating old town to visit but the pronunciation of its name always causes some confusion for it is 'Shrosebury' and not 'Shroosebury'. In ancient times it was known as Pengwern, being the seat of Cynddelyn, a sixth-century Powys chieftain who is mentioned in the poetry of Llywarch Hen. St Chad's Church is supposed to occupy the site of the Llys (palace) of the old Princes of Powys, prior to Saxon times. In later years the town became known as Amwythig and in the Domesday Book it is called Sciropisberrie.

It was in Shrewsbury that in 1283, Dafydd, the last of the Welsh Princes, was hung, drawn and quartered on Pride Hill at High Cross, after being sentenced by a Parliament summoned in haste by Edward I. Dafydd's head was then sent to the Tower of London, where it was crowned with ivy and placed alongside the head of his brother, Llywelyn the Last. One hundred and twenty years later the body of Hotspur was drawn and quartered at the same location. In July 1903, a temporary wooden cross was erected on the summit of Pride Hill to celebrate the 500th anniversary of the battle of Shrewsbury and it was later replaced by one fashioned in stone.

After visiting Shrewsbury I made my way to Battlefield, on the outskirts of the town, to see the church which was erected over the great pit where the dead were buried. It was initially built as a memorial chapel with financial aid from the King three years after the battle. Construction was undertaken by Roger Ive, priest of Leaton and rector of Allbright Hussey, which was replaced by this new church at Battlefield. Henry endowed the church with a college dedicated to Mary Magdalene and requested that masses be said at all times for the souls of the dead who lay in their thousands in the great pit beneath the church. Traces of the priests' cells have been found in the churchyard and a filled-in doorway in the wall of the church was once used by them.

The church was rebuilt in the Perpendicular style in 1460 and it consists of a square, embattled and pinnacled tower and a nave with an open-work roof. Restoration was undertaken in 1862 and the fine gargoyles representing knights and men-at-arms were renewed in memory of the men who fought in the battle.

Battlefield Church, is built over a massive pit in which thousands of soldiers killed in the battle of Shrewsbury were buried. It is quite a large Perpendicular building, the nave and chancel being continuous with a crenellated tower at the west end. It was repaired and restored in 1860. Of interest inside is a quaint wooden figure of the Virgin Mary with the dead Christ on her lap.

ST. MARY MAGDALENE, BATTLEFIELD.

THIS CHURCH IS MAINTAINED BY THE REDUNDANT CHURCHES FUND, WITH MONEY PROVIDED BY PARLIAMENT AND THE CHURCH OF ENGLAND, AND BY THE GIFTS OF THE PUBLIC. ALTHOUGH NO LONGER USED FOR REGULAR WORSHIP, IT REMAINS A CONSECRATED BUILDING.

This statue of Henry IV in his battle armour stands in a niche over the west window. His crown sits firmly on his head and he wears a dagger at his hip. He gazes towards the distant ridge of Houghmond to which many of Hotspur's men fled.

Inside (on the hammer beams) can be seen shields which display the coats of arms of the knights who took part in the battle. On the north side they represent Henry IV, Earl of Dunbar, Sir Hugh Stanley, Sir John Cockayne, Sir Nicholas Gousel, Sir Hugh Mortimer, Sir Hugh Sirley, Sir Robert Malveysin, Sir Madoc Kynaston, Sir Richard Sandford, Sir Edward de Rowson and Sir Francis Bromley. On the south side are those of Henry, Prince of Wales, Sir John Clifton, Sir Walter Blout, Sir Robert Gousel, Sir Thomas Wendesley, Sir John Massey, Sir Reginald Mottershed , Sir Jenkin Hanmer and Sir Richard Hussey.

A statue of King Henry IV in his battle armour stands in a niche over the east window. His crown is on his head and he wears a dagger at his hip. He gazes towards the distant ridge of Houghmond to which many of Hotspur's men fled.

Many years ago, a drain was being dug under the walls of the church and the workmen revealed the edge of the huge pit, exposing piles of bones in the mass grave. It is significant that this is the only church in England that serves as a war memorial.

When the Duke of Wellington returned to the site of the battle of Waterloo, he apparently exclaimed "They have ruined my battlefield!" Well, the same thing could be said today of the site of the battle of Shrewsbury, for it has also been disfigured. A railway embankment carrying the branch line from Shrewsbury to Whitchurch has cut it in half. When the two armies faced each other here in 1403, it was a field of growing peas.

The name of Owain Glyndŵr has been blackened by a tradition that he cowardly watched the battle of Shrewsbury from the branches of a tall oak on the Welsh road from Shrewsbury and made no attempt to strike at Henry from the rear. Well, if anyone did watch the battle from the Shelton Oak, it certainly wasn't Owain Glyndŵr, for at that time he was a hundred miles away in Carmarthen. He was also totally ignorant of the movements of Henry Percy, whose defeat at Shrewsbury was disastrous to the cause of the Welsh. After losing all hope of assistance from his northern ally, Owain found it necessary to enter negotiations with the French which did not prove very effective.

In the grounds of Shelton Oak Priory near the Oswestry Road once stood a massive tree known as the Shelton Oak. There is a tradition that Owain Glyndŵr watched the progress of the battle of Shrewsbury from its branches. They say that he sat high in the tree and looked across the flooded Severn to the low lying ground beneath Houghmond Hill. The tree was 42 feet in girth and hollow. In later years it was referred to as Glyndŵr's Oak. As late as 1824 it was still standing and described 'as much decayed with a hollow at the bottom sufficient to hold with ease half a dozen persons...' However there is no historical evidence that Owain was even in the vicinity of Shrewsbury at this time. It is more likely that he was attacking castles in Carmarthenshire, over one hundred miles away.

In early July, Owain took Llandovery Castle and then marched on Llandeilo Fawr. Then, instead of heading towards Brecon, as was expected, he turned west and continued to Dryslwyn. His forces tried to take Carreg Cennen Castle, but only succeeded in inflicting severe damage on its walls.

Standing in solitary grandeur on an isolated limestone crag one hundred metres above the River Cennen, this castle is a splendid sight, particularly when seen in moonlight or swept by a wild storm. Its history stretches back into the realms of legend for it is said that it was once the home of Urien, Lord of Is-Cennen reputed to be one of King Arthur's Knights of the Round Table. The ruins of the present day castle date from the time of Edward II and its walls are aligned to the cardinal points of the compass. Surprisingly built without a keep, its most fascinating feature is a long corridor lit by slits in the cliff face, leading for fifty metres to reach a spring which served the garrison during a siege and is now used by visitors as a wishing well.

Owain's forces found this castle a very hard nut to crack and even laid siege to it for more than a year in an attempt to starve the garrison into submission. On 5 July, John Scudamore, the Constable of the castle, wrote to John Fairford, the Receiver at Brecknock:

> He (Owain) lay last night at Dryslwyn with Rhys ab Gruffydd, and there I was and spoke to him upon Wales and prayed for a safe conduct under his seal, to send home my wife and her mother and their company and he would none grant me.

Owain reached Carmarthen on 5 July, and the following day he set fire to the town and killed fifty men. He destroyed the title deeds and documents of the Priory as well as others deposited in the town. Next day the castle was surrendered to him by the Constable. Glyndŵr then moved on to take Llanstephan and Newcastle Emlyn.

That night Richard Kyngeston, the Archdeacon of Hereford and also a royal chaplain received the news of the fall of Carmarthen. He immediately sat down and wrote to King Henry to come at great haste. His letter ended with the following postscript:-

> For God's Love my liege, Lord, think on yourself, and your estate, or by troth all is lost else; but and ye come yourself with haste, all other will follow after. On Friday last, Carmarthen town is taken and burnt and the castle yolden by Ro. Wygmor and the castle Emlyn is yolden, and slain of Carmarthen more than fifty persons. Written in right haste on Sunday; and I cry your mercy and put me in your high grace that I write so shortly; for by my troth that I owe you, it is needful.

Carreg Cennen Castle stands in solitary grandeur on the top of a limestone crag rising one hundred metres above the valley. It has been described as the most romantic castle in Wales and it is indeed a very impressive sight, particularly when seen in moonlight or swept by a wild storm. In July 1403 Owain Glyndŵr's forces laid siege to the castle and surrounded it for more than a year. They inflicted severe damage on its walls, but failed to gain possession. In the cliff below the castle is a cave known as Ogof Dinas (Castle Cave). Many years ago a local farmer claimed to have entered it and found the sleeping figure of Owain Llawgoch – waiting like Arthur to be summoned to aid his country in a time of great danger (Owain Llawgoch is sometimes confused with Owain Glyndŵr).

Newcastle Emlyn was attacked by Owain Glyndŵr in 1403

Laugharne Castle in West Wales

After the fall of Carmarthen, Owain proceeded westwards to St Clears and Laugharne, but a large detachment of his army (consisting of 700 of his men) was defeated in this area on the 12th July by the Lord of Carew.

During this campaign it is said that Owain paid a visit to a bard called Hopcyn ap Thomas ab Einion of Ynystawe, He consulted him on his likely destiny and was told by the old man that he would be captured between Gower and Carmarthen. Owain, being a very superstitious man, immediately left the area so that there was no chance of the prophecy being fulfilled.

In August, Henry IV was at Pontefract Castle and he wrote to the sheriffs of thirty-five shires commanding:-

> All knights, esquires and yeomen of those counties who, by grant of King Edward III, the late King Edward late Prince of Wales, or the king's father, confirmed by the king, or of the king himself yearly take any fees, wages or annuities of the king or one of his livery or retinue, shall under pain of forfeiting such fees etc. and all else which they may, cease every excuse and hasten to draw towards the town of Worcester, every man well furnished and arranged as his estate demands.

By 8 September, 1403, the King reached Worcester and prepared for his third invasion of Wales. With his army he rode via Hereford, Brecon and Llandovery to reach Carmarthen. But he met no opposition and by October he had returned to Hereford leaving Carmarthen Castle under the command of the Earl of Somerset. But it was soon retaken by the Welsh.

In November a French fleet commanded by Jean d' Espagne sailed to the North Wales coast and tried to take Caernarfon Castle but failed. Henry IV received notification of their intentions in a letter sent by the Constable of Chester:

> ...Robert Parys, the Deputy Constable of Caernarvon Castle, has informed us through a woman, for neither man nor woman dare carry letters on account of the rebels of Wales, whom Owen Glyndŵr, with the French and all his other power, is raising up to assault the town and castle of Caernarvon...And in the castle there are not in all more than twenty-eight fighting men which is too small a force, for eleven of the abler men, who were there at the last siege of the place are dead...

One of Owain's most bloodthirsty battles was fought on a hill to the east of Cowbridge. It became known as Stallington which in due course was changed to Stalling Down and is also known as Bryn Owain. The great Roman highway along the coast of Glamorgan runs over this hill where the forces of Glyndŵr and Henry IV once fought a most violent battle.

The two opposing armies met in a ravine running at right-angles and called Pant-y-Wenal (The Swallows' Hollow). Henry IV and his 34,000 men had previously set up camp on Kingshill to await the arrival of Glyndwr and his French allies.

Aided by men from the hills of Glamorgan, Owain inflicted an appalling defeat on his Anglo-Norman enemies and the battle, which lasted eighteen hours, was said to have been so terrible that 'the blood was up to the fetlocks of the horses.'

One of Owain's lieutenants during this battle was Cadwgan Lord of Glyn Rhondda, who led the men of Glamorgan waving his battle axe wildly in the air. Owain is said to have shouted across to him, "Llyfna a dy Fwyall, Cadwgan !" – "Harrow them with thy battle axe Cadwgan!"

Cadwgan lived at Aberochwy at the confluence of the Farch brook with the Rhondda, near the settlement now called Treorchy. For the remainder of his life he was known as Cadwgan 'of the battle axe.'

Stalling Down, near Cowbridge in Glamorgan, is also known as Bryn Owain and it is the site of a long and bloodthirsty battle fought between the forces of Owain Glyndŵr and Henry IV. It lasted eighteen hours and Owain inflicted an appaling defeat on his Anglo-Norman enemies.

In 1896 an oak plank was prised up in the floor of the south chapel of Llanblethian Church. A flight of stone steps was revealed leading down into a crypt with a groined roof. Inside the crypt was found three hundred male skeletons, laid one on top of the other. The crypt measures seventeen feet long by about fifteen feet wide and it was lit by three small openings which were covered up with earth on the outside. It is arched with stone from east to west and at the crown of the arch it is seven feet high.

There were no signs of coffins nor any clue of the date when the bones were laid there. They were subsequently removed and deposited in one large grave in the churchyard. One theory put forward to explain the existence of three hundred male skeletons in this crypt was that a great battle may have taken place long ago in the neighbourhood and the bodies of the slain were hurriedly deposited here. Such a battle of course took place about three miles away, in 1403, on Stalling Down Common, otherwise known as Bryn Owain.

It is relevant that in the clerks' pew is a defaced inscription to the effect that this church was the burial place of the Sweeting family *before the war with Owen Glyndŵr*.

146

East and West Orchard Castles, near St Athans, were built by the Berkrolles family to defend two celebrated orchards one of which was once visited by Henry I. A story is told of how Owain once came to East Orchard Castle disguised as a French gentleman and accompanied by Sir Edmund Mortimer, dressed as a servant, in order to ascertain the feelings of the owner about his cause. Sir Lawrence Berkrolles spoke violently of Owain and expressed his wish to have him in his clutches. He commented that his guest "might be lucky enough to see the great Owain Glyndŵr brought to the castle as a prisoner, for he was known to be in the neighbourhood and my tenants are searching for him everywhere." The next morning on his departure Owain produced his seal, which so frightened Sir Lawrence that he was struck dumb and remained so for the rest of his life. He probably had a stroke which left him semi-paralysed.

Inside St Athan's Church is a fine canopied tomb with two elaborately sculptured figures representing a knight and his lady. These were members of the Berkrolles family, but by local people they were known as the king and queen of East Orchard.

There is a tradition that Owain Glyndŵr presided at an Eisteddfod held at Pen Rhys, above Llwyn y Pia in Glyn Rhondda, to celebrate Glyndŵr's success at the battle of Stalling Down. The story is preserved in the name of Pantsteddfa Farm to the south of Ystrad and Owain at the time is believed to have been based at Llantrisant, about 8 miles away. It is significant that many of his followers, led by Cadwgan, came from the Rhondda Valley. The remote Cistercian cell at Pen Rhys was dissolved by Henry V in about 1415 as a punishment to the monks for supporting Glyndŵr.

The defeated English army retreated through Cardiff hotly pursued by the Welsh and French allies. The weather was appaling and the flooded rivers made their journey very hazardous.

Shakespeare had Owain Glyndŵr say:

> Three times hath Henry Bolingbroke made head
> Against my power; thrice from the banks of the Wye
> And sandy-bottomed Severn, have I sent
> Him bootless home, and weather-beaten back.

By the end of 1403, Glyndŵr's army had increased considerably and he attacked all the castles along the coast from Beaumaris to Cardiff, and only three castles proved too strong to be taken. But Owain now knew that it would not be long before he was was in complete control of Wales.

Eight
A Triumphant Year

We have now reached the year of Glyndŵr's triumph, the year which raised him from the footing of a local rebel and formidable outlaw to that of a ruling prince.

Prof. J.E. Lloyd

In January 1404, the English Parliament met and criticised the King for making severe financial mistakes, particularly in regard to the cost of the war in Wales. They decided to formally place Prince Henry in charge of the operation in Wales to defeat Owain Glyndŵr. Henry was given the assistance of Edward, Duke of York, and Thomas, Earl of Arundel. However, the young prince was not provided with any of the money which he needed so badly.

The following letter dated 21 April was sent to Henry IV from Shrewsbury:–

> Most excellent and mighty Lord, we humbly beseech your highness that you may hear how your loyal lieges of your county of Salop are in great doubt and despair from day to day at the malice (and mischief) which your Welsh rebels and their adherents are purposing to do and sooner or later will do with all their might in your said county, threatening your said lieges with the destruction of their goods and chattels... Most excellent lord, may it please you to show grace and favour to your said lieges, and to send them some of the men-at-arms and archers who have come into these parts with our most redoubted lord the Prince. Your said rebels and the French, knowing that this county is less well quartered than your other counties adjoining your marches of Wales, were intent on a 'chevauchee' into your said county before the coming of our lord the Prince... Most mighty lord, a third of your said county has been destroyed and devastated by your said rebels, and your lieges formerly living there have left to gain their meat and sustenance elsewhere in your realm.

In April, the Bristol ship masters were ordered to set sail to the bay of Cardigan to deliver provisions to the castles of Cardigan, Aberystwyth (Lampadarn) and Caernarfon. At the end of the month Prince Henry at last obtained agreement for reinforcements and 'some' money from the Council. It was decided that he should have in his service five hundred men-at-arms and two thousand archers for three weeks, and for the following three weeks, three hundred men-at-arms and two thousand archers.

A force commanded by Richard Beauchamp, Earl of Warwick, and nephew of the Lord of Abergavenny, was sent by the King into Monmouthshire in August. It would seem that he came into the county over the pass of Bwlch and fought a battle against Owain's men at Mynydd Cwmdu near Tretower on the eastern edge of Breconshire. Things did not go well for Owain on this occasion for his banner was captured and he nearly fell into enemy hands himself. Owain fell back into the Lordship of Usk and pursued Beauchamp to turn the tables in a hard fought battle.

On the outskirts of Monmouth is the conical hill of Craig y Dorth, where Glyndŵr's men later caught up with Richard Beauchamp. On this spur of the Trellech ridge, overlooking the Trothy Valley, above the village of Mitchell Troy, they gained a victory and managed to push the English forces to the very walls of Monmouth town.

On May 10 Owain sent from Dolgellau his chancellor, Gruffydd Yonge, Archdeacon of Merionydd, and his wife's brother, John Hanmer, as ambassadors to the French court. The treaty was signed at Paris on July 14 by James de Bourbon and Count de la Marche on behalf of Charles VI. The alliance does not appear to have been of much advantage, though the French forces reached Caernarfon more than once. In a letter of Reynolde de Boyldon, an officer of Conwy Castle, addressed to Sir Roger de Bresey, the Constable of Chester, it is stated that:

> The Frenchmen were makyn all the ordinance that thae mae or can for to assaele the towne of Carnaruan, in ale the haste that thae mae, knowin wel that the towne is more febil nowe then hyt was the last tyme that thae wer befurehyt, for as muche as a hepe o the beste that wer in Carnaruan that tyme bene-got betaghte setin; and as hyt seemethe to me hyt wer nedeful than thae had helpe in haste tyme. This letter was wrytyn in grete haste at Conwaye, the XXVJ daye of Fevuerzer, 1404.

Aberystwyth Castle fell, and then Owain captured Harlech, after a siege lasting several months, during which time the garrison had been reduced to twenty-one sick and starving men. He had tried three times to take this well defended stronghold and now decided to make it his headquarters. During the next four years he lived here in almost royal state with his wife, daughter, grandchildren and Sir Edmund Mortimer.

Owain was now in control of most of Wales. Only eight castles around the edge of North Wales were still held by the English. These were Caernarfon, Beaumaris, Conwy, Denbigh, Flint, Rhuddlan, Oswestry and Welshpool.

Craig y Dorth is a conical hill just outside Monmouth in Gwent. Two fields known locally as Upper Battlefield and Lower Battlefield, mark the location where Glyndŵr defeated an English force led by Richard Beauchamp, Earl of Warwick. The English soldiers were pursued to the gates of Monmouth.

The ruins of Aberystwyth Castle stand beside the original building of the town's university, the establishment of which would have been the fulfilment of one of Owain Glyndŵr's dreams.

During my travels in the footsteps of Owain Glyndŵr, I stayed one night in the Castle Hotel, which is directly opposite the gatehouse to Harlech Castle. Nearby, is a bronze figure of Bendigeidfran, bearing the body of his nephew Gwern, 'symbolising the sorrowful burden that love can be.' The significance of this Mabinogion tale is that there is a tradition that a lonely tower stood on this crag in ancient times. It was known as 'Twr Bronwen' – the residence of Bronwen – the white bosomed sister of 'Bran the Blessed,' and daughter of Llyr, Duke of Cornwall. This story is a lament over the folly and carnage of war. Bronwen, sister of Bendigeidfran, the King of Britain, departs from his court at Harlech to marry the King of Ireland. Their son, the boy King Gwern, is killed in the war which follows.

There is also a tradition that Maelgwyn Gwynedd built a castle here in the sixth century, as a place of refuge and about three hundred years later, the site was known as Caer Collwyn – 'the fortress of Collwyn,' after Collwyn ap Tango, who lived here in about 877. As head of one of the North Wales tribes, he was Lord of Y Gest and Eivionydd. His fortress, if it did exist, would, of course, have been more of a fortified camp than a stone castle as we know it today.

This striking bronze sculpture by Ivor Roberts-Jones RA was commissioned by the Welsh Arts Council and erected here in 1984.

Harlech Castle was captured by Owain Glyndŵr in 1404 after sickness and starvation had reduced the castle garrison to twenty-one men.

Certainly there are no signs of any earlier castle than the present one, which was built during the reign of Edward I as one of his ring of fourteen massive stone fortresses, designed to subjugate the Welsh during the last quarter of the thirteenth century.

This impressive fortress is magnificently situated on a rocky promontory, nearly two hundred feet above the green flats of Morfa Harlech (Harlech March) and the distant sea. It took seven years to build and the materials were delivered mainly by boats to a harbour which was at one time situated directly below the castle. Limestone, for example, was brought from Anglesey and Caernarfon and iron was conveyed from Chester.

The accounts for the project are still preserved in the Public Record Office and from them we can learn that 227 masons, 30 smiths, 22 carpenters and 546 labourers were employed here. The total cost was £58,392 9s 7d and the castle was completed by its builder, James of St George, a master mason from Savoy, in 1290. He was appointed as the first Constable of the castle and died at his Flintshire Manor of Mostyn in about 1309.

When Harlech Castle was captured by Owain Glyndŵr in 1404, the constable was William Hunte, who attempted to make a treaty with Owain's rebels, but he and two yeomen were seized. By January, pestilence and desertion had reduced the garrison to a mere twenty-one men (five Englishmen and sixteen Welshmen). In February, Owain himself had arrived on the scene and he managed to persuade the dispirited garrison to surrender the castle in payment of a sum of money.

I tried to picture the castle as it would have appeared in Glyndŵr's time, with just a few dwellings nearby, for the town of Harlech has largely grown up during the last three hundred years. An exhibition inside the castle tells the story of the castle's construction and the history of its occupation and final abandonment.

Owain and his family established their quarters in the great gatehouse, which contained the main living rooms of the castle where the Constable had previously resided. Edmund Mortimer and his family moved into the south-east tower, which still bears his name. For the next three years this was to be Owain's official headquarters and family home.

As I wandered around these noble ruins, I gave my imagination free rein and imagined myself standing where the great Owain Glyndŵr himself had once stood. In the Great Hall I conjured up his soldiers taking their meals and passing their leisure time there. Moving on to the adjoining chapel I pictured Owain and his family, giving thanks to God for the victories to date and praying for a successful outcome to the uprising.

High on the battlemented walls, I gazed across the green foreshore of Morfa Harlech and Traeth Bach, which in Glyndŵr's time was washed by the sea. Below now is a road, railway and a cluster of houses, a caravan park, school, playing fields and golf course. The whole area is now bounded by the grass covered humps of sand dunes, whilst the sea is half-a-mile away.

At one time the waves must have dashed high against the rocks at the foot of the castle and a once heavily-fortified stairway descends two hundred feet down the west side of the castle rock. It was built to provide access to the water gate and the harbour to which ships once brought essential supplies. There was a landing stage to which boats could be moored, and the stairway cut into the solid rock, covered with a natural arch, led up to the courtyard. I gazed across Tremadoc Bay, with the whole of the Llyn Peninsula before me and picked out Criccieth Castle standing proud. To the east rose the high craggy mountains of Snowdonia, gently bathed in the warm glow of the setting sun. Returning to the gatehouse I pictured Owain and his family residing there and imagined roaring fires in the now empty fireplaces, providing meagre heat in these rooms during the misery of a long cold winter.

The Great Gatehouse of Harlech Castle in which Owain Glyndŵr and his family took up residence in 1404.

For three years Harlech Castle became Owain's capital and he used it as his family residence and also held his parliament at this location. It is said to have been convened in a building in the town known as Ty Mawr (Big House), which survived until the late 19th century. The ruins were then demolished and two new houses appropriately named Ty Mawr and Glyndŵr were built on the site.

From Harlech I travelled south to Machynlleth, in order to renew my acquaintance with the location where Owain summoned his first Welsh Parliament. Situated in Maengwyn Street, the original building was a modest half-timbered house, which eventually collapsed and was replaced by the present building, now known as the Owain Glyndŵr Institute. It certainly incorporates remains of the former building and was erected in honour of this fifteenth century Welsh statesman. Inside is a fascinating exhibition which tells the story of Owain Glyndŵr's uprising and I found it a moving experience to visit the place from which, for a brief time, Wales was ruled as an independent country.

Parliament House in Maengwyn Street was built in the sixteenth century on the site where Owain Glyndŵr called the first Welsh Parliament. The original building was a modest half-timbered house which eventually collapsed and was replaced by the present building erected in 1912 by David Davies MP in honour of Owain Glyndŵr. Today, Parliament House is surrounded by a complex of buildings known as Canolfan Owain Glyndŵr which house an Owain Glyndŵr exhibition and the local Tourist Information Centre.

Owain Glyndŵr held his first Parliament in Machynlleth

Having successfully repulsed Henry IV, for the time being at least, Owain decided that Machynlleth was the most convenient meeting-place for representatives to attend from all parts of Wales. He summoned from every cantref four principal persons. There were even representatives from Scotland, France and Spain present and this Parliament was very different from the Council that had been called by Llywelyn the Great two centuries before. That had only been attended by princes, whereas Owain's Parliament was really an imitation of the English one.

In a characteristic lawyer's search for precedent, Glyndŵr modelled his Parliament on firm foundations. In the 10th century Hywel Dda had temporarily united the warring tribes of Wales under his rule. He had codified and improved Welsh law and set up the rudiments of a national Parliament. Owain wisely took up this concept.

The only English King (between the Conquest and the reign of Henry VIII) who had summoned members from Wales to his Parliaments was Edward II. In 1322 when he was at the very height of his powers, twenty-four representatives were summoned from South Wales and twenty-four from North Wales. His last Parliament was held in 1326 and the three counties of North Wales were represented by eighteen Welshmen and their boroughs by six Englishmen.

Owain's intention was that his Parliament would discuss matters concerning the welfare of the realm and, by united and peaceful action, to weld the whole of Wales into one solid state that was at peace within its own borders and governed by its own laws and statutes. It was here at Machynlleth that Owain Glyndŵr was crowned Prince of Wales in a colourful ceremony that probably took place in the open air.

Now bearing the royal title Owinus Dei Gratia Princeps Wallia ('Owain by the grace of God Prince of Wales'), he was treated by foreign potentates as sovereign of an independent country. He had his own flag, Great Seal, Privy Seal and his courts of law. Undoubtedly, he was a diplomat and a statesman, who wrote letters to other rulers and sent ambassadors to their courts.

From the time of his coronation, Owain used a seal which depicted himself seated in a high backed chair, holding a sceptre in his right hand and a globe in the left. On the obverse side it showed him as an armed warrior mounted on a horse. Pennant mentions an extant deed which he had seen to which that seal was attached, granting a pardon to John ap Howel - 'Anno principatus nostri VI datum apud Cefn Llanfair X die Jan. per ispsum principem.' The names of the four witnesses are Gruffydd ap Owen and Maredudd ap Owen, Gruffydd Yonge the Chancellor, and Rhys Tudur of Pen y Mynydd.

A seal is a piece of wax, lead or paper, attached to a document as a guarantee of authenticity or affixed to an envelope or receptacle to ensure that the contents may not be tampered with other than by breaking the seal. The piece of stone or metal upon which the design is engraved, and from which the impression is taken is called the *matrix*.

Sovereigns and magnates generally use a Privy Seal (privatum sigillum) to authenticate warrants to their clerks who would then issue documents on their master's behalf under a Great Seal. A Personal Seal (secretum) was used for private matters.

The Great Seal of the Realm was two-sided, with a different device on each side. The principal side (obverse) depicted the enthroned sovereign and the reverse his equestrian figure.

Parliaments were also held at Dolgellau, which is a town with streets so narrow and crooked that it has been suggested that it was built before the days when streets were invented. It has also been described as an "ugly but attractive town" for the buildings are solidly constructed of large blocks of hewn stone, which give it a dark and sombre appearance, particularly when seen on a wet day.

Owain's last parliament was assembled here on May14, 1404 in a building which used to stand near the Royal Ship Hotel. It was here that Owain is said to have signed a treaty of alliance with Charles VI of France. The wording of the document began in regal style:

'Owinus Dei Gratia Princeps Wallia'
and concluded
'Datiem Apud Dolgelli.'

Owain Glyndŵr on his throne

Owain Glyndŵr's seal depicts the only known portrait of the man, showing him with his forked beard, seated in a chair, holding the sceptre in his right hand and the globe in his left. The half body of a wolf forms the arms of his chair on each side and the background is ornamented with a mantle semée of lions held up by angels. The inscription is *Owenus … Princeps Walliae.* On the reverse, Owain is represented on horseback, in armour; in his right hand, which is extended, he holds a sword, and in his left a shield, charged with, quarterly, four lions rampant; a drapery, probably a *kerchief de plesaunce*, or handkerchief, won at a tournament, pendant from his right wrist. Lions rampant also appear on the mantle of the horse. On his helmet, as well as on his horse's head, is the Welsh Dragon. The inscription on this side is *Owenus Dei Gratia … Walliae.* The original seal is in the Bibliothéque National in Paris.

159

The Royal House in Machynlleth is believed to have belonged to Owain Glyndŵr at one time and in later years Charles I once stayed there.

This stone and timber building can be seen at Dolerw, Newtown, but it used to stand in Dolgellau where it was known as the Old Parliament House. It was purchased by Sir Pryce-Jones in 1885 and he had it transported to Llanllwchaiarn in a 32 truck train specially hired for the purpose. It was re-erected at Dolerw and has served as a Quaker meeting house.

Nine
The Tide begins to Turn
1405

A slaughter of the Welsh on Pwll Melin Mountain, near Usk, where Gruffydd ab Owen was taken prisoner. It was now the tide began to turn against Owen and his men.

Gruffydd Hiraethog

At the end of February, Rhys Gethin raised a mighty army in Glamorgan and then marched through Cardiff and Newport to attack the castles of Caerleon and Usk, which had been regained by the English.

Reaching Grosmont in northern Gwent, Rhys Gethin's men plundered and burnt the town until it was a smouldering ruin. It was devastated to such an extent that it never recovered and traces of the ruined streets can still be seen. At that time Grosmont was one of the largest and most prosperous towns in Gwent and, in South Wales, only Carmarthen and Abergavenny were greater in size.

Rhys Gethin no doubt assumed that Grosmont Castle, like most similar fortresses, was held by just a handful of men who were barely able to defend its walls and hardly likely to advance beyond them. However, he was in for a shock, for Prince Henry, based at Hereford, sent a small but well disciplined force to Grosmont, under the command of Sir Gilbert Talbot, Sir William Newport and Sir John Greynder.

In a compact body, brandishing swords, they fell upon the disorganised groups of Welshmen, taking them completely by surprise. Before long eight hundred corpses lay on the ground, whilst the remainder fled in confusion.

The King had given his son this commission, thinking that it would provide him with some military and political experience, while the task should be easily accomplished within a fortnight. But this assessment of the situation was wide of the mark, for the young, Monmouth born Prince of Wales, was to be occupied with this outbreak of Welsh patriotism for the next ten years.

Among those taken prisoner were Owain's secretary, Owen ap Gruffydd ap Rhisiant and his brother-in-law, John Hanmer. They were both taken to the Tower of London. The following is an extract from a letter that Prince Henry sent to his father, the King:-

Most dread sovereign, Lord and Father. In the most humble manner that I may in my heart devise, I recommend myself to your Royal Majesty, humbly praying your most gracious blessing.

On Wednesday, the 11th March, your rebels drew together the number of eight thousand men and burned part of your town of Grosmont, and there by the aid of the blessed Trinity, your son won the field (by fair reckoning upon our return from pursuit) some say eight hundred and some a thousand, upon being questioned upon pain of death.

Now such amends hath God ordained you for the burning of your hundred houses in your town aforesaid.

Victory is not in a multitude of people but in the power of God... Prisoners there were none taken, save one, a great chieftain among them; whom I have sent you, but he cannot yet ride at his ease.

Grosmont Castle, in northern Gwent, was the birthplace of Henry IV's grandfather, Henry, the first Duke of Lancaster. In 1405 the castle was occupied by a small but well disciplined force which defeated Rhys Gethin when he raided the town of Grosmont. His men were taken completely by surprise and about eight hundred of the Welshmen were slaughtered by English soldiers commanded by Sir Gilbert Talbot, Sir William Newport and Sir John Greyndor.

Prince Henry was only a teenager but his services in dealing with the Glyndŵr uprising were so highly regarded by the House of Commons that the King was requested to order the Prince to remain in the neighbourhood to deal with the border hostilities.

Following their defeat at Grosmont, the Welsh survivors re-grouped near Usk where an English force had re-taken the castle. John ap Hywel, the Cistercian Prior of Llantarnam Abbey, who for long had given stern warnings to his countrymen of the evil results that would follow from their unrepented wickedness, was also present. He wandered among the troops before the battle inspiring the men to defend their homes, their wives and their children. He promised that all who fell in the fight to come, "would sup that night in heaven." When he later attempted to flee from the battle he was heard to say that he himself was forced by his pledge of abstinence on a fast day to be absent from the feast.

Owain's eldest son, Gruffydd, led the attack, which was to cost him his freedom, on 15 March. It was a fierce battle fought on a hill called Mynydd Pwll Melyn (Hill of the Yellow Pool) behind the Castle. The garrison had come out of the castle led by Richard Grey, Lord of Codmor, Sir John Oldcastle (later Lord Cobham) and Sir John Greyndor. Overwhelmed by superior numbers, his men falling about him, fighting desperately to the last, Gruffydd was struck down and taken prisoner from the bloodstained field, where fifteen hundred of Glyndŵr's men were killed, including his brother Tudor. It was a bloody battle and a grievous defeat. It was reported with glee that Glyndŵr himself had been killed. With the death of their leader the Welsh would surely abandon their struggle for independence.

However, on closer examination, it was found that such thoughts were somewhat premature for, although the brothers' resemblance was very striking, a mistake of identity had been made. A wart over the eye, which distinguished the 'great Owain' was not in evidence on the body and it was then realised that it was Tudur and not Owain who had fallen in the conflict.

The remnants of the Welsh army were pursued through the river Usk into Monkswood and those who escaped fled into the Welsh mountains. Three hundred captives were beheaded and their bodies thrown into a pool behind Usk Castle. Gruffydd ap Owain was taken to London where he was imprisoned in the Tower. Statements of sums of money allowed for his maintenance appear occasionally in the Rolls. The sum of three and four pence a day is named for his rations and those of Owen ap Gruffydd of Cardiganshire, another Welsh captive taken prisoner at the same battle. Gruffydd ap Owain died in the Tower of the plague in 1410.

The battle of Mynydd Pwll Melyn was fought on the hillside behind Usk Castle in 1405, when Gruffydd, the eldest son of Owain Glyndŵr, led an attack on the fortress. During the conflict, fifteen hundred Welshmen were killed, including Owain's brother Tudur, and Gruffydd was taken prisoner.

The battle of Mynydd Pwll Melyn was later described by Adam of Usk in his *Chronicon Adae de Usk* which is a valuable chronicle of the events of his age:–

> For these lords (Lord Grey de Codnor and Sir John Greyndor), sallying forth manfully, took him (Gruffydd ab Owen Glyndŵr) captive, and pursuing his men to the hill country of Upper Gwent through the river Usk, there slew with fire and the edge of the sword many of them, and above all the abbot of Llantarnam, and they crushed them without ceasing, driving them through Monkswood, where the said Gruffydd was taken. And their captives to the number of three hundred they beheaded in front of the same castle near Pontfold.

Not daring to push his advantage further, Prince Henry marched back to the English border. Later that month, the inhabitants of the Honddu Valley in the Black Mountains ('Hothney, Slad Ffowothog, Y Glyn, Olghan and Stadewy'), realising now that Glyndŵr's cause was looking unlikely to succeed, made a mass submission and this also happened on a wide scale in both Gwent and Brecknock at this time.

In March of this year Owain was at Caerffili Castle, where the Constable, Countess Constance Despenser (whose husband had been executed by Henry IV at Bristol in 1399) formed a scheme to liberate the young Earl of March from the King's custody. She was herself of royal blood and a Plantagenet, being the daughter of Edmund Langley, who was Duke of York and Earl of Cornwall and therefore brother to Prince Edward, the Black Prince of Wales. Lady Despenser managed to reach the apartment at Windsor, where the young princes were being held and, by means of a false set of keys, succeeded in getting them safely out of the castle. She rode hard with the boys towards Wales, where their uncle, Edmund Mortimer, was waiting to receive them, but their escape was discovered and they were captured near Cheltenham within striking distance of the Welsh border.

On being interrogated by the Council, Lady Despenser stated that her brother, the Duke of York (the notorious Rutland who betrayed everybody and who had now succeeded his father in his title and estates) was behind the scheme. York was immediately arrested, but he protested his innocence, and after a few months confinement in the Castle of Pevensey, he was released and restored to his rank and property. The courageous Countess was pardoned, but the unfortunate blacksmith who had made the false keys had both his hands severed and was then executed.

Lady Despencer's lands were restored to her, in spite of her act of treason, in June 1406 and she held them until her death in 1416, when she was buried in state in Reading Abbey. Her son Richard died in October 1413, ending the male line of the Despencer family.

In May, the Earl of Northumberland, pardoned after the battle of Shrewsbury, was in rebellion again. Mowberry and Lord Bardolph who acted as Owain's envoys, were captured by a royal force, whilst two Welsh bishops, Byford and Trefor, escaped with Northumberland to Scotland.

The defeats at Grosmont and Usk were a major blow to Owain, who was now pinning his hopes on assistance from the French. On July 14, 1404, after a month of negotiations, a formal treaty of alliance between France and Wales had been concluded at the home of Arnaud de Corbie, the French Chancellor. In it Owain was referred to 'as the illustrious and most dreaded Owen, prince of the Welsh.'

Their common enemy was described as 'Henry of Lancaster'. Neither party was to make peace without the consent of the other and looking ahead to a vigorous campaign the French allies were supplied with a list of harbours and details of the route along which their armies should march. In January 1405, the treaty was formally ratified in Wales:-

In testimony wherof we cause these to be made our letters patent. Given in our castle of Lambadarn on the 12th day of January, AD 1405 and the sixth of our rule.

Owain was encouraged by the news, in late July, that a force of nearly three thousand Frenchmen commanded by Jean de Rieux, Marshall of France and Brittany, had just set sail for Wales in one hundred and forty ships. They disembarked in early August at Milford Haven. Among the Marshall's lieutenants were some very fine soldiers - Jean de Hangest, Lord of Avenscourt, Sire de Hugueville, grandmaster of the Crossbows, and Robert de la Heuge - who bore the nickname Le Borgne 'The One Eyed'.

Milford Haven is one of the finest natural harbours in the world. A fiord penetrates inland for about 20 miles, providing about 10 miles of safe anchorage. It was from this harbour that Richard II set sail for Ireland in 1399. The French army sent to assist Owain Glyndŵr landed here in 1404 and later in the same century Henry Tudor disembarked here with his 2,000 Norman and Breton force under the command of Philibert de Shaunde.

Unfortunately, the French had suffered rough weather in the Channel and most of their horses had died through a lack of fresh water. But the number of foot soldiers was considerable for the force consisted of eight hundred men-at-arms, six hundred crossbowmen and twelve hundred troops. The French first laid siege to Haverfordwest and set fire to the town, but failed to take the castle.

They then marched to Tenby and commenced a siege. Lord Berkeley and Henry Pay, the Warden of the Cinque Ports, however, entered the harbour and managed to set fire to fifteen of their ships. The French then pushed on to the east and managed to capture Carmarthen.

Henry IV was in Pontefract, Yorkshire, when he received news of the French landing in West Wales. On August 7, he wrote to the Sheriffs of eighteen shires and ordered them:

> ...to cause proclamation to be made, that all knights, esquires, yeoman and other fencible men...hasten to draw to the city of Hereforde, to march with the king and manfully resist the king's enemies; as now newly it has come to the king's ears that the seigneur de Hungervyle and a great number of his enemies of France with a fleet of ships has landed at Milforde Haven to reinforce the Welsh rebels, and with them are purposing to invade the realm and the marches of Wales, and to do what mischief they may to the king and his lieges.

The rumour that Owain was intending to invade England quickly spread and it is recorded that the monks of St. Albans were so concerned that they hung notices on the walls of their abbey – 'God save us from Glyndŵr.'

The French joined forces with Glyndŵr and the two armies marched through Morgannwg and Gwent towards England. Crossing the border, they plundered the hostile country as they went. Owain's soldiers sang songs of victory and marched proudly with their banners flying and trumpets sounding. Never before had so great an army marched behind a Welsh prince towards England. This was also the first time that a body of French soldiers had penetrated into the very heart of the island which had sent many an army into France.

By 22 August, they were just ten miles from Worcester and a camp was set up on Woodbury Hill in the parish of Whitley. This was the furthest point reached by an invading force in English history, since 1066. Glyndŵr and the French were installed on an ancient British fort crowning the summit of Woodbury Hill. Still known as 'Owen's Camp' it is surrounded by a deep fosse, which curves around the summit of the hill in the form of a crescent. Below the fort is an ideal arena for a battleground.

On a ridge to the north they glimpsed the fluttering pennons of the King's army coming into sight. The western sun was sinking and no doubt Owain's men strained their eyes trying to gauge the size of the opposing force.

Behind the King's army came an immense train of baggage and provision wagons. This sight was of particular interest to Glyndŵr's army, for he had made no provision for a lengthy campaign in this hostile country and when all his army's food was consumed they would either have to retire or live off the enemy.

The King took up his position on Abberly Hill, one mile to the north, and the two armies sat and gazed at each other from the opposing hills.

Both camps were strongly positioned and defended, and the numbers appeared to be evenly matched. But who would be the first to attack?

For eight days the two armies sat and waited with neither daring to take the initiative. Only small skirmishes were undertaken, which resulted in the death of about two hundred men from each side.

William Camden visited Woodbury Hill at the end of the 16th century and remarked:

> About seven miles below Temebury, the river (Teme) passeth under Woodberry-hill, remarkable for an old entrenchment on the top, vulgarly called Owen Glendower's camp; which notwithstanding is probably of greater antiquity.

Eventually, Owain retreated with his Franco-Welsh army back to the Welsh border. King Henry did not pursue them for his force was not large enough. Instead, he established a base in Worcester and made preparations to invade Wales once more. By the beginning of September, he had moved his headquarters to Hereford.

Had Owain won a victory at Woodbury Hill then he might have taken and sacked Worcester, but that would have been all that he would have dared accomplish, so far from his own lands. It is likely that such an action would have stirred the English people into such fury that King Henry would have been furnished with an army stronger than he had ever commanded before.

The French were disappointed that there had been no battle and that they had not had the chance to wreak vengeance on the English. A decision was made to sail back to France to winter in their own land. However, Sieur de Hugueville with some seventeen hundred men remained in Wales. They settled in companies at various castles, where they could rest comfortably during the winter and by their presence strengthen the garrisons of those fortresses.

On 10 September, Henry, at the head of a large force, commenced his fifth invasion of Wales. He entered Glamorgan and succeeded in relieving Coity Castle. He then left for the border as the rains came down – pursued by the Welsh, who attacked the rear of his army and stole the supply wagons. In total he lost forty wagon loads of provisions and a large quantity of jewels. The King reached Hereford on September 29 and five days later he was back at Worcester.

Coity Castle in the Vale of Glamorgan was besieged by Owain Glyndŵr's forces in 1405 and Parliament had to send a relief force in September of that year.

In August 1405, Owain Glyndŵr and his French allies set up camp on Woodbury Hill, ten miles from Worcester. The location is still known as 'Owain's Camp' and Henry IV with his large army took up a similar position on the opposite side of the valley. But surprisingly no battle took place and the Franco-Welsh army retreated to the Welsh border.

1406

The Tripartite Indenture

On 24th February an important meeting was held at the far end of the Llyn Peninsula, where Dafydd Daron, the Dean of Bangor, was lord of the manor, and was in possession of a house in the remote village of Aberdaron. He was descended from Caradoc ap Iestyn, one of the princes of South Wales, and firmly believed that justice for Wales could only be achieved through national independence. Dafydd's house, built of stone, to resist the blast of the winds sweeping from the west, was situated on the edge of the sea. It overlooked the mysterious island of Bardsey, which has become known as the island of twenty thousand saints.

The purpose of this meeting, which in later years became known as the Triple Confederacy, was to discuss how Henry IV's territory in England and Wales, could be divided between Owain Glyndŵr, the Earl of Northumberland and Edmund Mortimer. William Shakespeare in Act III of his play Henry IV, Part One, describes the scene in the Dean's house at Aberdaron. In his version, those present are the Archbishop of Bangor, Edmund Mortimer, Henry Percy (Hotspur) and Owain Glyndŵr. Holding up a map, Edmund Mortimer says:

"The Archdeacon hath divided it
Into three limits, very equally:
England, from Trent and Severn hitherto
By south and east, is to my part assigned,
All westward, Wales beyond the Severn shore,
And all the fertile land within that bound
To Owen Glendower:– and dear coz (ie Percy) to you
The remnant northward, lying off Trent
And our indentures tripartite are drawn."

However, Shakespeare made a mistake here for Henry Percy (Hotspur) could not have been present for he had been killed at the battle of Shrewsbury in 1403 and this meeting took place in 1406. It was the father of Hotspur - the Earl of Northumberland, Owain Glyndŵr and Edmund Mortimer, who met here on 28 February of that year. It was held in this remote corner of Wales because the Earl of Northumberland, being a fugitive, was anxious to conceal his whereabouts.

An ancient prophecy of Merlin fortold to remind the three men of its significance. He told how the 'mole accursed of God' should come to destruction, that a dragon and a wolf should have their tails plaited together and prevail, and that with them they should unite the lion, and these three would divide the kingdom possessed by the mole.

For the symbolic purpose of fulfiling this ancient prophecy, Glyndŵr assumed the role of the dragon, Percy the lion and Mortimer the Wolf. The mole of course was King Henry IV.

The following is a relevant extract from the actual wording of the Tripartite Agreement.

...the same lords, Owain, the earl and Edmund, shall henceforth be mutually joined, confederated, united and bound by a true league and true friendship and a sure and good union.

Again between the same lords, it is unanimously covenanted and agreed, that the aforesaid Owain and his heirs shall have the whole of Cambria or Wales, within the borders, limits and boundaries undermentioned, from Loegria, which is commonly called England; namely from the Severn Sea, as the river Severn leads from the sea, going to the north gate of the city of Worcester, and from that gate directly to the Ash Tree, commonly called in the Cymric or Welsh language Onnen Mangion*, which grows on the highway which is commonly called the old or ancient road, direct to the head or source of the Trent; thence to the head or source of the river, commonly called Mersewy, thence, as that river leads to the sea in going direction, within the borders, limits and boundaries afore-mentioned. And the aforesaid earl of Northumberland and his heirs shall have the counties written below, namely Northumberland, Westmorland, Lancashire, York, Lincoln, Nottingham, Derby, Stafford, Leicester, Northampton, Warwick and Norfolk. And the lord Edmund shall have the remainder of the whole of England to him and to his successors.

Again should any battle, riot or discord befall between two of the said lords (may it never be) then the third of the said lords, inviting to himself good and faithful counsel, shall duly correct such discord, riot or battle, whose approval or sentence the parties quarrelling shall be bound to obey. Also they shall defend the kingdom against all men, saving the oath on the part of the aforesaid Owain, given to the most illustrious prince, Lord Charles, by the grace of God, King of the French, in the league and covenant made and completed between them.

* Onnen Mangion (the ash tree at Meigen) is a reference to the location of the Battle of Meigen, where Cadwallon led the Welsh to victory in 632. On today's Ordnance Survey map it is near the village of Six Ashes to the south of Wolverhampton.

Owain himself had probably compiled the agreement, for he had trained in his youth at the Inns of Court in London. There he had acquired a knowledge of the law and knew how to frame such an important document.

Wales was all that Glyndŵr ever desired and the boundaries would merely be extended to the rivers Severn and Mersey. Otherwise he would rule Wales as she had always been. Northumberland could have what he wanted in the north, and a list of English shires was set down as his share. The remainder of the country would go to Edmund Mortimer, who openly avowed that he would hold it in trust for his nephew, the rightful heir to the throne, and only claim it for himself should the boy and his brother be murdered by Henry IV.

In March 1406 the last of Owain Glyndŵr's Parliaments was a council of Welsh magnates and clerics which met at Pennal, about 4 miles outside Machynlleth. In a letter addressed from Pennal and dated 26th March 1406,, we find Owain telling the French king that his aims were: to create a Wales territorially free, to create an independent Welsh Church and to create two Universities, one for North and one for South Wales. Many scholars believe that Owain's Chancellor, Gruffydd Yonge (Bachelor of Laws, Doctor of Degrees, Archdeacon of Merioneth and later Bishop of Bangor) was the architect of the Pennal Policy.

At this time there were two rival popes, one at Avignon and supported by Owain's ally Charles VI of France and the other one at Rome. Charles had requested that Owain should support the Avignon pope. The Welsh Parliament discussed this matter and agreed to the French King's request, but laid down four conditions:

1. That the Welsh Church should henceforth be independent of Canterbury, with St David's Cathedral as an Archbishopric. The Welsh metropolitan area was to include the Bishoprics of Exeter, Bath, Hereford, Worcester and Lichfield.

2. That only Welsh speaking Welshmen should be appointed to church duties in Wales.

3. That the Welsh Church should take possession of all church property in Wales, so that none of its revenues could be transferred to English churches and monasteries.

4. In order to provide for the adequate education of the Welsh clergy, Wales was to have two universities, one in the north and the other in the south, so that Welshmen should not have to go to the English universities.

Pennal Church, near Machynlleth

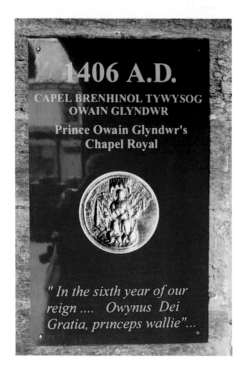

The Pennal letter, written on goatskin parchment, is in two parts: one a letter declaring Owain's intention to give obedience to the pope of Avignon and the other a formal document sealed with his great seal, setting out the terms of his allegiance.

Translation of the Pennal Letter

Most serene prince, you have deemed it worthy on the humble recommendation sent, to learn how my nation, for many years now elapsed, has been oppressed by the fury of the barborous Saxons; whence because they had the government over us, and indeed, on account of that fact itself, it seemed reasonable with them to trample upon us. But now, most serene prince, you have in many ways, from your innate goodness, informed me and my subjects very clearly and graciously concerning the recognition of the true Vicar of Christ, I, in truth, rejoice with a full heart on account of that information of your excellency, and because, inasmuch from this information, I understand that the lord Benedict, the supreme pontifex, intends to work for the promotion of an union in the Church of God with all his possible strength. Confident indeed in his right, and intending to agree with you as far as is possible for me, I recognise him as the true Vicar of Christ, on my behalf, and on behalf of my subjects by these letters patent, forseeing them by the bearer of their communications in your majesty'e presence. And because, most excellent prince, the metropolitan church of St David's was, as it appears, violently compelled by the barbarous fury of those reigning in this country, to obey the church of Canterbury, and de facto still remains in this subjection. Many other disabilities are known to have been suffered by the church of Wales through these barbarians, which for the greater part are set forth full in the letters patent accompanying. I pray and sincerely beseech your majesty to have these letters sent to my lord, the supreme pontifex, that as you deemed worthy to raise us out of darkness into light, similarly you will wish to extirpate and remove violence and oppression from the church and from my subjects, as you are well able to. And may the Son of the Glorious Virgin long preserve your majesty in the promised prosperity.

Dated at Pennal the last day of March (1406).

Yours avowdly

Owain, Prince of Wales.

Endorsement: To the most serene and most illustrious prince, lord Charles, by the grace of God, King of France.

To the most illustrious prince, the lord Charles, by the grace of God, King of the French, Owain by the same grace, sends the reverence due to such a prince with honour. Be it known to your excellency that we have received from you the articles following, brought to us by Hugh Eddowyer, of the Order of Predicants, and Morris Kerry, our friends and envoys, on the eighth day of March, A.D. 1406, the form and tenor of which follow:

In the first place they express the cordial greeting on the part of our lord the king, and of his present letter to our said lord the prince. In this manner, our lord the king greatly desires to know of his good state and the happy issue of the negotiations. He requests Owain, that he will write as often as opportunity offers, as he will receive great pleasure, and he will inform him at length, concerning the good state of the said lord, the king, of the queen, their children, and of the other lords, the princes of the royal family have and intend to have sincere love, cordial friendship, zeal for his honour, the prosperity and well-being of the state of the said prince, and in this the said prince, can place the most secure faith.

They also explain to the same lord, the prince, how our lord, the king, who esteems him with sincerity and love, greatly desires that, as they are bound and united in temporal matters, so also will they be united in spiritual things, that they may be able to walk to the house of the Lord together. My lord, the king, also requests the same lord, the prince, that he wishes him to consider, with a favourable disposition, the rights of my lord, the pope, Benedict XIII, the supreme pontiff of the universal church, that he might himself learn and cause all his subjects to be informed. Because my lord the king, holds that it shall be to the health of his soul and of the souls of his subjects, to the security and strength of his state, and that their covenants shall be laid in a stronger and more powerful foundation in the advantage of faith and in the love of Christ. Again, even as all faithful Christians are held to keep themselves well informed concerning the truth of schisms. Princes, however, are so held even more than others, because their opinion can keep many in error, especially their subjects, who must conform with the opinion of their superiors. It is, also, even to their advantage, on account of their duty, to keep themselves informed in all things, that such a schism may be entirely removed and that the Church may have unity in God. Because, he who is the true Vicar of Christ, should be known to have by nefarious means usurped the holy apostolic see, shall be expelled and cast aside, by all the faithful, as anti-Christ. To this purpose they should bind themselves to strive, to their utmost, according to the decrees of the holy fathers. To which purpose the said lord, the king, has striven, not without great burdens and expense, and will strive unweariedly.

175

Following the advice of our council, we have called together the nobles of our race, the prelates of our Principality and others called for this purpose, and, at length, after diligent examination and discussion of the foregoing articles and their contents being thoroughly made by the prelates and the clergy, it is agreed and determined that we, trusting in the rights of the lord Benedict, the holy Roman and supreme pontiff of the universal church, especially because he sought the peace and unity of the church, and as we understood daily seeks it, considering the hard service of the adversary of the same Benedict, tearing the seamless coat of Christ, and on account of the sincere love which we specially bear towards your excellency, we have determined that the said lord Benedict shall be recognised as the true Vicar of Christ in our lands, by us and by our subjects, and we recognise him by these letters.

Whereas, most illustrious prince, the underwritten articles especially concern our state and the reformation and usefulness of the Church of Wales, we humbly pray your royal majesty that you will graciously consider it worthy to advance their object, even in the court of the said lord Benedict:

First, that all ecclesiastic censures against us, our subjects, or our land, by the aforesaid lord Benedict or Clement his predecessor, at present existing, the same shall by the said Benedict be removed.

Again, that he shall confirm and ratify the orders, collations, titles of prelates, dispensations, notorial documents, and all things whatsoever, from the time of Gregory XI, from which, any danger to the souls, or prejudice to us, or our subjects, may occur, or may be engendered.

Again, that the Church of St David's shall be restored to its original dignity, which from the time of St David, archbishop and confessor, was a metropolitan church, and after his death twenty-four archbishops suceeded him in the same place, as their names are contained in the chronicles and ancient books of the church of Menevia, and we cause these to be stated as the chief evidence, namely, Eliud, Ceneu, Morfael, Mynyw, Haerwnen, Elwaed, Gwmwen, Llewdwyd, Gwrwyst, Gwgawn, Clydawg, Aman, Elias, Maelyswyd, Sadwmwen, Cadell, Alaethwy, Novis, Sadwmwen, Drochwel, Asser, Arthwael, David II, and Samson; and that as a metropolitan church it had and ought to have the undermentioned suffragan churches, namely, Exeter, Bath, Hereford, Worcester, Leicester, which see is now translated to the churches of Coventry and Lichfield, St Asaph, Bangor, and Llandaff. For being crushed by the fury of the barbarous Saxons, who usurped to themselves the land of Wales, they trampled upon the aforesaid church of St David's, and made her a handmaid to the church of Canterbury.

Again, that the same lord Benedict shall provide for the metropolitan church of St David's, and the other cathedral churches of our principality, prelates, dignitaries, and beneficed clergy and curates, who know our language.

Again, that the lord Benedict shall revoke and annul all incorporations, unions, annexions, appropriations of parochial churches of our principality made so far, by any authority whatsoever with English monasteries and colleges. That the true patrons of these churches shall have the power to present to the ordinaries of those places suitable persons to the same or appoint others.

Again, that the said lord Benedict shall concede to us and to our heirs, the princes of Wales, that our chapels, &c., shall be free, and shall rejoice in the privileges, exemptions, and immunities in which they rejoiced in the times of our forefathers the princes of Wales.

Again, that we shall have two universities or places of general study, namely, one in North Wales and the other in South Wales, in cities, towns, or places to be hereafter decided and determined by our ambassadors and auld nuncios for that purpose.

Again, that the lord Benedict shall brand as heretics and cause to be tortured in the usual manner, Henry of Lancaster, the intruder of the kingdom of England, and the usurper of the crown of the same kingdom, and his adherents, in that of their own free will they have burnt or have caused to be burnt so many cathedrals, convents, and parish churches; that they have savagely hung, beheaded, and quartered archbishops, bishops, prelates, priests, religious men, as madmen or beggars, or caused the same to be done.

Again, that the same lord Benedict shall grant to us, our heirs, subjects, and adherents, of whatsoever nation they may be, who wage war against the aforesaid intruder and usurper, as long as they hold the orthodox faith, full remission of all our sins, and that the remission shall continue as long as the wars between us, our heirs, and our subjects, and the aforesaid Henry, his heirs, and subjects shall endure.

In testimont whereof we make these our letters patent. Given at Pennal on the thirty-first day of March, A.D. 1406, and in the sixth year of our rule.

Endorsement: The letter by which Owain, Prince of Wales, reduces himself, his lands, and his dominions to the obedience of our lord the Pope Benedict XIII.

Translation from *Welsh Records in Paris* (T. Matthews, Carmarthen, 1910)

It is of interest that in 2000, on the 600th anniversary of Owain Glyndŵr's uprising, the Pennal letter written to King Charles VI of France was loaned for six months by the French Ministry of Culture and Archives Nationales in Paris and put on display at the National Library of Wales, Aberystwyth, as part of an exhibition celebrating the life and achievements of Owain Glyndŵr.

The idea of a Welsh university was one of Owain Glyndŵr's dreams. But Wales had to wait five centuries before a Parliament sitting at Westminster established the University of Wales in 1893! Scotland had St Andrews University in 1413, but Wales had to wait another 459 years before a university was opened at Aberystwyth in 1872. In 1883 a college for South Wales was opened at Cardiff. The following year Bangor College was opened in an old hotel building. But these colleges were not permitted to confer degrees. It was not until 1893, after prolonged discussion and opposition from both Houses of Parliament, that the three colleges received their charter and were incorporated as the University of Wales. Owain's proposals in 1405 certainly show that he was a man with high ideals ahead of his time.

The revival of the independence of the Welsh Church was the old dream of Giraldus Cambrensis in the twelfth century. Llywelyn the Great had sympathised with the movement, but no Welsh prince before Owain had thought of associating the Church with the State in Wales as it was associated in England. The burning of Bangor and St Asaph shows what Owain thought of the Church of his time which had been much affected by the gradual conquest of Wales.

At the time when the Pennal Policy was drawn up, Owain was staying at Cefn Caer, where the 14th century Lay House is still standing, on the site of a first century Roman fort. The document was sent, with its accompanying letter, to the French King Charles VI and the Avignon Pope Benedict XIII on 31 March 1406 and delivered by Owain's envoys Hugh Eddouyer, a Friar preacher, and Maurice Kerry. A facsimile of this important medieval document (held in the Archives Nationales, Paris) was sent back to Pennal in 1984 and it is on display in Pennal Church as part of the parish's novocentenary celebrations.

Pennal Church was founded in the sixth century by St Tannwg and St Eithrias. It was re-dedicated sometime between 1092-1120 by the Normans. It originally came under the jurisdiction of St Padarn's mother church and later the Parish church at Tywyn, but in 1683 Pennal became an independent parish. By the end of the 17th century it had been extensively rebuilt and again in 1769 at a cost of £1,270, utilising bricks from the 1st century Roman fort at Cefn Caer. It was rebuilt yet again in 1810 and finally restored by the Victorians in 1873.

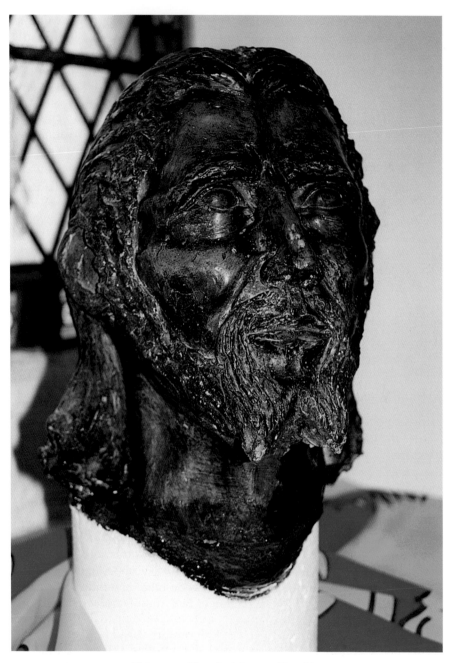

This carved head of Owain Glyndŵr
made by Doug Nicholls can be seen inside Pennal Church

In the Spring of 1406, Owain arranged ships for De Hugueville and his men to return to France. The last division returned in March, but friendly relations were maintained between Owain and the French government. However, Owain had now reached the end of the road and his power and influence went into steady decline. Throughout Wales people were now longing for a peaceful settlement and the resumption of the quiet life which, since war had swept over the land, was now but a distant memory. Even the most stalwart supporters of Glyndŵr were starting to admit that the struggle for independence was but a dream, and that Wales would have to yield to England's power as she had centuries before.

Despite the failure of the uprising, the name of Owain Glyndŵr had still not lost its potent spell, for wherever he appeared, timid tenants took courage, and thronged about him, shouting their support. The magic of his presence never failed – but he could not be in every part of Wales at the same time. He rode from place to place to strengthen and seek support for his cause, but once he had left the scene, rumours of defeats in other areas soon had a demoralising effect.

Bad news came in time after time. Anglesey was the first to fall away, suddenly returning to its old submission to the English King, and suing for that pardon which Prince Henry was always holding out to those who would agree to lay down their arms and return to the old fealty. Gower and Cardiganshire quickly followed.

Owain Glyndŵr and his family, Mortimer, Northumberland, David Daron and others were outlawed without hope of reconciliation. But Prince Henry's policy for the common soldier was one of clemency and mercy. Those who laid down their arms and submitted to English rule were neither fined nor punished. Instead, they were received graciously and promised the protection of the English castles if threatened by Glyndŵr's roving bands. Prince Henry obviously strove to prove that he cared just as much as Owain for the welfare of his Welsh subjects.

Most of the grievances of the peasants had wisely been redressed, and they no doubt longed for the time when they could till their fields in peace, unmolested by the armies of either friend or foe. Owain's high ideals were beyond the comprehension of the illiterate labouring classes upon whom he had depended for his strength and they now deserted in hundreds from his camp.

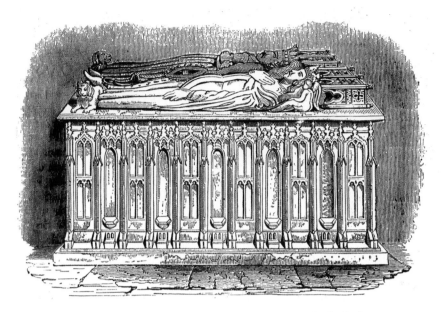

Henry IV's effigy on his tomb in Canterbury Cathedral.

King Henry had suffered a stroke at the end of 1405 and between April and September of 1406 his health began to fail so seriously that the question of settling the succession became urgent. On April 24 he addressed two letters from Windsor to the Council. In the first - written, it would seem, early in the day – he tells them that he should not be able to fulfil his purpose of being at Westminster on that day. Some ailment had attacked his leg, and he was also suffering from ague. Consequently his physicians considered that it would be dangerous for him to travel on horseback. However, he intended to be at Staines that night; from Staines he would journey by water to London, where he hoped to be in the course of three or four days. The second letter was written later in the day. By that time his illness had so much worsened that he had to give up the idea of travelling altogether. The Council would have to go on with public business without him.

On June 7, the House of Commons voted an address of thanks to the Prince, which was to be forwarded to him in Wales. At the same time, Parliament passed an Act declaring that the succession to the throne was in the Prince of Wales and the heirs – made of his body lawfully begotten and failing these to the other sons of the King and their heirs in succession. Six months later this was amended by another Act, which abolished the restriction to heirs – male.

1407

Aberystwyth Castle Falls

Today, Aberystwyth Castle is a sad and scanty ruin but it was once a strong and well sited castle, commanding a fine view over Cardigan Bay, while forty miles to the north, Snowdon can be seen on a clear day. Surprisingly, the first castle built by the Normans in this locality was actually constructed on another site. It stood on a hill above the River Ystwyth near Tan y Bwlch, but all that remains now is a well defined mound. The Welsh had managed to capture this fortress on several occasions, so, after putting up with such problems for nearly a century, the Normans decided to look for another site.

They selected the location where the present ruins stand and began to build their new castle in 1210. Protection was provided by the sea on one side, while marshland ensured a natural hazard on the other. However, two Welsh chieftains still managed to demolish the castle in the same year that it was first built.

Undaunted, the Normans built again but the Welsh soon destroyed the fortress for a second time. In 1277, Edward I, thoroughly irritated by the lack of progress, sent his brother to Aberystwyth to strengthen the building. In due course a town grew up around it.

Aberystwyth Castle was captured by Owain Glyndŵr in 1404, but retaken by Prince Henry after a long siege in 1407.

Owain Glyndŵr had captured Aberystwyth Castle in 1404 and Prince Henry now set out to recapture it. He made his way to Aberystwyth, accompanied by some of the best commanders in the English army – the Duke of York, the Earl of Warwick, John Oldcastle, Francis Court, John Greyndor, Audley of Monnington, Thomas, Lord of Carew of Pembroke, Admiral Thomas and Lord Berkely, who was the engineer in charge of timber work.

Great stores of bows, arrows, stone-shot and sulphur were collected at Hereford. Woods on the banks of the Severn were cut down to make siege machinery and a team of carpenters from Bristol were despatched to erect scaffolding, siege towers and scaling ladders in preparation for the storming of this formidable fortress.

Six large guns were also brought from Pontefract in Yorkshire via Bristol Port, and from Nottingham was transported a massive piece of equipment known as the 'Kinge's Gunne'. It weighed 4.5 tons and with it came 538 lbs of powder, 971 lbs of saltpetre and 303 lbs of sulphur. This was the first time in history that big guns were used to attack a British castle.

Initially, Prince Henry was convinced that Owain Glyndŵr was inside the castle. However, it was under the command of Rhys ap Gruffydd ap Llywelyn ab Ieuan Fychan of Ceredigion (better known as Rhys Ddu) and a fairly large garrison. They managed to withstand the Prince's attacks on the castle for some time but in due course their food and ammunition ran very low. Owain, who was busy trying to raise support in North Wales, had not come to their aid and they were practically starving, so on September 12, they agreed to a parley.

An indenture was drawn up and signed with both parties accepting a six weeks' armistice. The Welsh agreed that if by the seventh week on All Saints Day (Nov 1) Owain Glyndŵr had not arrived to assist them they would surrender the castle, on the condition that all lives would be spared. In the meantime, the armistice was to be observed on both sides and the Welsh were free to leave and enter the castle.

Prince Henry, no doubt satisfied with these terms, left Aberystwyth and returned to Hereford with most of his army, but leaving behind one hundred ant twenty men-at-arms and three hundred and sixty archers at Ystrad Fflur (Strata Florida Abbey) to await developments. According to the issues of the Exchequer dated 16 November, 1407, their role was 'to keep and defend the same from the malice of those rebels who had not submitted themselves to the obediences of the Lord the King, and to ride after and give battle to the rebels, as well in South as in North Wales.'

There was an English garrison stationed at Strata Florida up to the very last year of Owain Glyndŵr's life for it is recorded that in 1415, 'forty men-at-arms and eighty archers shall be placed at Strata Florida for the safe ward of these parts of Wales.'

Rhys Ddu travelled north to seek Owain and inform him of the situation at Aberystwyth. Owain was very angry and considered that the garrison had been treacherous. He threatened Rhys with death unless he ignored his promises to the English and let him into the castle with reinforcements. One dark night, Owain returned with a thousand men to Aberystwyth Castle. No English troops were there to prevent his approach for they lay snug and warm in their quarters at Ystrad Fflur, expecting to possess the castle within the week.

A terrible winter followed the relief of Aberystwyth Castle. Snow began to fall at Christmas and it seemed as though it would never cease. Then came the frost and North Wales lay frozen beneath a solid sheet of ice for three long months. Sheep perished upon the hills and cattle died in the valleys. People starved and froze to death for lack of food and firewood. Sickness and famine decimated the land. During this long cold winter, the heart of the nation failed and the power of resistance ebbed away. With the advance of spring came provisions from the English King and Prince of Wales, with offers of help and sustenance to all who would return to their allegiance. Seed-corn for their farms, stock for their pastures and above all, peaceful possession of their lands so long as they remained true to the King. As a result large numbers of people flocked to the English border and sought protection and safety at the great fortresses.

Glyndŵr's coffers were empty and his resources completely exhausted. Even his French allies had deserted, worn out by the rigours of winter. The land lay desolate and men were now talking with wistful regret of that hundred years of peace and growing prosperity which these wars had interrupted and destroyed. Some even began to curse the name of Owain Glyndŵr. He received a further set-back when the Duke of Orleans, his contact at the French court, was murdered and England and France soon afterwards signed a treaty.

No doubt, by now Owain had begun to realise that his dream of an independent Wales was not to be, for England would obviously not yield in the struggle as he had hoped she might. England would regard Wales as an alien nation with an independent prince, separated from her by no natural boundary, and an impossible neighbour.

Prince Henry returned to Aberystwyth in the summer, with a large force and directed operations against the castle himself and sent Gilbert, Lord Talbot, and Lord Furnival to attack Harlech Castle.

The huge cannons belched forth fire and smoke and hurled large round stones and huge balls of hot metal at the walls of the castle. However, these massive weapons had their problems for if they were fired more often than once in an hour they were likely to burst open and deal death and destruction to all who were standing near. One cannon was nick-named 'The Messenger' from its ability to hurl fiery messages. It burst open during the siege and killed or maimed a large number of men who were standing near it.

Siege towers on wheels provided platforms, beneath which men could undermine the walls and foundations. The Prince's force totalled 2,400 archers and men-at-arms, and a sum of £6,825 had been made available for their pay over a period of six months.

Owain had to resist the impulse to direct the defence from within the castle. It was better that he was on the outside where he could watch the attack and defence and endeavour to bring relief to those within, should the struggle prove too long or severe.

Rhys ap Gruffydd, who was conducting the defence, vowed that he would slay every man in the garrison himself rather than submit, and let the English eat their hearts out before empty walls; for he boasted that the castle of Aberystwyth could defy an army, even were there but ten men left alive within its walls.

The English swept round from the south. They came by land mainly but also by sea, hovering about the coast to make sure that no advantage was lost, and that no reinforcements or stores could reach the castle by sea. By the end of the summer Aberystwyth had fallen and Prince Henry allowed the garrison to march out unpunished.

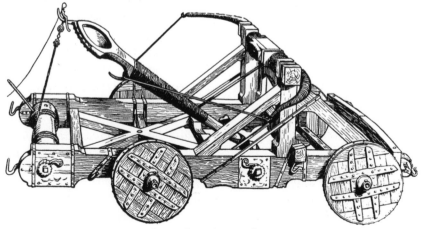

Stone throwing engine

1408

Harlech Castle Under Siege

Prince Henry had sent Gilbert and John Talbot to besiege Harlech Castle, where Glyndŵr's family were known to have their home. King Henry had expressed his determination that this fortress and its occupants should be captured at all costs. In the absence of Owain, the governor of the castle was Edmund Mortimer, whose courage was undaunted and his only hope was to hold the fortress until relief arrived, hopefully in the spring. Inside the castle were Owain's wife Margaret, two of his daughters and three grandchildren, including his grandson Lionel Mortimer. Owain himself had managed to escape with his son Maredudd and a few followers, no doubt believing that, on the outside, he could do more to assist his family.

Days merged into weeks and all the rigours of another winter were added to their privations, but still no relief reached them. The English had surrounded Harlech, from the water as well as the land. With the winter storms lashing the coast and the English vessels blockading the castle harbour, it became impossible for Glyndŵr to bring supplies to his besieged family. Twice he made desperate attempts to break through the blockade on the landside, but failed.

Harlech Castle

A brass cannon called the 'Kinge's Doughtir' (King's Daughter) burst during the siege and a claim for compensation was later made to Henry IV's Council by Gerrard Spong, who, it was revealed, had received no payment for the metal used in the manufacture of the cannon. He also requested payment for the cannon called 'The King's Messenger', which had burst at the siege of Aberystwyth Castle.

An assortment of cannon balls can be seen inside Harlech Castle. They were perhaps intended to be fired by the 'King's Messenger', a monster cannon which was used during the siege of 1409. The diameter of the largest ball is twenty-two inches, which is four inches larger than the biggest shells made in Britain during the First World War!

The garrison under the command of Edmund Mortimer was rapidly diminishing in numbers, for his men were dying or sickening daily from the effects of famine and long captivity. There were scarcely enough soldiers to man the walls and keep adequate watch, while outside the castle were Gilbert and John Talbot with an army of well fed men, one thousand strong.

"Within the sheltering walls were Glyndŵr's own family, bravely defended by ardent friends. Possibly he was there himself during this crisis, but he may have left to seek help, to no avail. He may have been urged to leave by those who loved him, as they knew that there could be no mercy if he should be taken. While Glyndŵr remained free, there was still hope."

D. Helen Allday 1981

1409

The Fall of Harlech Castle

In January, Sir Edmund Mortimer died of starvation and exhaustion and the garrison finally surrendered to the Royal forces. Owain's brave son-in-law had defended the castle to the bitter end during a siege which had lasted eight long months. Llywelyn ap Madog ap Llywelyn the commander of the castle's defences was killed.

Glyndŵr's family – his wife, two daughters and the Mortimer grandchildren – were captured by Gilbert Talbot of Goodrich Castle and taken as prisoners to the Tower of London. Catrin Mortimer, her small son and two of her daughters died there in 1413 and they were buried in St. Swithin's Churchyard. A note written by the Exchequer Clerk and dated December 1413 records:

> To William del Chambre, valet of the said Earl (Arundel). In money paid to his own hands, for expenses and other charges incurred for the burial and exequies of the wife of Edward (meaning Edmund) Mortimer and her daughters, buried within Saint Swithin's Church London... £1.

It is also recorded that the Crown allocated the sum of £30 a year for the upkeep of Margaret Glyndŵr and the other prisoners. Only the son Mareddudd now remained with Owain. What subsequently happened to Margaret Glyndŵr and her grandson Lionel Mortimer is not known.

It is of interest that in 1460 Harlech Castle had to endure another famous siege during the 'Wars of the Roses' when it was besieged by Yorkists for eight years. The castle was held for the Lancastrians by Dafydd ap Ifan ap Einion and he was besieged by forces under the command of Sir Richard Herbert, brother of the Earl of Pembroke. The starving garrison were eventually granted honourable terms of surrender and they came out with flying colours, inspiring the well known tune 'The March of the Men of Harlech'.

During the Civil War the castle changed hands more than once, being finally taken by Mytton. It was the last castle to hold out for the King, just as it had been the last castle to hold out for Owain Glyndŵr during his uprising and for the House of Lancaster during the 'Wars of the Roses'.

Harlech Castle was captured by Owain Glyndŵr after a siege lasting several months. For four years he lived there in regal style with his wife, daughters, grandchildren and Sir Edmund Mortimer. Prince Henry recaptured the castle in 1409 after an eight month siege.

About five hundred years after Glyndŵr's four year occupation of Harlech Castle an interesting discovery was made when the middle ward was being cleared in 1923. Somebody noticed something glinting in the soil. When it was cleaned it was found to be a gilt bronze boss from a set of horse harness bearing *the four lions rampant quarterly counterchanged and gules* which was assumed by Owain Glyndŵr as his insignia for his role as Prince of Wales. This was an important find for it is one of the few surviving genuine relics of Owain's life.

The blaze of patriotic hope which had swept Wales from end to end after a century of tranquility, and which had called upon Owain Glyndŵr to be its champion and deliverer, had awakened in his spirit hopes and aspirations that could obviously never be fulfiled. His dream of ruling a united and peaceful Wales and seeing it grow and thrive to become a power in the world was finally over.

On February 1, Prince Henry was appointed guardian of the young Earl of March and his brother. These were two very important young men for they represented a rival claim to the throne. Later that month, Prince Henry was appointed Constable of Dover Castle and keeper of the Cinque Ports. After this time, no mention is made of the Prince's personal presence in Wales, though he continued to hold the office of Lieutenant of the Principality. He seems to have resided chiefly in London or at the seat of his new duties.

In St Nicholas's Church, Montgomery, can be seen two recumbent figures of knights in armour which have been brought here from Chirbury Priory. The larger one represents Roger Mortimer and the other is believed to depict Sir Edmund Mortimer, who once served as Constable of Montgomery Castle. After his defeat at the battle of Pilleth, he became Owain Glyndŵr's son-in-law on marrying Catrin Glyndŵr. He died during the long siege of Harlech Castle in 1409.

1410

The Shropshire Raid

Owain made one final attempt to turn the fortune of war in his favour by carrying out a raid on the Shropshire border, but it was doomed to failure. His force was easily routed by the Constable of Welshpool and three of Owain's faithful followers were captured. Rhys ap Gruffydd of Cardigan, known as Rhys Du (the Black), was taken to London for trial and execution as a traitor. His head was added to numerous other trophies barbarously displayed on London Bridge. Philip Scudamore of Troy, near Monmouth, suffered a similar penalty at Shrewsbury. Rhys ap Tudur of Penmynydd, a cousin of Owain, who had played a leading role in the capture of Conwy Castle in 1401, was executed at Chester. The Scudamore mentioned above was no doubt related to John Scudamore who married Owain Glyndŵr's daughter.

To prevent any further uprisings, the King ordered that troops should be stationed at various locations in Wales, in particular at Strata Florida and Bala. These forces, together with the castle garrisons, kept Wales in a state of subjection.

In 1410 the following Welsh prisoners were received at Windsor Castle: Howel ab Ieuan ab Howel, Walter ab Ieuan Fychan, Rhys ab Ieuan ab Rhys, Ieuan Goch ab Morgan, Dafydd ab Tyder, Rhys ab Maredudd, Madoc Bach, Jenkyn Bachen, Dafydd ab Cadwgan and Thomas Dayler. Also in this year, King issued his letters to Richard Grey of Codnor, Constable of Nottingham Castle, to deliver to the Constable of the Tower of London, Gruffydd ab Owain Glyndourdy and Owain ab Gruffydd ab Richard, his prisoners.

1411

The King Should Abdicate

During the latter part of his father's reign, after the Glyndŵr uprising had faded away, Prince Henry, despite still being Lieutenant of Wales, seems to have had little to do with Welsh affairs. The last record of his presence in the country is in a document, executed at Carmarthen Castle, and bearing the date September 23, 1408. He had now been in command for five and a half years. When he had been formally appointed to his office he was just nine months younger than the Black Prince had been at the battle of Crecy. There is no doubt that in those times youngsters came very early to their maturity.

On 28 February, 1409, Prince Henry was appointed Constable of Dover Castle and Keeper of the Cinque Ports, while he still continued to hold the office of Lieutenant of the Principality. Then on March 18, the King, having 'the fullest confidence in the circumspection and fidelity of his most dear son, Henry, Prince of Wales,' appointed him for the period of twelve years as Captain of the town of Calais. To be in command both at Dover and Calais, while still holding the Lieutenancy of Wales, was undoubtedly to be in a position of considerable trust.

In 1410, the Prince received from the King a grant for life of the palace of Coldharbour in the parish of Hayes in Middlesex. Parliament the following year made grants to the Prince for operations to be carried on at Calais and also for the continued defence of Wales.

The Prince in a later Parliament of that year expressed his desire that King Henry should resign his kingdom, being incapable, by reason of ill-health, of performing his duties. The King refused to do so, and the Prince and his Counsellors then withdrew from the Parliament.

A chronicle written by a monk of the Abbey of Malmesbury states that in the thirteenth year of King Henry IV 'a convention was made between Henry Beaufort, Bishop of Winchester, and almost all the Lords that one of them should speak to the king, desiring that he should resign the crown and permit his eldest son to be crowned, seeing that he was so horribly afflicted by leprosy; and that this being told to the king, he, being unwilling so to resign his crown, by the advice of some of his Lords rode through a great part of England, notwithstanding the said leprosy.'

Sixteen years later Henry Beaufort, the Bishop, was put on trial for high treason, being accused of having stirred up the King, when Prince of Wales, to bring about the resignation of his father. However, no evidence was offered in support of the charge and the Bishop was acquitted.

Monstrelet tells us that:

> He (Henry IV) was so sorely oppressed at the latter end of his sickness, that those who attended him, not perceiving him to breathe, concluded that he was dead, and covered his face with a cloth. It was the custom, whenever the king was ill, to place the royal crown on a cushion beside the bed, and for his successor to take it at his death. The Prince of Wales, being informed by the attendants that his father was dead, had carried away the crown; but shortly after, the king uttered a groan, and his face was uncovered, when, on looking for the crown, he asked what had become of it? His attendants replied 'My lord the Prince has taken it away.' He bade them send for the Prince, and at his entrance the king asked him why he had carried away the crown. 'My lord,' answered the Prince, 'your attendants here present affirmed to me that you were dead; and as your crown and kingdom belonged to me as your

eldest son, after your decease, I took it away.' The king gave a deep sigh, and said. 'My fair son, what right have you to it? For you well know I had none.' 'My Lord,' replied the Prince, 'as you have held it by the right of your sword, it is my intent to hold and defend it the same during my life.' The king answered, 'Well act as you see best; I leave all things to God, and pray that he will have mercy on me'.

This account was written by a Yorkist partisan, who no doubt introduced it into his chronicle to suggest that the dying king confessed his wrongful tenure of the crown.

In the Parliamentary records of 1411 it is stated that the Prince of Wales desired of the King that he should resign the kingdom, as being incapable, by reason of ill-health, of performing his duties, that the king refused to do so, and that thereupon the Prince and his counsellors withdrew from the Parliament.

Henry IV depicted on his tomb at Canterbury Cathedral

1412

The Capture of Dafydd Gam

During one of Owain's last campaigns in 1412 he managed to capture Dafydd ap Llywelyn (known as 'Gam' from a cast in one eye). He was the grandson of Howel Fychan of the manor of Park Llettis near Llanover in Gwent, and fourth in descent from Einion Sais who served in the battles of Crecy and Poitiers. His father Llywelyn purchased the estate of Penywaun near Brecon and it was there that Dafydd was probably born.

Henry IV sent orders to John Tiptoft, Constable of Brecon, to pay the 'seven hundred marks' (about £360) ransom for Dafydd Gam. He was released by Owain after taking a solemn oath not to bear arms, or otherwise oppose him. But no sooner was he free than he violated his oath in every way. He betrayed the intentions of Owain to Henry and attacked Owain's followers when he met them. Owain, then angry and exasperated, burned Dafydd Gam's house near Brecon to the ground.

Dafydd Gam once owned a house at Llantilio Crosseny in Gwent and his presence there is confirmed by an inscription in a window in the north wall of the nave of St Teilo's Church. Translated from the Latin it reads:

'David Gam, golden-haired knight, lord of the manor of Llantilio Crosseny, killed on the field of Agincourt in the year 1415.'

1413
The King is Dead. Long Live the King!

By now most of Owain's once faithful followers had largely deserted him, won over by the promises of pardon held out to them by Hugh Huls, Baron of the Exchequer, and Chief Justice Hankford, who had been sent by Henry IV to North Wales to enquire into the conduct and pardon of rebels, who were prepared to submit and pay an appropriate fine to secure their freedom.

King Henry was now dangerously ill. He had a tumour under his nose, and it was said that he was dying of leprosy, but it was more likely to have been some form of skin disease such as eczema, which can itself be a revolting sight. It would seem that for the last five years his flesh had been rotting away and it is interesting that Adam of Usk had observed that Henry's hair was thick with lice at the time of his coronation. Even when he was just twenty, he had been prone to sores, pimples and boils and was frequently sick.

His condition was probably very exaggerated and there were even rumours that his toes and fingers had rotted away. The Scots even believed that his body had shrunk to the size of a twelve-year-old child. However, Henry continued to carry out his duties as ruler of the land, but was constantly accompanied by his confessor, the Dominican friar, John Tille.

In December, the King's health seriously deteriorated while he was residing at his Eltham palace. For a while it even appeared that he had passed away, but surprisingly he recovered and it is recorded that he 'kept Christmas with such festivity as he might'.

But the following March he collapsed whilst praying in the Confessor's Chapel at Westminster Abbey. His attendants carried him into the Abbot's house, nearby. But he did not come round and died that evening in a room called the Jerusalem Chamber. His death in this room strangely fulfilled a prophecy that Henry of Bolingbroke would die at Jerusalem. His death on March 20, St Cuthbert's Day, at the age of 47, ended a troublesome reign of fourteen years. His body was taken to Canterbury for burial. But during the journey by water, a storm arose and the superstitious sailors threw the King's body overboard. Another body was substituted, which means that Henry IV was in fact buried at sea and the tomb in Canterbury Cathedral contains an impostor.

Parliament was immediately dissolved on the demise of the Crown; but the prelates, peers and representatives of the Commons assembled in an informal manner. For the first time in English history, without waiting for the solemnities of coronation, the gathering spontaneously offered homage to the new sovereign.

Twenty-five-year-old Henry was crowned king of England and France and Lord of Ireland in Westminster Abbey, on 10 April, 1413. It was the Sunday before Easter, and the king was escorted by fifty new knights that he had created that day, and the most important men of his kingdom. The procession fought its way through a blinding snowstorm down Chepeside to Westminster Palace.

The new king celebrated his accession to the throne by pardoning all the rebels in Wales, and in the autumn of that year, Hugh Huls of Walford and Chief Justice Hankford were despatched to North and South Wales officially to receive the rebels' submission. Gwilym ap Tudur and Henry Don were among the first to make their submission and receive their pardon. Their example was followed by many other Welshmen who had fought with Glyndŵr.

The young Earl of March, who was still regarded by some as the rightful heir to the throne was released from imprisonment, to which the superstitious fears of Henry IV had condemned him. Henry V, whilst a prince, had been the guardian of the young earl's estates and he seems to have discharged the trust with fidelity. The Earl of March repaid him with affection and loyalty.

Another hereditary enemy was treated in the same generous fashion. The heir of the Percys, son of Hotspur, who fell on the battlefield at Shrewsbury, had been carried by his grandfather into Scotland. Henry V, in the second year of his reign, restored him to his title and estates.

In addition, Henry decided to carry out the wishes set down in Richard II's will, seeking to make amends for his father's severe actions, as the deposed king had always been kind to him when he was a boy. Richard had asked to be buried next to his wife Anne, in Westminster Abbey, in the tomb that he had designed himself. So on 4 December, 1413, the remains of King Richard were brought from Langley, Herefordshire. The body was then removed from its sheaf of lead and placed in a coffin of elm and conveyed to London, where it was buried in royal style in Westminster Abbey.

Funeral of Richard II

Ten
Owain Glyndŵr's Final Years

And no one has ever been loved as the common people of Wales loved Owain Glyndŵr. Llewelyn is a figure in history, but Owain Glyndŵr is as if he were still alive with the nation, and it is no wonder that like Moses and Arthur, the location of his grave is not known. The poets sang their longing for his return, and the common people awaited his coming. They believed that they would encounter him again on their way, that he would lead them to a higher freedom; they would not have it that he was dead.

Sir Owen M. Edwards

Success had vanished like a dream of the night and Owain Glyndŵr was now a hunted man, who hid from his enemies and never spent much time in any one particular place. He wandered in peril of his life and liberty through the heart of the country over which for fifteen years he had ruled as Prince. Apart from honour, he had lost everything; his lands had gone, his home – the one-time centre of renowned hospitality – was now a burnt out ruin. All his sons had been captured and had died, save only Maredudd, who now shared his downfall.

Owain Glyndŵr's final movements are obscured in a veil of mist for he appeared to seek obscurity, probably roaming through Wales in disguise, perhaps talking to his countrymen and seeking their feelings on the failure of the uprising. In appearance he probably now resembled a strange wild figure, who looked more like a prophet and seer than a warrior and a prince. Men who clung to the old cause no doubt still regarded him as a hero and an idol, and prayed for his restoration to power, whilst others shook their heads sadly, weary of the long, fruitless struggle.

In July 1415, just before he sailed for France, Henry V again offered a pardon to Owain Glyndŵr and any of his men who still followed him. A state document issued from Portchester Castle, and dated 5 July, 1415 stated that :

> ...full powers are given to Sir Gilbert Talbot to treat with Owain, and to offer him and his followers a free pardon if they should so desire it.

Sir Gilbert Talbot, of Grafton, Worcestershire, a faithful counsellor of Henry V, had fought against Owain on the battlefield and no doubt had a strong respect for his Welsh adversary. However, it would seem that Owain was either too proud or too ill to accept the offer of a pardon. It was perhaps impossible for him to recognise defeat and he preferred to fade away into history.

By 1416, King Henry had still heard no word from Glyndŵr, so on February 24 he made another attempt to offer him a pardon. On this occasion, he sent Owain's son Maredudd as an intermediary. Such an action suggests that Owain was thought to be still alive and that Maredudd knew where he was hiding.

Maredudd was offered a pardon in 1415, and 1416, but he was obviously reluctant to accept a pardon for himself without the agreement of his father. However, on 6th April 1421, he eventually accepted the King's pardon and he obviously knew that his father had died. To know that Owain was deceased, he must have had knowledge of his whereabouts, or at least had contact with someone close to him.

Owain Glyndŵr, just like King Arthur, died in some unknown location, the identity of which is one of the great mysteries of Welsh history, although the legends and theories are numerous. Some maintain that he was buried hurriedly at night with his sword and shield and that later he was removed from the shallow grave and taken to another secret place for a second burial, the location of which has never been revealed.

Iolo Morgannwg claims that Owain Glyndŵr spent his last years living the life of a hermit under the name 'Sion Goodfellow the mine' in Coed y Marchog (Knight's Wood) on the lower slopes of Mynydd Coch near Welsh St Donats. Upon his death he was buried beneath the sanctus bell in Welsh St Donat's Church.

There is another belief that he was buried near the Priest's Door of Corwen Church. Above the door is a stone lintel bearing the mark of his dagger (see page 59). This stone is probably an old gravestone dating from around the eleventh century, which used to be in the churchyard, before it was incorporated into the fabric of the church.

Glyndŵr is also said to be buried beneath the great window of the south aisle in Bangor Cathedral. However, according to Archdeacon Coxe, 'Humphrey, a late Bishop of Bangor and a great antiquary, did not credit this report, but firmly believed, from a passage in Giraldus' Itinerary, that it was the mausoleum of Owain Gwynedd, Prince of North Wales, AD 1138.'

In West Wales there is a tradition that Glyndŵr is buried near the village of Wolf's Castle. But the earthen mound in question, which stands close to the road, is more likely to be of military than sepulchral origin.

Another theory claims that Owain died 'upon the top of Lawton's Hope Hill' which is near Dinmore in Herefordshire, whilst another tale in the same county maintains that he perished in Haywood Forest, near Callow, just outside Hereford.

Just like King Arthur, there are also stories that Glyndŵr is not dead but merely sleeping in a cave. Such a tale maintains that he and his men lie 'sleeping in Ogof-y-Dinas, buckled in their armour, waiting for the day to rise and fight for Wales again.'

Pencoed Woods Cave, near Bridgend in Glamorgan, is said to have been used by Owain Glyndŵr as a hiding place.

The tomb of Owain Gwynedd in Bangor Cathedral was at one time mistakenly thought to be the tomb of Owain Glyndŵr.

High on the east side of the Irfon Valley, to the north-east of Llanwrtyd Wells, is a rock shelter known as Twll Rhys Gethin. There is a local tradition that Rhys Gethin, Owain Glyndŵr's loyal general at Pilleth, used the cave as a hiding place.

Near the village of Llanbrynmair in Powys is a tumulus above Cwm Carnedd (Valley of the Stones) which is said to mark the grave of a robber called Owain who lived in this area. It is said that he was eventually killed at Pwll-y-Warthal – 'The Stirrup Bog' – where his stirrups broke and he was captured. His pursuers buried him here and erected a cairn to mark the grave. It is unlikely that this person was Owain Glyndŵr but this is a good example of how such mounds situated in remote places obtain their names.

Another interesting story is one which describes how Owain died in the mountains of Mid Wales. He was accompanied by just one faithful friend, who buried him on a bleak hill top. The grave is remembered as Cefn Bedd Owain on the west side of the Cerdin. A hill on the eastern side of the Cerdin valley near Llanwrtyd Wells is called Disgwylfa (lookout). The idea of a small band of followers hiding with Owain in this valley certainly seems to make sense and of interest is the local legend of a brigand named Rhys Gethin, who once lived here in defiance of the English King. He was an outlaw, who survived by rustling livestock, and it is significant that on the hillside above the entrance to the valley is a small rock shelter called Ogof or Twll Rhys Gethin.

The 1863 volume of *Archaeologia Cambrensis* provided me with the following piece of interesting information:

In Hengwrt MSS 133 (a manuscript of about the reign of Henry VIII) are inserted two vellum leaves of much older date, containing what appears to be a portion of a register of remarkable events. On one of these is the following notification of the death of Owain Glyndŵr:-

Obitus Owain Glyndŵr die sancta mathei apostali anno domini millimo CCCCXV' (1415)

Then appears a notification of an eclipse of the sun in 1433; and then one of the death of Henry V.

All these entries appear to be contemporary with the foregoing events; and, if I recollect, it is the only authentic record which has come to light of the death of Glyndŵr.

W.W.E.W.

Adam of Usk makes an interesting comment:

Died Owen Glendower, after four years he had lain hidden from the face of the king and the realm; and in the night season he was buried by his followers. But his burial having been discovered by his adversaries, he was laid in the grave a second time; and where his body was bestowed may no man know.

Any search for the grave of Owain Glyndŵr must take into account the possibility that Margaret, Owain's beloved wife, survived her imprisonment in the Tower of London, and, after Owain's defeat, was allowed to return to Wales, or its borders to spend her last days at the home of one of her daughters.

If this was the case then, assuming that Owain was fit enough to make the journey, it would have been quite natural for him to have headed in the same direction. The question is, which daughter was the chosen one?

Four of Owain's daughters had married into Herefordshire families:

Alice the eldest married Sir John Scudamore of Kentchurch
Janet married John Croft of Croft Castle
Catrin married Sir Edmund Mortimer of Wigmore
Margaret, the youngest, married Roger Monnington of Monnington Court and Sarnesfield.

Well, for a start, I could dismiss Catrin, who, after being taken prisoner at Harlech Castle, had died in the Tower of London and was buried with her children in St Swithin's Churchyard, London.

Alice had married Sir John Scudamore in 1410 and they resided in the Scudamore family home at Kentchurch, near Pontrilas. The Scudamores have a long history for they came over with William the Conqueror in the eleventh century. The spoils awarded to his followers, after the defeat of King Harold in 1066, included the demesne of Sancta Keyna, afterwards called Penchirche which over the years was changed to Kentchurch. From that day to the present time it has been the seat of the main line of the Scudamore family.

The family became divided into two lines – the Scudamores of Kentchurch and the Scudamores of Holme Lacy. It is of interest that the Holme Lacy Scudamores opposed the Welsh uprising and, in 1402, Sir John Scudamore of that place was defending the Castle of Carreg Cennen against Glyndwr, whom he referred to as a 'false traytor.'

The Scudamores of Kentchurch, on the other hand, appear to have sympathised with the Welsh in their troubles and their persecutions for many generations and possibly the situation of Kentchurch had much to do with this, seated as it was, on the borders of Wales. Sir Philip Scudamore, for example, was one of Owain's principal generals and he was taken prisoner in 1409, sent to London and beheaded.

For more than twenty years Sir John Scudamore of Kentchurch kept his marriage to Owain Glyndŵr's daughter a secret, but in 1432, it probably came to the notice of Henry VI, who relieved him of his honours as steward and constable of Monmouth, Grosmont and Whitecastle.

Kentchurch Court is approached through an avenue of elms and to the south east of the court is a moated site, where the earlier fortified house of Penchirche once stood, with a history going back to 1066. It is quite remarkable that the line of the Scudamores has continued without a break as owners of this estate since the Norman Conquest. There are few family houses with a longer history.

The Court was enlarged and partly rebuilt in the seventeenth century and then remodelled in 1824 by John Nash the architect of Buckingham Palace. It is a noble house, surrounded with parkland, where deer browse amid the oaks and beeches, giving a peaceful air of repose to the location.

A massive and battlemented corner tower is the oldest part of the house and it is known as the Glyndŵr Tower. It is fourteenth century and dominates the L-shaped house. The work of the architect John Nash is evident, especially in the top storey with its battlements, windows and round turret. An old drawing shows the tower before his alterations, with a pyramidal roof.

Kentchurch Court in Herefordshire has been the home of the Scudamore family since the Norman Conquest. The oldest part of the house is known as the Glyndŵr Tower and inside is a panelled room which is said to be the bedroom used by Owain when visiting his daughter Alice, who was married to Sir John Scudamore.

The 'Glyndŵr Tower' at Kentchurch Court dating from the fourteenth century is the oldest part of the house and contains a bedroom which is said to have been used by Owain Glyndŵr.

Inside the tower is a panelled room, which is said to have been the bedroom used by Owain Glyndŵr when he visited his daughter Alice. The room is certainly over five hundred years old and such stories are coloured by stirring accounts of dark and windy nights, when the wind blows from the Black Mountains and a mysterious ghostly figure can be seen emerging from a recess in the wall. This closet is reputed to have been Owain Glyndŵr's hiding place. Hanging over the fireplace in this room is a picture which is the only known portrait of Owain Glyndŵr. It is a sketch drawn from his seal and shows a dignified man wearing a full length robe.

If indeed Owain did spend time at Kentchurch Court during his final years then he would no doubt have often looked across at Grosmont and pondered with anguish on the disaster of 1405 when Rhys Gethin lost eight thousand men, during his fateful visit to that town. If only his lieutenant had been more careful on that fateful day then Owain's fortunes may well have taken a different direction.

Another portrait hanging in Kentchurch Court is of particular interest. It has been dated by the National Gallery as c.1400 and it is said to depict Sion Cent, who is otherwise known as Jack of Kent. He is a mysterious figure about whom numerous strange and magical stories have been woven. Sion was a strange mixture of a Celtic Bard, a learned monk and an historical figure. Some writers have even suggested that he was really Owain Glyndŵr in disguise, living here in hiding during his final years.

This portrait, painted in oils, shows Sion Cent as a grim looking monk dressed in monastic robes. He holds an open book in his hand and scowls out of the original pegged oak picture frame. In the background is a ruined castle on a hill and a castellated house, approached by a bridge. When you look at the painting with its subject staring back at you with sad and hypnotic eyes, you get the feeling that this mysterious monk must still haunt the old house.

It has also been suggested that Sion Cent was a monk who, being a supporter of the Lollards, was forced to seek refuge at Kentchurch, which at that time was a very remote place. Also it has been considered that alternatively, the portrait may depict Sir John Oldcastle, who was Herefordshire's Lollard martyr.

Research into the background of Sion Cent revealed to me that he was probably born in about 1300, of humble parentage at Cwm Tridwr near Eglwysilan in the Senghenydd area of Glamorgan. His uncle was a priest, who lived as a hermit at Llwyn Dafydd Ddu in Pentyrch, Glamorgan. He instructed Sion in Welsh, English, Latin and Barddoniaeth (the science of Welsh versification). When he became a young man, Sion went to Kentchurch to work as a stable boy to Squire Scudamore.

This portrait painted by Jan Van Eyck, a Flemish Master Painter, is said to depict Sion Cent, who was a mysterious figure about whom many strange stories have been woven. It has been suggested that he was really Owain Glyndŵr in disguise. Verses composed by Sion Cent on his death bed are to be found in the Iolo Manuscripts and a list of his poetical pieces is contained in the Welsh Charity School Manuscripts, quoted in The History of the Literature of Wales by Charles Williams (pp 50-59). Part of the poem which he wrote on his death bed reads:

> *The torment of subduing vengeance*
> *Alas is afflicting me*
> *Woe to the one, woe to the many*
> *Who shall endure a portion of my torture*
> *Hear my groaning and sorely complaining,*
> *Like a wolf on a chain.*
> *Do not heavenly Lord I beseach thee*
> *Take me from the world in a state of burning.*
> *God of heaven forgive me the sins*
> *I have committed so long;*
> *Before dying – before the fierce summons of death*
> *My day it is approaching.*

Sir John Scudamore quickly realised that the lad was very intelligent and he paid to have him properly educated. Sion was sent to Oxford, where he obtained a degree and was ordained.

On his return to Kentchurch, Sion became chaplain to the Scudamore household. He also acted as secretary to Sir John and taught his children. Later, Sion joined the Franciscan order and spent some time abroad. Returning after a few years, he took up his duties again as chaplain and tutor. In his spare time he wrote poetry and translated the bible into Welsh.

Stories of the deeds of 'Jack of Kent' in the character of a wizard who practiced sorcery are very much a part of the folklore of this area. He was made responsible for all sorts of strange undertakings and it was claimed that he had made a compact with the Devil in order to obtain supernatural assistance. It is interesting that Owain Glyndŵr, too, was credited with such powers. William Shakespeare had him say:

> I can call spirits from the vasty deep
> And teach thee to command the devil.

We are told that Jack of Kent sold his soul to the devil in return for his supernatural powers, on the condition that whether he was buried inside or outside a church then Satan could claim his body. However, crafty Jack pulled a fast one on the devil by arranging to be buried half in and half out of Grosmont Church, and a stone jutting out from beneath an exterior wall is said to cover his grave. A similar story is also associated with the church at Kentchurch.

This stone beneath the outside wall of Grosmont Church is reputed to cover the grave of Jack of Kent.

There is is a half-finished stone effigy inside Grosmont Church, which local people at one time claimed to be a representation of Jack of Kent. However, it obviously depicts a knight bearing a large shield and was probably intended to be one of the early lords of Grosmont Castle.

Inside Kentchurch Church can be seen the figure of a seventeenth century John Scudamore and his family. He lies reclining in armour, holding a book with his wife, Amy, beside him. At their sides are the kneeling figures of their nine children and a tenth child is depicted in swaddling clothes. This John Scudamore was 37 years of age when he died in 1616. Above the monument is an inscription which reads:-

> Here lyeth the body of John Scudamore of Kentchurch in the Countie of Hereford Esq., who married Amy the daughter of John Starkie of Darlie in the Countie Palatine of Cheshire Esq., by whom he had issue nine children … eight sonnes and one daughter leaving her with child of the tenth.

d... March
Anno Safutio 1616
Actatis 37
His mournful widowe to his
worth still debtor
Built him this tombe but in
her heart a better.

When the earlier John Scudamore married Glyndŵr's daughter Alice in 1394, they had a son who was also named John and a daughter Catherine, who in turn married Thomas Cavendish, ancestor to the Dukes of Devonshire, who to this day quarter Scudamore arms, consisting of three stirrups. John Scudamore, grandson of Owain Glyndŵr, died at the battle of Agincourt in 1415, and his sister Catherine died in 1489, and was buried at St Botolph's Church, Aldersgate.

In the Wars of the Roses, the Scudamores of Kentchurch espoused the cause of the Lancastrians, as did those at Holme Lacy, and in the defeat of the Red Rose at Mortimer's Cross in 1461, Sir John Scudamore (son-in-law of Owain Glyndŵr) died with his three sons. Sir Henry, Sir James and Sir William, with their father Sir John, were beheaded on Candlemas Day, 2 February, 1461 and the Moccas part of their estates was confiscated and bestowed on the Herberts.

St. Mary's Church, Kentchurch

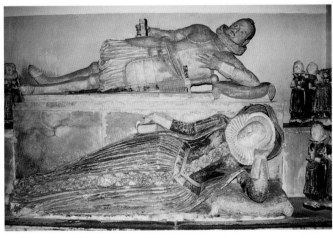

Inside the church at Kentchurch can be seen the effigies of a seventeenth-century John Scudamore and his family. He lies reclining in armour with his wife beside him and at their sides are the kneeling figures of nine children. This John Scudamore, who died in 1616, was a descendant of the Sir John Scudamore who married Alice Glyndŵr.

My next destination was Croft Castle which has been inhabited by the Croft family since Domesday, apart from a period following 1746, when the estate was sold because of debts. It was bought by Richard Knight of Downton Castle. In 1923, the trustees of Sir James Croft bought the property from the owners at that time and in 1956 the National Trust took over the freehold.

A long drive leads up to the castle and one passes between long lines of ancient beeches and oaks through gently rising parkland. These grounds are well known for their venerable and impressive trees and a celebrated chestnut grove is said to contain some of the finest specimens of the Spanish chestnut tree in England. It is claimed that they are the product of nuts taken from one of the vessels of the Spanish Armada by Admiral Sir John Croft.

Croft Castle, apart from a brief period, has been inhabited by the Croft family since the eleventh century. In 1396 a Sir John Croft married Janet Glyndŵr and no doubt her father Owain was an occasional visitor to the castle during his latter years.

St Michael's Church in the grounds of Croft Castle

The tomb of Sir Richard Croft (the great-grandson of Owain Glyndŵr) and his wife Eleanor.

It was a much earlier Sir John Croft who married Janet Glyndŵr in about 1396, when she was aged about seventeen. Their son and heir, William Croft, was born two years later. The date of Sir John's death is not known, but he was certainly alive in 1417 because it is recorded that he was 'appointed Attorney to deliver seisin of land 10 March 1410.' It would also appear from the Abbey of Oseny Chart ('William son and heir to John 1421-23') that William succeeded his father in 1421, which indicates that Sir John Croft outlived his father-in-law, Owain Glyndŵr.

Just like Owain Glyndŵr, the Croft family can claim descent from Cadwaladr - the last Welsh King of Britain.

Croft Castle, with its four round towers, was built early in the fourteenth century, but it has of course been much altered and restored at various periods. The interior is mainly eighteenth century.

In the grounds of the castle is the church of St Michael and All Angels. Inside can be seen the impressive tomb of Sir Richard Croft, the great grandson of Owain Glyndŵr. Depicted in the armour that he wore in the battle of Tewkesbury, Sir Richard lies here with his wife Eleanor who was the widow of Sir Hugh Mortimer. She acted as governess to the sons of Edward IV in Ludlow Castle and died in 1520. Sir Richard Croft, her husband, fought in the Wars of the Roses and died in 1509.

Above the canopied tomb, in one of the window panes, is an heraldic sun representing the parhelion which appeared in the sky on the cold Candlemas day in 1461, when Sir Richard donned his armour and rode off to fight alongside Edward, Duke of York, the future Edward IV.

The Rev. Thomas Thomas, in his 'Memoirs of Owen Glendower' published in 1822, tells us that Owain's 'fifth and youngest daughter, Margaret, was married to Roger Monnington of Monnington, in the County of Hereford.'

At one time it was assumed that this couple resided at Monnington-on-Wye, where an old stone house stands on the north bank of the River Wye. To the west of the house, a long avenue of Scots pines stretches towards Brobury Scar and they are reputed to mark the route of Owain's flight back to Wales, when his enemies once came here in search of him. Certainly, he would have been screened by the trees as he galloped away to hide in the Radnor Hills, but these trees were in fact planted to commemorate the election of William Tomkyns as MP for the Weobley Division in 1628.

Browne Willis, in his *History of the Bishop of Bangor* claimed that Owain Glyndŵr, passed away and was buried at Monnington, on 20 September, 1415.

In 1680 claims were made that the grave of Owain Glyndŵr had been discovered in Monnington-on-Wye churchyard and the following is an extract from a manuscript (6832) in the Harleian Collection held at the British Museum:-

About the year 1680, the church of Monnington was rebuilt, in the churchyard of which, stood the trunk of a sycamore, in height about nine feet, and two and a half in diameter, which being in the workmen's way was cut down: a foot below the surface of the ground was laid a large grave-stone without any inscription; on its being removed there was discovered at the bottom of a well stoned grave, the body (as it is supposed) of Owen Glendower, which was whole and entire and of goodly stature, but there was no appearance of any remains of a coffin; where any part of it was touched, it fell to powder; after it had been exposed for two days the stone was again placed over it and the earth cast upon it.

Monnington Court at Monnington-on-Wye was held by the Audley family during the time of Owain Glyndŵr and they were certainly not sympathisers with his cause.

It was once believed that an unmarked slab of stone near the porch of the church at Monnington-on-Wye in Herefordshire, covered the grave of Owain Glyndŵr. It would seem, however, that this place has been confused with Monnington Straddel, a few miles away.

The error of placing Owain Glyndŵr's place of refuge at Monnington-on-Wye has been repeated by one writer after another. During my research into this matter, I visited Hereford Reference Library, where I studied with interest the 1933 Journal of the Woolhope Naturalist Club. The Hon. Secretary of the club, during a visit by its members to Monnington Church, made the following comment:

> I wish once more to kill the tradition that the celebrated Owen Glendower was buried here. The statement was first made in 1679, when in the rebuilding of the church a large sycamore obstructed the work and was cut down. Beneath was found a stone coffin lid, pointed at the lower end and possibly of thirteenth century date, and still to be seen just to the north of the porch. This lid covered a stone-lined grave containing a skeleton and someone thereupon suggested it might be the remains of the Welsh Chieftain, no doubt having in mind that one of Glyndwr's daughters was said to have married Sir Richard Monnington of Sarnesfield and confused the family name - Monnington with that of the place. However, a cursory glance at the descent of the manor would be sufficient to dispose of any such connection, and show that the selection of such a spot as a retreat by the rebel is too important to be entertained.

John Duncombe's *History of Herefordshire* revealed to me that Monnington Court at Monnington-on-Wye was in fact, at the time of Owain Glyndŵr, held by the Audley family who being anti-Welsh were certainly not supporters of his cause. The Manor of Monnington had been in the possession of Sir John Gifford in 1287 and on his death in 1309 he left two daughters, the elder of whom, Katherine, a widow of Sir Nicholas Audley, succeeded to Monnington.

The Manor remained in the Audley family until the death of Nicholas Audley in 1392, when it passed to his three sisters. One of these was Joan, who had married Thomas Touchet. He was summoned to Parliament as Baron Audley and fought for the King against Owain Glyndŵr. It is, therefore, hardly likely that Owain would have sought shelter at the manor of one of his chief opponents, with whom he had no family ties whatsoever. Thus it becomes obvious that the story of Owain's supposed burial in the churchyard, beneath a grey unmarked slab is highly unlikely.

On consulting J.E. Lloyd's book *Owen Glendower* published in 1931, my attention was drawn to Monnington Straddel, which is on the east side of the Golden Valley and also in Herefordshire. There has obviously been confusion between Monnington-on-Wye and Monnington Straddel.

This Valley of the Dore is so named because the Normans confused the Welsh 'dwr' from the name of Ystradwr (Valley of water) with the French d'or (gold) and accordingly it became known as the Golden Valley.

Staddel or Straddel was the name of an ancient territorial division, later part of Webtree Hundred, between Ewias, Ergyng (Archenfeld) and the River Wye. The name Straddel stems from the Welsh Ystrad, which can mean Vale and also street. The latter meaning is not inappropriate here, since the Roman road from Abergavenny to Kenchester crossed the valley near Abbeydore.

Dore Abbey was rebuilt by Sir John Scudamore of Holme Lacy. He also built a rectory there and presented ground for a churchyard. He endowed the church with tithes from his property and it was dedicated on Palm Sunday, 22 March, 1634, by the Bishop of St David's.

From Vowchurch Common, I followed a narrow lane and drove through deep puddles to reach Monnington Court. Gazing up at the brick mansion, I realised that it was obviously built on the site of a much earlier building. I knocked at the door several times, but failed to get any response, so I wandered around looking for someone. But the place was deserted. Feeling quite disappointed, I returned to my car and headed back up the lane.

On an impulse, I stopped at Holsty Farm and knocked on the door. After a few moments, I heard the sound of a door banging and heavy footsteps. The front door opened and an elderly gent (Colonel Cleghorn) stood before me.

I explained my interest in local history and asked him if he knew any stories relating to Owain Glyndŵr or his daughter living at Monnington Court further up the lane. Quite frankly I expected him to either shake his head with disinterest or possibly even shut the door in my face. However, he took me by surprise by saying abruptly:

"Yes, I know all about Owain Glyndŵr, I even know where he is buried – but I am not going to tell you for I am sworn to secrecy – it's not far from here."

He paused and I said encouragingly, "That is really fascinating, I wish you could tell me more."

"Glyndŵr was found in a sad and sorry state up in the Welsh hills and brought here to spend his last days. He was buried with his sword and his shield. Someone, an expert on the matter, has shown me the exact spot, but I have given my word that I will tell no one where it is."

"Is it true that Owain lived here with his daughter during his final days?" I asked.

"Yes, Owain Glyndŵr spent his last days at Chapel Farm, which is an ancient ruin, just below the Court. It is being restored at the moment by the Prudential Assurance Company, who now own the building. Owain lived there during his last few years with his wife. That is all that I am prepared to tell you."

Monnington Court at Monnington Straddel, just off the B4348, in the Golden Valley, Herefordshire, stands near the site of an earlier building which in the time of Owain Glyndŵr was the home of his daughter Margaret, who married Roger Monnington. It is quite likely that Glyndŵr may have spent his last days at this location.

Close to Monnington Court is an oval mound which is probably the remains of either a motte or a moated manor house. It stands on a broad natural terrace surrounded by a ditch which was possibly the outer defence of a crescent-shaped bailey, to the west of the mound. This may well be the site of the fortified home of Roger Monnington and his wife Alice, the daughter of Owain Glyndŵr.

Realising that it was pointless to press Colonel Cleghorn any further, I decided to leave the matter for the time being. So I thanked him for such fascinating information and returned to my car. Turning it around I drove back up the lane to Monnington Court, with a new sense of purpose.

On foot, I continued up the lane doing my best to avoid sticky red mud and deep puddles, to reach Chapel Cottage, which I then photographed. At that time the cottage was being rebuilt and all the skeleton timbers of the ancient building were exposed. There were large piles of building materials scattered around and it was obviously a very expensive project.

On my return to the Court, the farmer arrived on his tractor. He stopped the engine, and in a friendly manner, asked me what I was doing. I quickly explained, and then asked him if he knew any local traditions concerning Owain Glyndŵr.

"Yes I do," he said, and proceeded to tell me a local story that had been passed on to him. "There is a field near Chapel Cottage which is still known as the bloody field. It is the site of a battle where Owain was killed. They say that he is buried in that mound covered in trees." He pointed to a clump of trees behind a barn.

"The estate is now owned by the Prudential Assurance Company. They are spending about £100,000 in renovating Chapel Cottage and it is to be let for holidays. I am their tenant, for they own my house as well."

The farmer told me that his name was Richard Stokes and he gave me permission to wander around and take any pictures that I needed. I replied that I had all that I needed for the time being, but would return on another day when the light was better.

Another visit to Hereford Reference Library provided me with further information on the Manor of Monnington Straddel. The tree-covered mound is a moated site surrounded by a ditch with a crescent shaped bailey on its west side. It was probably a fortified site in Glyndŵr's time and where no doubt his daughter and son-in-law were living.

I also found a description of Chapel House (Chapel Cottage):-

Chapel House, now three tenements at Monnington Straddle one and a quarter miles E.N.E of the church, is of two storeys, timber-framed and plastered; the roofs are covered with stone slates. It was built probably in the 16th century on an L-shaped plan with the wings extending towards the west and south. Early in the 17th century a wing and porch were added on the east side of the south wing. The timber framing is mostly exposed, and the 17th century wing has moulded barge boards and a shaped apex post to the gable. There are some old battered doors and panelling. The front door has ornamental strap hinges and scutcheon-plate.

Chapel Cottage, near Monnington Court, dates back to the 16th century, but stands on the site of an earlier building. Its name confirms that there was once a chapel at Monnington Straddel which was probably a Chapel of Ease attached to Vowchurch Church, about 2 miles twest of here, near the road to Hereford. There is a local tradition that Owain Glyndŵr died at Chapel Cottage, near Monnington Court and it is of interest that Thomas Pennant in his *Tours of Wales* states that: "It is said that he (Owain Glyndŵr) was buried in the churchyard of Monnington, but there is no monument, nor any memorial of the spot that contains his remains." Subsequent writers decided that Pennant was referring to Monnington-on-Wye and ignored Monnington Straddel.

The 28,000 acre estate in which Monnington Court Farm stands is now owned by the Duchy of Cornwall. Very significantly it was purchased by Prince Charles, the present day Prince of Wales, on the eve of the 600th anniversary of Owain Glyndŵr's uprising.

Chapel Cottage, near Monnington Court

DESCENDANTS OF OWAIN GLYNDŴR

Even today there are many living descendants of Owain Glyndŵr through his daughters, who within a few years of his death, were allowed to retain or recover a portion of his prescribed estates, though his possessions in North Wales were lost. The Scudamores of Kentchurch, for example, are descended from Alice Glyndŵr, who married Sir John Scudamore in 1410. Their daughter, Catherine, married Thomas Cavendish, ancestor of the Dukes of Devonshire. Catherine died in 1489 and was buried at St Botolph, Aldersgate. Thomas and Catherine had a son and heir who was also named Thomas, and his descendants, the Dukes of Devonshire, to this day quarter the Scudamore arms, consisting of three stirrups.

But it is the Crofts who can claim to have the nearest descent from Glyndŵr, for the head of the family at the present time, Sir Hugh Croft, of Croft Castle, twelfth baronet, is fourteenth in direct male descent from William Croft, who being the son of Sir John Croft and Janet Glyndŵr, was a grandson of Owain Glyndŵr. All of Glyndŵr's sons died without issue, so it is the Croft family that quarter his arms.

> *His grave is beside no church, neither under the shadow of any ancient yew. It is in a spot safer and more sacred still. Rain does not fall on it, hail nor sleet chill no sere sod above it. It is forever green with the green of eternal spring. Sunny the light on it; close and warm and dear it lies, sheltered from all storms, from all cold or grey oblivion. Time shall not touch it; decay shall not dishonour it; for that grave is in the heart of every true Cymro. There, for ever, from generation unto generation, grey Owen's heart lies dreaming on, dreaming on, safe for ever and for ever.*

Owen Rhoscomyl 1905

EPILOGUE

I first started working on this book in 1980 but after five years' research I moved on to other projects. The uncompleted manuscript lay untouched, on a shelf in my study, for the next ten years, during which time I worked on several other books including one which I co-authored with David Pykitt, entitled *Journey to Avalon – The Final Discovery of King Arthur*.

An article published in the *Western Mail* on Thursday 5 January 1995 re-awoke my interest in Owain Glyndŵr and I then with some urgency went back to work on this book. Welsh correspondent Clive Betts had written a report on 'new evidence which appeared to solve the mystery of what happened to the Welsh patriot Owain Glyndŵr when he mysteriously disappeared after his last battle.'

I spoke to Clive on the telephone and told him of my research carried out ten or more years previously and it became obvious that he too had followed the same trail that led to Monnington Straddel in Herefordshire. Clive, for example, had also carried out research in Hereford City Library and had interviewed Richard Stokes, the farmer who lived at Monnington Court.

As a result of that conversation, I renewed my interest in the subject and undertook further research to complete this book for publication as soon as possible.

I returned to Monnington Court and spoke to Richard Stokes again. He remembered my visit about ten years previously and had seen the article in the Western Mail, but there was nothing more that he could add to the information that he had previously given me. Besides, he had no time to spare chatting for he had to get on with his harvesting. He suggested that I might like to talk to his wife instead.

Mrs Stokes listened to my story with interest and took me around to the back of the house to show me evidence of an earlier stone building on the site, which was perhaps there in Glyndŵr's time. She suggested that I might like to go and talk to Richard Stokes Senior who had lived at the Court previously, having taken over the farm from his father. He was now retired and lived in a new bungalow, a short distance along the road to Hay. She also told me that Colonel Cleghorn was still alive and was now living in a house on the Hereford Road.

I thanked her for her help and drove off to see Mr Stokes Senior, whose bungalow is very appropriately called 'Glyndŵr'. Before long I was sitting in his living room and asking him if he could tell me about the local traditions concerning Owain Glyndŵr.

"Well, all I can tell you is that Owain Glyndŵr is reputed to be buried in the old motte, which is surrounded by the traces of a moat, up at Monnington. I remember, in about 1932, when I was about twelve years of age, two archaeologists from North Wales spent a week or so excavating the top of the mound. Hughes and Rowlands were their names, but they must be dead by now. They dug about six feet down right in the centre of the mound, but found nothing at all.

"The story is that Owain Glyndŵr is supposed to have come down from the Black Mountains and fought his last battle here, and the field next to Chapel Cottage is still called the Bloody Meadow, named I suppose due to the fact that there was so much blood shed in the fighting."

"Where did the story of this battle come from, for it is certainly not mentioned in any of the books about Owain Glyndŵr?"

"It is just a local tradition I suppose."

"What do you know about Chapel Cottage?"

"Well it must have been an old chapel at some time because the two fields adjoining it are called Chapel Meadow and Chapel Close. Those old names still persist until now, as local names. It is possible that the cottage was originally a chapel and it was later converted into cottages."

"How long did you live at Monnington Court?"

"I was born there."

"So your father was farming there before you."

"Yes, that's right."

"Did he talk much about the local traditions of Owain Glyndŵr?"

"No, my mother was much more interested in history. All that Father really cared about was his horses and the farming."

I thanked Mr and Mrs Stokes for their hospitality and returned to my car. Within a short time I was knocking on the door of the house where I had been told that the Colonel was now living. An elderly woman came to the door, and she was obviously his wife. I explained that I was interested in local history and would be grateful if I could talk to her husband. She replied to the effect that he had not been very well, but she would go and find out if he would see me.

She returned a few minutes later and told me that he would be along shortly. Waiting in the hall for several minutes I began to wonder if he was ever coming, and then I heard the shuffling of feet. A long thin walking stick then stabbed through an open doorway at the end of the hall and the figure of an elderly man slowly followed behind it. He shuffled up the flag-stoned hall and told me to go into his study on the left.

Sitting in a comfortable armchair, beside an impressive book case, I glanced at some of the titles and was immediately aware that the Colonel had a deep interest in history. He obviously did not remember my calling on him at his farm ten years previously, so once again I asked him if he could tell me anything about the local traditions concerning Owain Glyndŵr.

"Owain Glyndŵr looked upon himself as a sort of King. He had two daughters – one who married a Scudamore from Kentchurch and one who married Lord Croft. Eventually, when Glyndwr was on the run, he fell ill up in the Black Mountains and was taken to Chapel Cottage at Monnington, where he died.

There have always been tremendous arguments as to whether he was buried at this Monnington or Monnington on Wye. But the Scudamore family are practically certain and all I can say is that I **know** that he was buried at Monnington Straddel.

Chapel Cottage was originally pre-Domesday – it features in the Domesday Book and I have reason to believe that the foundations of the present Chapel Cottage go right back to the seventh century."

"Would there have been a chapel on the site in Glyndŵr's time? It must have been called Chapel Cottage for some reason", I commented.

"Not in his day. It may have been put up in memory of him of course."

"Like a shrine" I said.

"Of some sort, I suppose. The present building is in brick and half-timbered. It is much more recent than the earlier stone building on that site. It was there that he died, and I have reason to think that he was buried nearby. I am not going to say more than that."

"There appears to be some confusion as to whether Monnington Straddel was the home of Roger Monnington who was married to Margaret Glyndŵr, or was it in the ownership of the Scudamore family?"

"I know the Scudamores well, and John's grandmother also maintains that Glyndŵr was found in the Black Mountains and taken to Chapel Cottage.

In the tower at Kentchurch Court is a room about twice the size of this one, where Owain Glyndŵr lived for quite a while when visiting his daughter."

"There is a sort of hiding place there I believe?"

"Yes, but there are many, for in the whole house there are hidden ways – from room to room to room. It is a fascinating house but it gives some people the creeps."

"I know what you mean, for I once took a party there from the Hill College in Abergavenny, on a weekend tour of historic places, and a certain lady in the group refused to go into the house, insisting that it was haunted. Earlier that morning she had also refused to enter the Skirrid Mountain Inn, for the same reason."

"At Kentchurch Court, underneath Owain Glyndŵr's tower, there is a dungeon known as Glyndŵr's Dungeon, where everyone he didn't like was thrown into. I know it intimately for I dug 40 or 50 tons of mud out of that damn dungeon, when the flood took place."

"What do you think of the idea that John of Kent was really Owain Glyndwr in disguise?"

"I can give you a positive **no** to that suggestion. Some years ago I took a certain man to Kentchurch to find out quite a lot about John of Kentchurch and his ill-doings, and he was shown the portrait of John of Kent. That picture is painted by two different artists. The background is painted by one artist and the figure by another and it definitely does not show Glyndŵr."

"How can you be sure of that?"

"'This man who can do things that I cannot pretend to do, wasn't told a thing about the picture. He maintained through his powers that it has been painted by two different people. He was pointedly asked if it could have been Owain Glyndŵr and the answer was a definite no. "

" This chap presumably had dowsing abilities?"

"Yes, quite amazing ones!"

"Do you have proof that Owain Glyndŵr is buried at Monnington Straddel?"

"What do you call proof?"

"Have you seen something?"

"All I can tell you is that I took this same man to a certain place, and he left me for certain reasons and went to a particular place. He then came back and said that there was nothing of importance there. We were walking back to my farm, when he suddenly said. 'I have told you a lie. Come back with me.' We went back and for various reasons - all he said was, 'A royal person is buried here. He is in peace.' I said, 'How do you know that he is a royal person?' He replied, 'Because he is buried with his sword and his shield and only royalty used to be buried in that manner.' That is the only proof I have."

"Did he dowse with a pendulum?"

"No he always used rods – once you put him on to a certain line – set him on a course – it just poured out of him."

"Do you know anything about the so-called 'Bloody Meadow' near Chapel Cottage?"

"Yes, but I don't think that it has anything to do with Owain Glyndŵr. It would appear that a battle was once fought there, for bits and bridles have been found and also slain horses have been found in lines, presumably killed by the winning side in a bloodthirsty battle. But it probably occurred after Glyndŵr's time."

"I have been told by someone that an excavation was carried out on top of the mound many years ago."

"Yes, there have been several. People have dug here and there, looking for the grave of Owain Glyndŵr. But he should be left in peace."

"I quite agree. He was the greatest Welshman who ever lived."

****

So it would appear that there is a strong tradition that Owain Glyndŵr spent his last days at Monington Straddel and that his grave is there. In 1999 the Scudamore family revealed that the secret of Glyndŵr's final resting place had been passed on to the family heir through the centuries and that he is indeed buried at Monington Straddel. Yet somehow I am not fully convinced, for with the 600th anniversary of Glyndŵr's uprising approaching, the family were being pestered by the media and it is possible that this statement was made in order to regain a quiet life.

A new book by Alex Gibbon titled *The Mystery of Jack of Kent and the Fate of Owain Glyndŵr* (Sutton Publishing) is due to be published later in 2004 which may shed new light on the possible location of Glyndŵr's grave. The author, whilst carrying out research into the identity of Jack of Kent, claims to have found evidence that the man known by that name, who once resided at Kentchurch Court was in fact Owain Glyndŵr.

Alex has, quite understandably, not been prepared to reveal his conclusions to me, before the publication of his book, but he has indicated that he believes that Glyndŵr was buried inside an existing church in Wales. If his theory can be proved correct then he will have solved one of the greatest mysteries in Welsh history.

> *Throughout Wales, his name is the symbol for the vigorous resistance of the Welsh spirit to tyranny and alien rule and the assertion of a national character which finds its fitting expression in the Welsh language... For the Welshmen of all subsequent ages, Glyndŵr has been a national hero, the first, indeed, in the country's history to command the willing support alike of north and south, east and west, Gwynedd and Powys, Deheubarth and Morgannwg.*
>
> J.E. Lloyd

APPENDIX I
The Final Years of Henry V

In 1415 Henry V set sail on an expedition to France. He took with him nine hundred men at arms and five thousand archers, the royal seals and a piece of the 'True Cross' - six inches long and one inch wide, to bring him good luck.

On October 25 of that year, the English and French armies met in a field, about twenty miles inland from Boulogne to do battle. Henry's army was in a poor state, weakened by hunger and dysentery. They faced an army fifty thousand strong and, to make matters worse, the night before the battle it rained in torrents, with the result that the ploughed fields separating the two armies turned into a quagmire.

As the French infantry squelched awkwardly through the mud, Henry ordered his archers to shoot. A devastating shower of arrows fell onto the French, causing enormous casualties. Fighting hand to hand, the English swung axes against the French swords and a wall of bodies rose between the two armies. For two hours they fought until the French cavalry charged, but fell back under a sky full of deadly arrows. The survivors turned and fled. That day seven thousand Frenchmen died and the English losses were less than one hundred. The twenty-eight year old king had won a great victory.

At the end of the battle Henry enquired the name of the castle to be seen in the distance and was told that it was Agincourt. He immediately cried "Then, since all battles ought to be named after the nearest castle, let this henceforth and lastingly bear the name of the battle of Agincourt!"

Henry then called together the clergy and ordered them to perform a service of thanksgiving on the field before the whole army. They chanted the 114th Psalm and on the first verse of the 115th Psalm, every man knelt on the ground. They then sang the *Te Deum*, and so closed the now famous battle of Agincourt.

Of all the battles ever fought by France up to that time none had ever been so fatal as that of Agincourt. *Never did so many and so noble men fall in one battle*, says the French chronicler, Monstrelet. It was a wholesale slaughter of France's princes and nobles and amongst the men who fell that day, were one marshal, thirteen earls, ninety-two barons, fifteen hundred knights and eight thousand gentlemen. There were fourteen thousand prisoners left in the hands of the English, amongst whom were the Dukes of Orleans and Bourbon, the Marshall Boucicault, the Counts of Eu, Vendôme, Richemont, Craon, and Harcourt.

The highest estimate of the English killed puts it at sixteen hundred, while Elmham contends that it was only one hundred, and other contemporary writers state that it was only forty. The only persons of note who fell on the English side were the Earl of Suffolk and the Duke of York.

It is said that when Henry left the harbour of Calais to return to England the inhabitants of the town showed their delight at his departure by ringing the church bells. On hearing this joyful sound, Henry immediately put back to harbour and confiscated the offending bells. He brought them back to England and presented them to his native town to be hung in the tower of the parish church of St. Mary the Virgin. This unlikely story probably arises from a misreading of a medieval inscription on one of the bells:

Habeo nomen Gabrielis missi de Coelis

It would seem that 'Coelis' (Heaven) was mistakenly read as 'Calais'.

The two hundred foot spire of St. Mary's Church is a notable landmark, but the 'Calais bells' which once hung in the tower were recast in 1706.

In 1417 Henry attacked Normandy and three years later he concluded peace with the French. By the Treaty of Troyes he was acknowledged to be heir to the throne of France. On the same day that the treaty was finally ratified, Henry became betrothed to Princess Katherine, the nineteen-year-old daughter of King Charles of France, in the church of Notre Dame at

Henry V   Katherine

Henry V was described by a contemporary writer, Titus Livius of Friuli:-

> In stature he was a little above the middle size; his countenance was beautiful, his neck long, his body slender, and his limbs most elegantly formed. He was very strong; and so swift, that, with two companions, without either dogs or missive weapons, he caught a doe, one of the fleetest of animals. He was a lover of music, and excelled in all martial and manly exercises.

Before the betrothal the young couple went together to the high altar, where the articles of peace were read aloud, and both affixed their seals to them. Taking Katherine's hand, Henry placed on her finger the ring worn by the queens of England at their coronations. The Duke of Burgundy took an oath to obey Henry as Regent of France, so long as King Charles should live, and after the latter's death, to acknowledge him as his liege-lord. Nine days later, Henry and Katherine were married and the young King of England had now satisfied his ambitions. He was now Regent and heir of France and the husband of the fair Katherine. The young queen was crowned at Westminster and they set off on a tour of England so that Henry could show off his beautiful bride. Sadly they were only to have two years together.

Just before the birth of her child, he was forced to return to his army in France and whilst he was besieging Meaux, news was brought to him that Katherine had given birth to a son at Windsor.

A few months later Henry was struck down with dysentery at Bois de Vincennes outside Paris, whilst travelling to assist his ally the Duke of Burgundy, and he died at the age of 34, just after 2.00 am on Monday, 31 August,1422. His heir, who became Henry VI, was barely 9 months old.

Queen Katherine had been summoned to attend her husband's death-bed but it was a long journey and she arrived too late. She was just twenty-one when she re-crossed the Channel with the body of her husband.

Henry did not come of a long-lived family although his great-grandfather indeed had reached sixty-five, an age which had only once before been reached by an English king. But his grandfather had died, worn out, at fifty-eight; his father, after years of suffering, expired at forty-seven; and his mother died in her twenty-fifth year.

The king's body was dismembered – the flesh boiled from the bones – and then bones and flesh placed in a casket with spices. The remaining parts were buried in the churchyard of St. Maur des Fosses.

From Vincennes it was first taken in great pomp, attended by his household, and a multitude of the people, to the church of Notre-Dame in Paris, where a solemn service was performed over it. From Paris it was removed with the same state to Rouen. Here Queen Katherine waited with the corpse until affairs were sufficiently settled before returning to England. This was not for some weeks, and it must have been about the beginning of November when the procession set out on the journey to Calais.

The coffin was placed in a cart drawn by four magnificent horses. Above it was an effigy of the king, made from boiled leather and dressed in royal robes. It was beautifully painted, with a crown of gold on its head. The right hand held a sceptre, the left a golden ball and the face looked up to the heavens. The effigy lay on a mattress, on which was a coverlet of vermilion silk interwoven with beaten gold.

The King of Scots followed as chief mourner; with him were Henry's kinsmen, the English nobles in France, and the officers of his household, while at the distance of a league behind followed the Queen with her ladies.

A halt was made at the church of St. Woolfran in Abbeville. There the coffin rested while rows of priests on either side chanted requiems unceasingly day and night. In every town through which the procession passed, masses were daily said from break of day to noon for the dead man's soul.

From Calais the body was transported to Dover. It was then carried through Canterbury and Rochester to London, which was reached on Martinmas Day (November 11). As the procession approached the city it was met by fifteen bishops clad in their episcopal robes, a number of mitred abbots and other dignified ecclesiastics, and many people of all ranks. The service for the dead was chanted as the procession passed over London Bridge and down Lombard Street, to St. Paul's Cathedral. The adornment of the horses which pulled the funeral carriage was notably significant. On the collar of the first was emblazoned the ancient arms of England; on that of the second, the arms of France and England quartered. These, the late king had borne in his life-time, as a solemn claim to the double crown; the third showed the arms of France simply; the fourth the traditional bearings of the invincible Arthur – for like him, Henry had never been vanquished on the field .

After a long service in St. Paul's Cathedral the body was transferred to its final resting place in Westminster Abbey. Never before, had preparations on such an impressive scale, been made for the reception of a deceased monarch. The relics which occupied the extreme eastern end of the Confessor's Chapel were removed to make room for the body of the great king. Over the tomb of Caen stone and Purbeck marble, was raised a chantry, where masses were to be offered up for ever for his soul, and an altar built in honour of the Annunciation.

The chapel later constructed here was built in the shape of the first letter of his name. It had been designed by Henry himself and took eight years to erect. Among the statues which adorn it are those of St. George of England and St. Denis of France, the two kingdoms which, for a time at least, he had united; the sculptures represent scenes of his life, his coronation, and his victories in France. The shield and the helmet placed above the tomb belong to Henry's time, but they are not, as they have been represented to be, his actual arms used at Agincourt, having been furnished by the undertaker as part of the funeral equipment.

On the tomb below may still be seen the effigy of the King, but sadly stripped of its ancient splendour, for the leather effigy which was carried from Rouen to London was substituted with a more permanent memorial. It is a figure cut out of heart of oak, covered with silver-gilt and with a head of solid silver, paid for by Queen Katherine. Two teeth of gold were stolen in the reign of Edward IV and the silver head was taken at the time of the Dissolution.

Henry's heir was his son, also named Henry, who was barely 9 months old. To his infant son, now Henry VI, was bequeathed the impossible task of retaining France and ruling the English nobles. He succeeded to the throne without being Prince of Wales.

Shrine of Henry V in Westminster Abbey

Tomb of Henry V in Westminster Abbey.

Queen Katherine later secretly married Owen Tudor, a descendant of small Anglesey squires. He was in the army of Henry V that fought the French wars, which includes Agincourt. After the wars, Owen had obtained a place at Court. He was then in his middle thirties and he and the Dowager Queen fell in love. At the time, he was 37 years of age, tall and good-looking. He was Clerk of the Wardrobe and it was his duty to guard the Queen's jewels, to discuss new clothes with her, and to buy the materials for her gowns. The affair was carried on in secret and it is not known exactly when they were married, but there must have been suspicions, because in the sixth year of the reign of Henry VI, a law was passed forbidding the marriage of a queen-dowager without the consent of the King.

They had three sons. The first was Edmund of Hadam, the second Jasper of Hatfield, the third Owen of Westminster, and in 1436 Katherine gave birth to a daughter who died within a few days.

Eventually news of Katherine's marriage with Owen Tudor leaked out and her three Welsh sons were taken from her by Order of the Council and placed under the care of Katherine de la Pole, the Abbess of Barking.

Owen Tudor was arrested and taken to Newgate and in 1437 whilst he was in prison his wife Katherine died. She was buried with pomp and ceremony in Our Lady Chapel in Westminster Abbey. At the age of 76 Owen Tudor led a Royalist army against the Yorkists and was defeated at Mortimer's Cross. He was beheaded in Hereford Market Place.

Years later, the two sons of Owen Tudor - half-brothers of Henry VI - were declared legitimate and accepted into the ranks of nobility. Edmund Tudor was created Earl of Richmond, and his younger brother, Jasper, was made Earl of Pembroke.

Edmund Tudor married Margaret Beaufort, heiress to the house of Somerset. At the age of thirteen she gave birth to a son at Pembroke Castle on June 26, 1456. This grandson of Owen Tudor and Katherine de Valois was to ascend the throne as Henry VII, the first of the Tudor Kings. Henry VII, had his grandmother's bones moved so that he could build his own chapel and for centuries Katherine's body, encased in lead, lay in a wooden chest where her face – the face of a Queen of England – was available for all and sundry to examine.

Weever in his *Funeral Monuments* describes it as he saw it in the time of Charles I :

> Here lieth Katherine, Queen of England, wife to Henry V, in a chest or coffin, with a loose cover, to be seen and handled of any who much desire it, and who, by her own appointment, inflicted this penance on herself, in regard to her disobedience to her husband, for being delivered of her son, Henry VI at Windsor, which place he forbode.

Samuel Pepys tells how he came here and on being showed the body... "I had the upper part of her body in my hands and I did kiss her mouth, reflecting that I did kiss a Queen, and that this was my birthday, thirty-six years old, that I did first kiss a Queen."

It was not until 1716, during the reign of George III that the bones of Queen Katherine were decently buried in the vaults of Westminster.

The 600th anniversary of the birth of Henry V at Monmouth Castle was celebrated in Monmouth during August 1987, when a whole month of celebrations was organised. A specially commissioned play about the life and times of Henry V was performed in St. Mary's Priory Church with the people of Monmouth participating on a massive scale.

Helmet, shield and saddle of Henry V.

233

The 15th century which had begun with Owain Glyndŵr's uprising closed with Welshman Henry Tudor (Henry VII) on the throne. The bards proclaimed him to be the heir of Cadwaladr and that at last the ancient prophecies had been fulfilled.

Part of an exhibition in Pembroke Castle commemorating the birth of Henry Tudor

The memory of the Welsh state which Glyndŵr created just two generations before Henry Tudor ascended the throne of England, on the threshold of the modern era, still inspires Welsh patriots.

Gwynfor Evans

APPENDIX II
Chronology of Events

1270	(7 December) Death of Gruffydd ap Madog, and northern Powys is divided among his four sons, Madog, Llywelyn, Owain and Gruffydd. The latter receives Ial and Edernion (including Glyndyfrdwy) as his share.
1354	(28 May) Birth of Owain Glyndŵr (according to Pennant) but the year is possibly 1359.
1367	Birth of Richard Plantagenet.
1370 c.	Owain studies law at the Inns of Court, London.
1376	Death of the Black Prince.
1377	Death of Edward III, and Richard II succeeds to the throne.
1382	Richard II marries Anne of Bohemia.
1383 c.	Owain marries Margaret, the daughter of Sir David Hanmer.
1385	Owain fights in Richard II's army at the battle of Berwick against the Scots.
1386	Owain gives evidence in suit of Grosvenor v Scrope at Chester.
1387	Owain is appointed chief squire to Admiral Arundel and fights in the naval battle of Cadzard.
	Death of Owain Glyndŵr's father-in-law, Sir David Hanmer.
1388	Reginald de Grey succeeds his father to the Lordship of Dyffryn Clwyd.
1394	Death of Anne of Bohemia.
1396	Marriage of Richard II to Isabella, daughter of Charles VI of France, cementing the truce established by Richard in the Hundred Years War.
1399	Death of John of Gaunt - Richard II sails to England - Henry Bolingbroke returns from France - Richard II is deposed and imprisoned in the Tower.
	Bolingbroke is crowned Henry IV.
	Owain Glyndŵr submits grievances to Parliament.
	Owain Glyndŵr is summoned to join Henry IV on Scottish expedition.
1400	Death of Richard II at Pontefract Castle.
	(16 September) Conspirators assemble at Glyndyfrdwy.
	Owain is declared Prince of Wales.
	(19 September) Ruthin is attacked.
	Henry IV receives news of the Welsh uprising.
	Denbigh, Rhuddlan, Flint, Hawarden and Holt are ravaged.
	(22 September) Oswestry is set on fire.
	Welshpool is attacked.

(24 September) Welsh forces suffer a defeat at Vyrnwy and retire to the hills.
(26 September) Henry IV reaches Shrewsbury.
(October) Henry IV arrives in Bangor.
(15 October)Henry IV returns to Shrewsbury having made a circuit of North Wales.
(8 November) Owain Glyndŵr's estates granted to John Beaufort, Earl of Somerset.

1401

(January) Parliament meets and shows concern over the situation in Wales.
(21 February) Commons represent to the King and Lords in Parliament that the Welsh are in a dangerous mood.
(1 April) Conwy Castle is captured by Owain's cousins, the Tudors of Anglesey.
(June) An agreement is reached at Conwy Castle.
Rhys Gethin defeats a large force at the battle of Hyddgen.
(2 October)Henry IV marches into South Wales
(9 October) Llywelyn ap Gruffydd Fychan of Caio is put to death at Llandovery Market Place.
Henry IV establishes his headquarters at Strata Florida.
Owain attacks Welshpool.
(2 November) Owain threatens castle and town of Caernarfon.

1402

(January) Owain attacks Lordship of Ruthin.
(February) A Blazing comet is visible in the sky.
(April) De Grey is captured and imprisoned in Dolbadarn Castle.
(27 April) Three armies assemble at Chester, Shrewsbury and Hereford
An attempt is made on Owain's life by his cousin Hywel Sele.
(22 June) Rhys Gethin is victorious at the Battle of Pilleth and Edmund Mortimer is captured. He later agrees to join Glyndŵr.
(August) Owain Glyndŵr enters Gwent and Glamorgan.
Cardiff, Llandaff, Abergavenny, Caernarfon attacked.
(23 July) Henry IV at Lileshall, Shropshire.
(2 September) Henry IV's army crosses border into Wales.
(7 September) Weather appalling,Henry IV's tent blows down.
Owain Glyndŵr invades Herefordshire.
(15 September) Henry IV leaves Hereford and goes to Carmarthen.
Caerphilly, Newport, Caerleon and Usk taken by Owain.
French land in Carmarthen.
(22 September) Henry IV returns with his army to England.

1403

(8 March) Prince Henry at the age of 16 is appointed royal deputy in Wales.

(May) Llandovery is attacked and Llandeilo burnt by Glyndŵr's army.

Henry Prince of Wales at Shrewsbury. He informs the king that Owain Glyndŵr, Prince of Wales, is about to invade England.

Dryslwyn Castle, Newcastle Emln and Dinas Powis Castles attacked.

Prince Henry marches into Wales and destroys Sycharth and Glyndyfrdwy.

(6 July) Surrender of Carmarthen Castle.

(9 July) Owain Glyndŵr at St. Clears.

(10 July) Hotspur raises the standard of revolt in Chester.

(12 July) Negotiations with Carew.

Owain Glyndŵr consults a soothsayer about his future prospects.

(21 July) Battle of Shrewsbury (Owain Glyndŵr at Carmarthen).

(8 September) Henry IV arrives at Worcester.

(November) Determined attack by Glyndŵr's forces on Caernarfon.

1404

(January) Parliament places Henry, Prince of Wales, in control of operations in Wales.

Glyndŵr captures Criccieth, Harlech and Aberystwyth Castles.

First Welsh Parliament is held at Machynlleth and Owain Glyndŵr is crowned Prince of Wales.

John Trefor, Bishop of St Asaphs gives his support to Glyndŵr

(10 May) Conference at Dolgellau.

Owain appoints Griffith Yonge as his Chancellor and John Hanmer, his own brother-in-law, as his special ambassader to conclude an alliance with the French.

Treaty with France.

Battle at Mynydd Cwm Ddu.

Battle of Craig y Dorth.

Coity Castle is attacked.

(10 June) Welsh attack on Archenfeld.

Harlech and Aberystwyth Castle are captured by Owain.

Bangor Cathedral is burnt by Glyndŵr.

A Parliament is held at Dolgellau.

(14 July) A formal treaty of alliance between Wales and France is signed by Gruffydd Yonge and John Hanmer on behalf of Glyndŵr and by Le Compte de la Marche, Louis Compte de Vendome, Arnaud de Carbie, Chancellor of Franc,e and by the Bishops of Arras, Meaux and Noyon on behalf of Charles VI.

(20 August) Henry Don led an attack on Kidwelli, assisted by
William and Gwyn ap Rhys Llwyd.
(October) Owain Glyndŵr occupies Harlech.
(14 November) An English army is sent to break the siege of
Coity Castle.
(25 November) Force assembled at Hereford under Prince Henry.

1405

(12 January) Owain Glyndŵr ratifies his treaty with the French
at Aberystwyth Castle.
(February) Lady Despenser attempts to abduct the Mortimer
heirs and bring them to Caerfilli Castle.
(27 April) Prince Henry is appointed Lieutenant in North Wales
with 500 men-at-arms and 3,000 archers under his command.
(11 March) A Welsh force led by Rhys Gethin is defeated at
Grosmont.
(May) Battle at Pwll Melyn, Usk. Glyndŵr's brother, Tudur is
killed and his eldest son Gruffydd is captured and taken to the
Tower of London.
(June) John Hanmer, Owain's brother-in-law is captured and a
reward of £26 13s 4d is given to the man who took him prisoner.
Gruffydd Yonge is also captured
(22 July) The French sail from Brest.
(1 August) Owain holds a Parliament at Harlech.
A large Welsh and French force marches on Worcester.
(10 August) King Henry IV reaches Worcester.
Owain holds a second Parliament at Harlech. It is attended by
ambassadors from Scotland, France, Brittany and Castile..
(10 September) Henry IV invades Wales again - enters
Glamorgan and relieves Coity Castle.
(1 October) Henry IV back at Worcester.
Owain Glyndŵr returns to Harlech.

1406

(12 January) Glyndŵr signs a treaty at Aberystwyth Castle
ratifying a Franco-Welsh treaty.
(28 February) Tripartite Indenture signed and sealed by Owain
Glyndŵr, Edmund Mortimer and the Earl of Northumberland,
their aim being to divide Henry IV's kingdom into three
separate principalities.
(31 March) Owain summons a Parliament at Pennal and a letter
is written to the King of France, pledging full support for Pope
Benedict XIII of Avignon. It is sent to Paris with several of
Glyndŵr's ambassaders.
(5 April) Prince Henry is appointed King's deputy in Wales.
Gower, Towi and Ceredigion submit to the King.

(10 November) A Royal Commission is opened at Beaumaris for granting pardons and assessment of fines.

1407	Little is known of Owain Glyndŵr's movements in first half of year.
	Henry IV's health starts to fail.
	Preparations are made to attack Aberystwyth and Harlech castles.
	Pestilence in Wales.
	Assault by Prince Henry on Aberystwyth.
	(September) Aberystwyth garrison makes terms.
	Prince Henry returns to England leaving 500 soldiers at Strata Florida.
	(October) Owain Glyndŵr slips into Aberystwyth Castle.
	(December) Severe weather until the end of March.
1408	
	(February)Earl of Northumberland and his allies defeated at the battle of Bramham Moor.
	(May) Glyndwr sends two envoys to Paris to make a desperate appeal for assistance.
	Aberystwyth Castle is captured by Prince Henry.
	Siege of Harlech Castle. Edmund Mortimer dies of starvation.
1409	Harlech Castle falls to the English. Owain's wife, two of his daughters and three of his grand-daughters are captured and taken to London.
	Glyndŵr is now without a base.
	Pardons are granted by the King to Howel ap Gwilym, Abbot of Conwy, and Lewis Byford, Bishop of Bangor.
1410	Owain makes a raid on the Shropshire border to obtain provisions. Rhys Ddu, Philip Scudamore and Rhys ap Tudur are captured and executed.
1411	A pardon is granted to Adam of Usk, who claimed to be a follower of Glyndŵr "against his will".
1412	Owain Glyndŵr seizes Dafydd Gam of Brecon and Llantilio Crossenny.
	(June) A ransom is paid to Owain Glyndŵr for the release of DafyddGam.
1413	Death of Henry IV and Prince Henry becomes Henry V.
	(May) Pardons offered to all Welsh followers of Glyndŵr.
1413	A Welshman who came to London is paid £1 for secret information regarding 'Ewain Glendourdy'.
1415	Owain Glyndŵr finds refuge at Monnington (?).
	(15 July) Gilbert Talbot is empowered by Henry V to offer Owain Glyndwr a pardon.
	(20 September) Supposed death of Owain Glyndŵr.

1416	Maredydd ab Owain makes a final attempt to rally opposition in north Wales, with the support of the Scots.
	(24 February) Maredydd ab Owain is sent with offer of a pardon.
	Celebrating the end of the war in Wales, Henry V makes a pilgrimage to St Winifred's Well, Holywell in North Wales.
1420	John, Duke of Bedford is empowered to treat with Meredydd ap Owain regarding the possibility of his serving under the King in Normandy.
1421	Maredydd ab Owain finally accepts a pardon from Henry V.
1430	Death of the chronicler, Adam of Usk.
1433	Sir John Scudamore, Glyndŵr's son-in-law is dismissed as Sheriff of Herefordshire.
1948	Parliament repeals certain Acts of Parliament that are deemed out of date. Among them is an Act against Owain Glyndŵr.
1956	Heraldic slab of Madog ap Gruffydd the great-grandfather of Owain Glyndŵr is found at Valle Crucis Abbey.

Llywelyn the last native prince of Wales is a figure of history, but Owain Glyndŵr is as if still alive with the nation, and it is no wonder that like Moses and Arthur, the location of his grave is not known. The poets sang their longing for his return. They would not have it that he was dead.

Sir O. M. Edwards

APPENDIX III
Recent Events

1996 – The Owain Glyndŵr Society was formed in Carmarthen with the following aims:

(1) To honour the contribution of Owain Glyndŵr to the history of Wales.
(2) To contribute to the development of the heritage of Wales.
(3) To attempt to find the grave of Owain Glyndŵr and to mark it appropriately.
(4) To erect a fitting memorial to Owain Glyndŵr at an appropriate place at the turn of the millenium.
(5) To endow a lasting academic memorial to Owain Glyndŵr.

1999 – In April a comet crossed the skies heralding the coming of the 600th anniversary of the uprising of Owain Glyndŵr.

The 28,000 acre estate at Monnington Court was purchased by the Prince of Wales's Duchy of Cornwall estate. It was significantly purchased by Prince Charles from the Prudential Insurance Company on the eve of the 600th anniversary of Glyndŵr's uprising.

Embassy Glyndŵr came into existence, following a decision by a group of exiles to search out the last resting place of Owain Glyndŵr's daughter and her children, who all died whilst imprisoned at the Tower of London in 1413. Embassy Glyndŵr has campaigned for the official recognition of Dydd Glyndŵr (Glyndŵr Day on September 16th) and in the promotion of Coffad (Commemoration) Glyndwr 2000-16-22. Embassy Glyndŵr is a non paid, voluntary, non profit making collective that has been established to promote knowledge of Owain Glyndŵr, his life and times and of the Great War of Independence. Embassy Glyndŵr aims to act as 'Owain's Embassy' to the world – an international link – to provide knowledge in regard to Owain Glyndŵr and his great struggle for an independent Wales from 1400-16.

In May, John Scudamore, a direct descendant of Sir John Scudamore and Alice Glyndŵr, revealed a family secret that just before his mother died in February 1999 at the age of 86, she told him the secret of the location of Owain Glyndŵr's burial place. The knowledge that he was indeed buried at Monnington Straddel had been passed down to the heirs through the centuries.

On November 28, Owain Glyndŵr was named as one of the Makers of the Millenium by some of the world's most powerful and influential people. He was named the seventh most influential person in a poll published in a Sunday newspaper. Those listed ahead of him were printing press inventor Johann Gutenburg, William Shakespeare, William Caxton, who brought printing to Britain, Leonardo da Vinci, Elizabeth I and Michael Faraday who discovered electricity. Also in the top ten, but behind Glyndŵr in the list were Sir Isaac Newton, Abraham Lincoln and Galileo. Owain Glyndŵr thus took his true place among the most influential people of the past 1,000 years.

2000 – In April, an Owain Glyndŵr exhibition was opened at the National Library of Wales, Aberystwyth. The exhibition included a series of paintings by the North Wales artist, Margaret Jones. She was commissioned to produce 14 original paintings depicting scenes in the life of Glyndŵr. The centre piece of the exhibition was Glyndŵr's Pennal letter which he entrusted his emissary Gruffydd Yonge to deliver to the French King in 1401. Attached to it is the only surviving wax seal of Owain Glyndŵr and the document was on loan from the Bibliotheque Nationale in Paris for a period of six months. Nearly 45,000 people from all over the world visited the exhibition and translations of the display were available in French, German, Spanish and Catalan.

In June, Nick Russell, Managing Director of the Cardiff based firm Terra Dat Geophysics and Geotechnology, conducted a scientific survey of the supposed burial site at Monnington Court Farm. The survey was financed by the Owain Glyndŵr Society and backed by Herefordshire County Council and English Heritage.

They concentrated on the mound area but found no evidence of a burial. However, they did find shadow traces of a building which could have been the church of the lost village of Monnington Straddel. The ancient structure appears to have had walls a metre thick and measured approximately 8 metres by 18 metres.

My own feeling is that, although the mound has long thought to have been the burial site, it is more likely that Owain was buried in the consecrated ground of the small church which once stood nearby. It served as a Chapel of Ease attached to Vowchurch which is about 1.5 miles to the west. Its existence is obviously connected with the name of Chapel Cottage, an old timber-framed house.

This part of Herefordshire was once in Wales for it used to contain the Welsh kingdoms of Ewias and Archenfield and the Welsh language was spoken in the area up to a century ago.

It should also be remembered that Owain's Tripartite Agreement signed at Aberdaron in 1406, together with Edmund Mortimer and Percy, Earl of Northumberland, gave Owain all the territory west of the Severn, which would of course include his possible burial site at Monnington Straddel. Straddel or Straddle was the name of an ancient territorial division, later part of Webtree Hundred, between Ewias and Erging (Archenfield) and the river Wye.

On September 16 a memorial to Owain Glyndŵr was unveiled at Machynlleth in the grounds of Y Plas (Celtica). It is appropriate that the monument should be sited in Machynlleth for this is where Owain held his first Parliament. It is approximately in the centre of Wales, at the meeting point of Ceredigion, Powys and Gwynedd.

The massive block of slate for the memorial was extracted from Penrhyn Quarry, Bethesda in North Wales and the sculptor was Ieuan Rees of Ammanford.

In his speech at the unveiling ceremony, Adrian Jones, President of the Owain Glyndŵr Society, said:

"Owain Glyndŵr gave us a concept of hope, against devastating odds and out of hope a dream and out of a dream a vision to an idea that lit a flame, inextinguishable. It became a legend and the legend a nation. He did not seek greatness and achieved immortality because of his love of his country. We must now show that not only do we love and cherish our past, but as the world looks at us today, we must prove that we are sufficiently mature as a nation to take our place in the world like the example set for us by Owain Glyndŵr."

The memorial was unveiled by Professor Rees Davies and Dafydd Iwan. Later that afternoon a banquet was held at the Owain Glyndŵr centre and in the evening a procession of people carrying Glyndŵr's Four Lions Rampant banner walked from the Parliament House to the memorial.

The proclamation of Owain Glyndŵr as Prince of Wales in 1400 was marked with a Holywood style letter sign on a hillside above the A40 between Llandeilo and Carmarthen. The letters, four feet high, were erected by members of the Welsh Heritage Campaign and the Owain Glyndŵr Society on land owned by Henry Jones Davies, Editor of Cambria magazine at Nantgaredig.

Embassy Glyndŵr campaigned for September 16 to be recognised as Glyndŵr Day. They consider that the same status should be afforded to this date as November 5 has in relation to Guy Fawkes. In recent years many Welsh patriots have adopted September 16 as a National Independence Day celebration. A flag has even been raised on the summit of Caerdrewyn near Corwen, where a small Welsh Freedom Army once rallied to Glyndŵr's banner prior to the attack on Ruthin on 23rd of September, thus commencing the 1400-16 War of Independence.

A public house in Cardiff was re-named the *Owain Glyndŵr* and its new menu included an item called "Owain's Battle Feast". This pub has also made available a bilingual booklet on the story of Owain Glyndŵr.

2000 – On 17 January, a plaque to commemorate the execution of Llywelyn ap Gruffydd Fychan was unveiled at Llanymddyfri (Llandovery) on the exact spot outside the castle gates where this brave man was brutally killed in the presence of Henry IV on October 9, 1401, having refused to betray Owain Glyndŵr.

Llwybr Glyndŵr – Glyndŵr's Way a 132 mile (212km) waymarked walk was granted National Trail status in 2000. Starting at Knighton, the route winds north-westwards through Abbeycwmhir and Llanidloes to reach Machynlleth. It then heads eastwards through Llanbrynmair, Llangadfan and Meifod to finish at Welshpool. It links with Offas Dyke Path at Knighton and Welshpool, providing the option of a circular route. Also, it links with the Severn Way at Llanidloes and Welshpool.

In June, at Cosmeston Medieval Village, near Penarth in the Vale of Glamorgan, the reconstructed medieval community was attacked by the forces of Owain Glyndŵr. Visitors were able to watch a full scale attack on the defended village.

A two-day re-enactment of the siege of Coity Castle was held to form the centre piece of the community's millenium celebrations. This was one of the longest campaigns of Owain Glyndŵr's revolt, for his men were encamped in a field here for a period of two years from 1404-06.

In September the Wye Valley Brewery produced a commemorative ale called 'Braveheart Bitter' in honour of Llywelyn ap Gruffydd Fychan. It was launched at the Castle Hotel, Llandovery, within sight of where the Welsh hero was killed.

The Owain Glyndŵr Public House in Cardiff

The Siege of Coity Castle was re-enacted in June 2000

This slate monolith, about 14 feet high was erected by the Owain Glyndŵr Society on September 16th, 2000 in the grounds of Y Plas, Machynlleth. It was designed by Ieuan Rees, whose work can also be seen in Westminster Abbey. The head of the monument bears a representation of Owain's Great Seal, thus symbolising his stature as a statesman. The main body of the memorial bears a representation of Owain as a knight in armour. At the base of the monument is an englyn composed by the poet Dafydd Wyn Jones:

> Owain, tydi yw'n dyhead - Owain,
> Ti piau'n harddeliad,
> Piau'r her yn ein parhad
> A ffrewyll ein deffroad.

> Owain, spring of our aspiring, - Owain
> Prince for our approving,
> Inspirer of our enduring,
> And scourge for our awakening.

On Sunday 16 September a memorial was unveiled to Catrin Glyndŵr (wife of Sir Edmund Mortimer) and her children who were taken from Harlech Castle and incarcerated in the Tower of London. It is not known how they died but their burial in 1413 at St Swithin's Churchyard in the City of London is recorded in documents of the time.

The ceremony included performances by three pupils from Ysgol Ardudwy in Harlech , who were present at the ceremony to symbolically represent the grandchildren of Owain Glyndŵr that were captured at Harlech Castle in 1409 and taken to London to die in the Tower. Also present were the London Welsh Choir, and actress Siân Phillips, who gave the inauguration speech to mark the occasion. She commented: "The memorial will create a focal point in London for people with Welsh connections and I am sure that it will become a natural venue for future events and celebrations."

The sculpture, 10ft high, which stands in a landscaped garden in Cannon Street (site of the old St Swithin's graveyard) was designed by Welsh artist Nic Stradling-John of Pontypridd, and it was carved from a 14 tonne block of Gelligaer bluestone by Bryn Chegwidden. It takes the form of a curving shape with a flowing line leading from the stone base to a bronze tip and is designed to suggest a mother protecting her child. It was carved by Richard Renshaw who is based at Cwmdu near Crickhowell in Powys. There are two inscriptions on the stone (in Welsh and English) by the writer Menna Elfyn.

It was Isobel Monnington-Taylor, a descendant of the Monningtons of Herefordshire, who co-ordinated the project. The Monningtons have owned land and held influence in Herefordshire since well before 1400. There were once Monningtons at Monnington-on-Wye, Sarnesfield and Monnington Straddel. Isobel Monnington-Taylor has researched her family history to find that she is descended from one of Owain Glyndŵr's daughters (Margaret) who married into the Monnington family.

In September, the National Playing Fields Association, with the support of the Welsh National Assembly and local Authorities created a scheme using Owain Glyndwr's name as a means of protecting playing fields throughout Wales. Once the fields have been dedicated it will not be possible to build on them.

Monmouthshire County Council became the first local authority in Wales to make a formal dedication of an Owain Glyndŵr playing field at the village of Llanelen, near Abergavenny. Pupils of Llanelen Church in Wales School helped Monmouth AM David Davies (himself a descendant of Owain Glyndŵr) to unveil a plaque marking the occasion.

This memorial to Catrin Glyndŵr and her three children stands in a landscaped garden in Cannon Street on the site of the old St Swithin's graveyard in London. It is the only known burial site of a member of Glyndŵr's immediate family.

Photograph by Clive Gardener

On 10 September, the four Lions Rampant flag of Owain Glyndŵr was presented by Embassy Glyndŵr to the National Assembly in a special ceremony. The flag is to be flown annually on Glyndŵr Day (September 16) at the National Assembly building in Cardiff Bay.

On October 6, a 16ft stainless steel statue to Llywelyn ap Gruffydd Fychan, (the "Welsh Braveheart") was unveiled on the north side of Llandovery Castle, overlooking the town car park and market area. It was exactly 600 years after Llywelyn's execution here in the presence of Henry IV.

This brave supporter of Owain Glyndŵr had led the King's army on a wild goose chase, supposedly taking them to a secret hiding place in the mountains. When Henry IV realised he had been tricked by a false claim, he had Llywelyn half-hanged, disembowled, beheaded and dismembered. The remains were then salted and sent to the main Welsh towns as a warning.

A competition had been held in order to obtain a suitable design for the memorial and five entries were considered. The Organiser Robert ap Steffan stressed that it had been a community project from the outset and he had wanted the sculpture to be absolutely stunning and a big talking point throughout Wales.

The winning design by Toby and Gideon Petersen was finally chosen and the majority of the £50,000 funding came from a National Lottery grant provided by the Arts Council of Wales. The Petersen brothers took four months to make this abstract figure which now stands like a 'guardian angel' over Llandovery town.

Llywelyn was from the commote of Caio so it was decided that a piece of stone from that area would be incorporated into the memorial. On this stone was carved the last verse of a poem by Carodyn in suitable innovative lettering.

2002 – On 22/23 June, a two day event was held to mark the 600th anniversary of the historic battle of Pilleth, when Owain Glyndŵr defeated Sir Edmund Mortimer on the slopes of Bryn Glâs Hill. The event helped to raise money for the restoration of Pilleth Church which stands near the battle site.

Memorial in stainless steel to Llywelyn ap Gruffydd Fychan, erected on the north side of Llandovery Castle on the 600th anniversary of his execution here in the presence of Henry IV.

Places relevant to the story
of Owain Glyndŵr

NORTH WALES

Aberconwy Parish Church is built on the site of the old Cistercian Abbey, which was founded by Owain Glyndŵr's illustrious ancestor Llywelyn the Great in 1184. He was buried, as founder, in front of the high altar. His son, Prince Dafydd, was also brought here from Aber for burial. When Gruffydd, Dafydd's half-brother, was killed whilst trying to escape from the Tower of London, the Abbot of Aberconwy persuaded Henry III to let him have the remains of his body for burial here as well. Llywelyn the Great was buried here in 1240, but in 1289 his remains were transferred to Maenan and later to Llanwrst.

Aberdaron, near the tip of the Lleyn Peninsula, is where Owain Glyndŵr, Edmund Mortimer and Earl Percy met in secret to divide England and Wales between them. This historic meeting was held at the house of Dafydd Daran, Dean of Bangor, who supported the uprising.

Bangor Cathedral was burnt by Owain's soldiers in 1402 because the Bishops supported Henry IV. Wherever Owain went he ruthlessly sacked the property of Henry IV's sympathisers and destroyed all buildings in his path that might assist the King's army. The Cathedral lay in ruins for nearly a century until re-building was commenced in 1496 by Bishop Dene. It continued for many years, with the last restoration being carried out by Sir Gilbert Scott in 1886. Gruffydd ap Cynan, Prince of Wales, was buried here. Owain Gwynedd, his son, was another valiant Prince of Wales, and his stone coffin, with a cross on its lid, used to be situated beneath a pointed arch, but this has been built up and concealed from view in the thickness of the wall. The bodies of Owain and his brother Cadwaladr were removed by the order of Archbishop Baldwin, because they had been excommunicated by Thomas a' Becket on the charge that their father, Gruffydd, had married his first cousin.

Beaumaris Castle is said to be the most perfectly designed castle, with a concentric plan, in Britain. It was built by Edward I in 1295 to strengthen his defence of the Menai Strait and to keep the Welsh in check. The castle was given to Henry Percy (Hotspur) by Henry IV in 1400 in recognition of his services in helping to set Henry on the throne, but later the gift was revoked.

Beddgelert Churchyard is where Rhys Goch Eryri, a bard and contemporary of Owain Glyndŵr, was buried. His patriotic songs nearly brought the vengeance of the English upon him. A nearby stone is referred to as the chair of Rhys Goch Eryri and here he apparently sat when he wished to compose one of his odes.

Bryn Saeth Marchog - 'Hill of the Seven Knights' is an eminence between the farms of Llwyn y Brain and Bryn. Here, on 30 January 1402, Owain Glyndŵr captured Lord Grey after a brief skirmish with his soldiers. There is a tradition that there were seven knights in the Earl's company.

Cachardy Owain at Carrog, near Corwen, was once the site of a fourteenth-century stone cottage which Owain Glyndŵr used as a prison house. It was demolished some years ago and new houses built in its place.

Caernarfon Castle was attacked by Owain Glyndŵr on several occasions. Aided by French soldiers, he first tried to take this great castle in 1401. They failed, for it was too well defended and he lost two hundred men, but the town and surrounding area suffered badly. He tried again in 1403 and also in 1404. At his last attempt he used the latest in siege techniques and machines, but the small garrison of 28 men managed to prevent the Welsh army from making any impression on the fortress. Prince Henry later established himself at this castle and in 1417 it was used as a state prison.

Carrog Uchaf, Glyndyfrdwy is believed to have once been a home of Owain Glyndwr.

Castell Dinas Brân, perched on a conical hill above Llangollen in the Dee Valley, was once the home of the Princes of Powys, from whom Owain Glyndŵr was descended through the line of Bleddyn ap Cynfyn. The castle was built by Gruffydd ap Madoc in about 1236. He was the son of the founder of Valle Crucis Abbey, where both he and his father are buried. The castle was besieged by Owain Glyndŵr in 1401, when it was defended by Thomas Fitzalan, Earl of Arundel.

Conwy Castle was originally known as Cynwy and the town resembles a Welsh harp in shape. The castle took eighteen years to build and was constructed by Edward I during his long and violent war with the native Prince of Wales - Llywelyn the Last. The town walls were built at the same time as the castle and defended by 21 massive semi-circular towers. Among the constables of the castle was Henry Hotspur, a descendant of Llywelyn the Great's daughter Gwladys, by her marriage with Ralph Mortimer. There is a statue in Lancaster Square of Llywelyn the Great. It is inscribed: 'Llywelyn ap Iorwerth, Founder of Conwy Abbey A.D. 1184'. The castle was captured during the first year of the uprising by Glyndŵr's cousins from Anglesey, Gwilym and Rhys Tudur, one Sunday whilst the garrison, apart from two men, were in church. Following a siege of three months and the payment of a 1,000 marks fine, the castle was later surrendered to Henry Percy ('Hotspur').

Corwen, a market town on the A5 has an Owain Glyndŵr Hotel and a modern statue of the Welsh patriot. A lintel over a doorway of the church is said to bear an impression of Glyndŵr's dagger, which he is supposed to have thrown in a fit of temper from Pen-y-Pegwn above the church. Corwen is one of the many places that have been suggested as a possible burial place for Owain Glyndŵr.

Criccieth Castle held out in the Glyndŵr wars under its constable, Ieuan ap Meredydd. In 1402, Prince Henry authorised the castle to be garrisoned by six men-at-arms and fifty archers. The castle was captured and destroyed by Glyndŵr in 1404.

Denbigh Castle was built in the reign of Edward I and was at one time the largest castle in Wales. The entrance is through a magnificent archway, once flanked by two large octagonal towers and the grounds inside once covered ten acres. The battered effigy above the gateway represents the castle founder, Henry de Lacy, Earl of Lincoln. In 1399, Denbigh castle became the headquarters of Henry Percy (Hotspur). It was destroyed by Owain Glyndŵr in 1402. The rocky hill behind the Crown Hotel is said to have been the site of a fortress used by the old Welsh princes.

Dolbadarn Castle is one of the royal castles of ancient Wales. It stands on a rocky knoll overlooking Llyn Peris and was built to guard the main route from Caernarfon to the upper Vale of Conwy and central Wales. It has been a fortified site since the sixth century, when it was first a stronghold of the Welsh princes. The ancient tower is said to have been constructed by Llywelyn Fawr who imprisoned his brother Owain Goch here for over twenty years. Lord Grey also languished here for several years, and Dafydd Gam, Owain's bitterest enemy, was kept here for a short time. This was the only medieval fortress to be built in the heart of these mountains.

Dolgellau - In St. Mary's Church is a stone effigy of Meurig ap Ynyr Fychan, a grandfather of Hywel Sele whom Owain Glyndŵr killed at Nannau. A Parliament was held at Dolgellau in May 1404, when Owain dispatched two envoys with a letter to Charles VI, which resulted in a treaty of alliance between Wales and France. The old Parliament House was taken down in 1882 and transported to Newtown, where it stands in Sir Pryce Jones's Park.

Ffestiniog is said to have been the birthplace of Rhys Goch Eryri - 'Red Rhys of Snowdonia'. He was an aged bard who lived during the reign of Owain Glyndŵr. (see Beddgelert).

Flint Castle in Clwyd stands forlornly beside the tide with its sightless eyes staring morosely across the sands of the Dee. It was among the first of the group of castles built by Edward I in Wales and was completed in about 1281. Richard II in 1399, after being ambushed by the Earl of Northumberland, was brought here to meet Henry Bolingbroke. Richard heard mass in the chapel on the upper floor of the Great Tower. From Flint he was taken to London, where the deed of abdication was signed.

Glyndyfrdwy is a small village in the Dee Valley, from which Owain Glyndŵr took his name. In the Owain Glyndŵr Memorial Hall can be seen several items of historic interest. These include a copy of a letter sent to Charles VI, King of France, from Pennal in March 1405. There are pictures of Owain's Parliament House in Dolgellau and Cachardy (Owain's prison house at Carrog) and a portrait of Owain Glyndŵr, drawn from his seal. Of particular interest is a copy of the document ratifying the 1404 Treaty between Charles VI, King of France, and Owain Glyndŵr, Prince of Wales. It was signed on 12 January, 1405 at Llanbadarn, Aberystwyth, and stamped with Owain Glyndwr's seal. There is also a copy of a letter confirming the appointment of John Hanmer, Owain Glyndŵr's brother-in-law, and of Gruffydd Yonge, his Chancellor, as Ambassadors to the French Court with proposals for alliance with France. The ensuing treaty was signed on 14 July, 1404 at the house of the French Chancellor. There are replicas of Owain Glyndŵr's seal (back and front) and a snuff box reputedly made from the hollow oak tree at Nannau, where Owain is said to have concealed the body of Hywel Sele.

Beside the A5 just beyond the village is a high circular Mound, which marks the site of Owain's second home. It is sometimes called Y Pigyn and also Owain Glyndŵr's Mount.

Gwrych Castle, near Abergele, is a picturesque and impressive building, but it is really a sham castle, having been built in 1815. Of interest are some tablets at the castle gateway, recording historic events which took place in this locality. One tablet tells of the ambush of Richard II by the Earl of Northumberland in 1399.

Hanmer lies in the furthest corner of Maelor Saesneg (English Maelor). In 1383 Margaret Hanmer married Owain Glyndŵr in the parish church, which is dedicated to St Chad, who was known as the Saint of the Midlands and became the Bishop of the Kingdom of Mercia. Margaret Hanmer's three brothers supported Owain's cause and John Hanmer acted as his envoy in Paris. During the Wars of the Roses, Hanmer Church was burnt down and then rebuilt in about 1500, but the tower was not finished until 1570. Another fire in 1889 destroyed the interior of this Tudor church, leaving only a shell. It was rebuilt in the old style and opened in 1892, but the chancel was not rebuilt until 1936.

Harlech Castle stands on a rocky outcrop 200 ft above the marshes of Morfa Harlech on the Traeth Bach estuary. It was built by Edward I between 1285 and 1290, at a cost of just over £8,000. This impressive concentric castle was designed by Edward I's military engineer, James of St George. Owain Glyndŵr laid siege to the castle in 1404 and it surrendered after sickness and starvation had reduced the garrison to twenty-one men. Glyndŵr then made it his headquarters and lived here with his family in grand style for four years. The castle was retaken in 1409 by a substantial English force of one thousand men led by John Talbot the Earl of Shrewsbury, after a siege which lasted eight months, during which Sir Edmund Mortimer died of starvation. Glyndŵr's wife, daughter and four grandchildren were taken prisoner.

Llanfaes Priory on Anglesey was built by Llywelyn the Great in 1237, over the tomb of his wife, Princess Joan. The priory was destroyed by Henry IV, who ruthlessly drove out the friars and plundered their church. Today there are no remains of the priory to be seen.

Llanrwst Church was built in 1470 on the site of a twelfth century church that was destroyed by fire. In the Gwydir Chapel (an annexe built on the south side of the chancel in 1633 by the Wynnes of Gwydir House), can be seen a huge coffin, which is believed to have once contained the body of Llywelyn the Great, who was first buried in the abbey he founded at Conwy. When it was dissolved by Edward I, the stone coffin was taken to Maenan Abbey. Following its dissolution in the time of Henry VIII the coffin was brought to Llanrwst. The roof of the chapel is composed of carved oak, which was brought here from the dismantled abbey at Maenan. In 1400, the town was depopulated following an attack by Owain Glyndŵr. The church was left a blackened ruin and for many years afterwards deer and goats grazed on grass growing in the centre of the deserted town.

Llys Bradwen below Cadair Idris was the court of Ednyfed ap Aron in the fifteenth century. There is little sign of the building constructed of boulders and roofed with slates that once stood here. It was a member of this family who assisted Owain when he sheltered in a coastal sea cave near Rhoslefaina.

Nannau, near Dolgellau, is said to be the 'highest gentleman's house' in Britain. The first house on this site was built by Cadwgan ap Bleddyn, Prince of Powys. Three hundred years later Owain's cousin, Hywel Sele, lived here. He tried to murder Owain, but failed in the attempt and was killed by Glyndŵr, who concealed the body in the trunk of a hollow oak tree, which became known as the 'Hobgoblin's Hollow Tree'. It kept its grisly secret for many years.

Ogof Owain, is about one mile from Tonfanau, near Tywyn, close to the mouth of the Dysynni in the parish of Llangelynnin (old Merionethshire). Owain is supposed to have sheltered in this sea cave whilst being pursued by his enemies in 1406. It should only be visited at low tide. He was secretly supported by Ednyfed ap Aron, who lived at Llys Bradwen near Cadair Idris.

Pennal Church, near Machynlleth, was founded in the sixth century by St Tannwg and St Eithrias. Inside can be seen a facsimile of the Pennal Letter, which was drawn up during Lent on 31 March, 1406 by Owain Glyndŵr and the Avignon Pope, Benedict XIII. It was delivered to the French King, Charles VI.

Plas Eglwyseg at World's End near Llangollen was once the site of a hunting lodge owned by Owain ap Cadwgan (d.1116), the grandson of Bleddyn ap Cynfyn, King of North Wales, who was killed in 1073. Bleddyn ap Cynfyn was the most important of Owain Glyndŵr's noble ancestors.

Plas Penmynydd is a sixteenth century mansion situated about three miles north-west of Llanfair Pwll on the island of Anglesey, just off the road from Menai Bridge to Llangefni. It is the ancestral home of the Tudors and the birthplace of Owen Tudor, the grandfather of Henry VII. The church in the village contains a Tudor Chapel with the monuments of Gronw Fychan and his wife, Myfanwy, who were the uncle and aunt of Owen Tudor and friends of the Black Prince. Through his mother, Gronw Fychan was a first cousin of Owain Glyndŵr.

Rhuddlan Castle was being visited by Edward I when news of the birth of his son at Caernarfon Castle came to him. Four months later the infant prince was brought here and shown to the people of Rhuddlan at the Black Friars House near Twt Hill and seventeen years later, on his birthday, Prince Edward accepted the homage of the local people at this friary. He was the first Prince of Wales who had no real right to the title. Parliament House in High Street is where Edward I held his Parliament in 1283. Here the Statutes of Rhuddlan were passed in 1284. Edward's policy was to establish the Norman shire system in Welsh Wales. This meant the substitution of English law for Welsh law, along with English administrative systems, English customs and English language. These laws swept away the old dynastic boundaries and gave Wales her first shires or counties; Anglesey, Caernarfon, Merioneth, Flint, Cardigan and Carmarthen. The rest of Wales was known as Marches and was not made into counties until the reign of Henry VIII.

Rug Hall once belonged to Owain Glyndŵr and was later a seat of the Vaughans. A table inside is said to have belonged to Llywelyn the Great. A staple sticks out of one leg, to which Llywelyn is said to have tied his dog. The manor was purchased from Henry IV by the Salisbury family, after being confiscated from Owain Glyndŵr. There used to be a dagger kept here with a knife and fork, all in one sheath, but each in a separate compartment. It was claimed that Owain always carried it with him.

Ruthin Castle, in the Vale of Clwyd, is situated on a red sandstone ridge, rising above the valley and was built in the late 13th century. During the time of Owain Glyndŵr, this was the home of his arch enemy, Reginald de Grey, Lord of Ruthin. What Glyndŵr failed to do, Cromwell accomplished when he demolished most of this fortress. However, after repair and conversion at the end of the nineteenth century, it is now one of the most luxurious hotels in North Wales.

Strata Marcella was a Cistercian monastery founded in 1172 by Owain Cyfeiliog. It took 80 years to build and had a nave 200 feet long, behind which was a choir and a presbytery. It was the second largest abbey in Wales. Owain Glyndŵr destroyed it during his uprising and today not one stone is left above ground. Its foundations have been revealed by excavation and surviving fragments of this building can be seen in the churches of Pool, Guilsfield and Buttington.

St. Asaph Cathedral stands on the site of a church founded by St. Elwy in 560. He was succeeded by Asa or Asaph, the grandson of Pabo-Post-Prydain. It is the smallest cathedral in England and Wales and the east window is a copy of one at Tintern Abbey. St. Asaph Cathedral lay in ruins for seventy years after Owain Glyndŵr destroyed it. The present building was constructed in the time of Henry VII. Interior roof painting and gilding was carried out in 1969 to celebrate the investiture of Prince Charles as Prince of Wales.

St. Peter's Church, Ruthin is reputed to be the burial place of Owain's enemy Lord Grey, (if the following lines are reliable), although his tomb is certainly not in existence:

> *A church there is at Wrythen at this day*
> *Wherin Lord Grey, that once was earle of Kent*
> *In tombe of stone, within the chauncel laye.*

Valle Crucis Abbey was founded in 1201 by Madog ap Gruffydd, Prince of Powys and cousin of Llywelyn Fawr. He was one of Owain Glyndŵr's ancestors and his lands stretched from the Berwyns to Chester. A memorial stone to Madog ap Gruffydd, the great-grandson of the founder and the great-grandfather of Owain Glyndŵr, can be seen here. The Abbey was well known for its patronage of the bards, and Iolo Goch, Owain Glyndŵr's domestic bard, and also Guto'r Glyn, a fifteenth century poet from Glynceiriog, were buried here. This was the abbey church of Powys Fadog and in North Wales it was second only to the great monastery of Aber Conwy, which was burnt by English soldiers in the thirteenth century.

A story is told of an occasion when the Abbot was walking in the Berwyn Mountains and he met Owain Glyndŵr, who appeared to be an old and dejected figure. Owain said 'Sir Abbot you have risen too early.' The Abbot replied, 'No, Owain it is you who has risen too early - by a hundred years!' This Abbey is yet another suggested burial site for Owain Glyndŵr.

MID WALES

Abbey Cwmhir was founded in 1143 and although it was was once the largest abbey in Wales it was never completed. Its fourteen bay nave was even longer than the naves of Canterbury and Salisbury Cathedrals, and twice as long as the nave of St David's Cathedral in Dyfed. In 1237 Henry II marched here to punish the abbey for supporting Prince Llywelyn ap Iorwerth. He would have burned the abbey, but accepted payment of three hundred marks instead. Llywelyn ap Gruffydd, the last Prince of Wales, is said to be buried near the site of the altar in the ruined nave. The Abbey was burned by Owain Glyndŵr in 1401. After the Dissolution of the monasteries, part of the nave arcades were taken to Llanidloes and incorporated in the church. The rood screen was possibly transferred to Llanonno.

Aberystwyth Castle is one of the seven remaining castles built by Edward I to enforce his supremacy over Wales. However, little is now left of the towering inner ward or the concentric walls of defence erected by the military engineer, James of St George. It was a typical concentric fortress built on a diamond-shaped site. The outer walls included the old town. Owain Glyndŵr captured this castle in 1404 and held it for three years, before it was retaken by the English. During the Civil War it was garrisoned for the king and shared the usual fate of such castles when it was dismantled by Oliver Cromwell in 1647.

Bleddfa, near Pilleth, is built on the site of an earlier church, which was destroyed by Owain Glyndŵr's army at the time of the battle of Pilleth.

Brecon Cathedral contains a wooden effigy of a lady which is the only remnant of the Gam family tomb. It was burned by Parliamentary troops during the Civil War. Dafydd Gam, who lived near Brecon, was not a supporter of Owain Glyndŵr.

Bronllys Castle was last fortified against Owain Glyndŵr. A Welsh bard named Bedo Brwynllys lived here in the mid fifteenth century.

Bryn Glâs Hill, Pilleth, is the site of a famous battle in which an English army suffered a massive defeat when they fought a Welsh force commanded by Rhys Gethin. He took Sir Edmund Mortimer, the English commander, prisoner and a large number of English soldiers were killed. The burial site of those who died in the battle is marked by a conspicuous grove of Wellingtonia trees, planted by Sir Richard Green-Price at the end of the nineteenth century.

Builth Castle, in Powys, was built by Edward I. It took five years to build and dates from 1277. At the time of Owain Glyndŵr's uprising it was in the charge of Sir John Oldcastle. The Welsh name of Builth Wells is Llanfair ym Muallt ('the Church of St. Mary in the hundred of Buallt'). It is recorded that £400 was spent on repairs in 1409, which were obviously needed as a result of damage caused by Glyndŵr.

Cefnllys Castle (Castell Glan Ithon) stands on a hill, about 2 miles east of Llandrindod Wells. In 1403 Henry IV ordered the castle to be provisioned against attack.

Dyfynog in Powys is where Henry IV signed a 'proclamation of pardon' in 1403. He then stayed the night at Sennybridge.

Hay-on-Wye Castle was considerably damaged by Owain Glyndŵr when he attacked it in 1400.

Hyddgen, on the northern slopes of Plynlimmon, was the site of Glyndŵr's base during the first year of his uprising and a battle against a large army of Flemish soldiers was fought here. It is commemorated by two white rocks known as Cerrig Cymafod Owain Glyndŵr (Owain Glyndŵr's Covenant Stones). The battle is also commemorated by a plaque, which can be seen on a stone plinth at the east end of the Nant y Moch Reservoir dam .

Knighton Castle was built by the Mortimers at the end of the twelfth century and destroyed by Owain Glyndŵr in 1401. The place is called Knighton (Knight's Town) after Sir Roger Mortimer. The Welsh name for the town is Tref-y-Clawdd - 'the town on the dyke' (Offa's Dyke).

Knucklas Castle stands on a lofty hill and was once known as Caer Godyrfran. It was built in 1282 by the Mortimers. Below the castle is the 'bloody field' where the battle of Beguildy was fought in 1146 between the Welsh and the Mortimers. The castle was destroyed by Owain Glyndŵr in 1402.

Llandovery Castle was built by the Normans in 1110 and almost immediately captured by the South Wales princes. It remained a constant source of strife amongst them, being taken and retaken until the days of Edward I. It was attacked by Owain Glyndŵr in 1403 and has been a ruin ever since. Henry IV rested here during one of his unsuccessful sorties into Wales and executed Gryffudd ap Llywelyn Fychan, the Squire of Caio, in the market place.

Machynlleth has an ancient building in Maengwyn Street which stands on the site of the traditional meeting place of Owain Glyndŵr's Parliament. The building was restored by David Davies, a wealthy industrialist who purchased it in 1906. He spared no expense and the work was completed in 1912. It is now known as the 'Owain Glyndŵr Institute' and houses an exhibition on the life and times of Owain Glyndŵr (Open Easter to September 30 or otherwise by appointment). Owain Glyndŵr's seal was adopted by the local Urban District Council as the design for their own. It depicts Glyndŵr with his forked beard, sitting on a chair, a sceptre in one hand and an orb in the other.

Royal House, Machynlleth, just north of the clock tower, is said to be where Owain resided when he held his Parliament in Machynlleth. It is called Royal House because Charles I stayed there in 1644 whilst travelling to Chester.

Mathafon, west of Cemmaes Road, only dates back to 1628, but a house stood on this site in Owain Glyndŵr's time and he apparently stayed there on various occasions.

Mathrafal is the site of the ancient court of the Princes of Powys. A tree-covered mound with banks and ditches can be seen on the east bank of the Banwy, just above its confluence with the Fyrnwy. This fortified site was established by Eliseg, Prince of Powys, in the eighth Century and it became an important seat of the Powysian royalty following the Anglo-Saxon conquest of the lowlands beyond Breidden by Offa, King of Mercia. In the 12th century the court was moved by Gwenwynwyn to Powis Castle. Mathrafal was destroyed by King John on 2 August 1212 during his campaign against Llywelyn the Great.

Meifod is the old ecclesiastical capital of Powys and the burial place of many of the Princes of Powys. The church dates from 1155 and at one time belonged to the Abbey of Strata Marcella. One of the Powysian princes buried here was Madog, an ally of Henry II in his wars against Wales.

Monaughty, near Pilleth, was once known as Mynachdy (The Monks' House or Monastery). It was given to Abbey Cwmhir by Roger Mortimer, 4th Earl of March, the elder brother of Sir Edmund Mortimer who was captured at the battle of Pilleth. The last Abbot of Abbey Cwmhir was permitted by Henry VIII to end his days here after the dissolution of his monastery. Rhys Gethin is said to have slept here the night before the battle of Pilleth.

Montgomery Castle was originally a motte and bailey fortress, known as Y Domen, built by Roger de Montgomery in 1072. It stood one mile north-west of the town and was later superseded by the present castle which was started by Henry III in 1223. Montgomery is the oldest borough in Wales, for its charter was granted by Henry III in 1227. This walled town was sacked by Owain Glyndŵr in 1402. He attacked the castle but the garrison held out against him. The town walls were never rebuilt after his visit and for two centuries the town remained in ruins.There are few traces remaining of the wall which once surrounded the town. It was flanked with towers and the entrances were defended by four fortified gates, which, according to Leland were called: 'Kedewen Gate, Chirbury Gate, Arthur's Gate and Kerry Gate.'

Montgomery Church contains an effigy believed to be that of Edmund Mortimer, son-in-law of Owain Glyndŵr and brother-in-law of Hotspur. He was at one time the Constable of Montgomery Castle but died during the long siege of Harlech Castle in 1409.

Mynydd Cwmdu near Crickhowell is the site of a battle where some of Owain Glyndŵr's forces were defeated in 1404.

Newtown - just outside is the old Parliament House which was used by Owain Glyndŵr at Dolgellau. This stone and timber building was purchased by Sir Pryce-Jones in 1885. He had it transported to Llanllwchaiarn in a 32 truck train specially hired for the purpose. It was re-erected at Dolerw and here it stands at the side of the road, where it has served as a Quaker meeting house.

Newton Farm, Brecon, was once the home of the Games family, who were descendants of Sir Dafydd Gam.

New Radnor Castle was originally called Trefaesyfed. It was once a fortress of considerable strength, built by Phillip de Breos at the end of the eleventh century. When the Mortimers became the great power in the Marches it came into their possession. The mound on which the castle once stood can still be seen, but the castle itself was destroyed by Owain Glyndŵr in 1401 and the stonework has long since been removed. He hanged the garrison of sixty men from the curtain walls. Human bones and skulls discovered during excavations for church rebuilding in 1843 were probably the remains of the unfortunate garrison. By 1405 Henry IV had re-possessed the castle and garrisoned it with thirty men-at-arms and one hundred and fifty archers under the command of Richard, Lord Grey.

Owain Glyndŵr's Way is a 130 mile waymarked walk established by Powys County Council. It starts at Knighton on Offa's Dyke and takes in the sites of many incidents associated with the rebellion, including Abbey Cwmhir, Plynlimmon, Machynlleth and Lake Vyrnwy. The walk finishes at Welshpool.

Oswestry was nearly destroyed by Owain Glyndŵr in 1400. It became known as Pentrepoeth - 'Hot town'. The English name of this town is derived from Oswald, the Northumbrian king who was killed in a battle fought here against Penda, King of Mercia. Just outside the town is St Oswald's Well. There is a legend that an eagle tore an arm from his martyred body, but the bird fell dead immediately and water sprang from the spot where it fell and was found to possess a miraculous cure for blindness.

Peytin Gwyn, on the Upper Chapel Road, just north of Brecon and in the Parish of Llandefaelog Fach, is the birthplace of Dafydd Gam. The castle that once stood here was purchased by Llywelyn, the father of Dafydd, from William Peyton - hence Pytin, a corruption of Peyton. An artificial mound can be seen here with a farmhouse near its base. There were in fact, three Peytins along this road - Peytin Du, Peytin Gwyn and Peytin Glas, named it is said after different soil colours. The houses all have their own fortified mounds and Dafydd Gam's father bought the three houses for three hundred marks from William Peyton. One account states that Dafydd spent his early years at Peytin Gwyn and another states that 'Owen destroyed Gam's paternal residence, the castle of Peytins.'

Powis Castle was first built by Cadwgan ap Bleddyn, in 1110. It was originally known as Castell Coch ('the Red Castle'). Cadwgan and his brothers Madog and Rhirid ruled Powys in three portions but the latter two brothers were killed in a battle with King Rhys of South Wales. It was Owen, the son of Cadwgan, who carried off Nest, the wife of Gerald of Windsor, to Plas Eglwyseg at World's End, near Llangollen. Cadwgan was murdered by his nephew, Madog, near Castell Coch. Later, Owen, the son of Cadwgan, captured Madog and put out his eyes. Powis Castle was attacked by Owain Glyndŵr in 1401, but its impregnable walls resisted all his assaults, so he withdrew after reducing the suburbs of Welshpool to ashes.

Powys was an ancient kingdom which stretched from the neighbourhood of Mold to the River Wye near Hay. It was founded by Cadell Ddyrnllug ('the black-fisted'). His family remained in power until Cyngen, the last ruling member, died in 854 on a pilgrimage to Rome. His nephew Rhodri the Great, who ruled in Gwynedd,later annexed Powys. By 1000 it had shrunk northwards to include only Montgomery shire and South Denbyshire.

Strata Florida Abbey was occupied in October 1401 by Henry IV and Prince Henry, after driving out the monks who had sided with Glyndŵr. The abbey was plundered by the English soldiers and used as a base during Henry IV's campaigns against Owain Glyndŵr. In 1402 it was placed in the custody of the Earl of Worcester, and in 1407 and 1415, it became a military outpost occupied by several hundred men-at-arms and archers, who were sent here to defend the abbey and use it as a base in the war against Glyndŵr. No less than eleven Welsh princes of the House of Dynefwr were buried here during the twelfth and thirteenth centuries.

Sycharth, near Llansilin, in the ancient commote of Cynllaith, is the site of Owain Glyndŵr's impressive fortified home, where he once lived with his wife Margaret and their large family. The site can be found in the steep-sided valley of the Cynllaith, a tributary of the Tanat, near the English border, south-west of Oswestry. The main feature is a flat-topped mound, surrounded by earthworks. A fascinating description of Glyndŵr's estate is provided by his household bard, Iolo Goch.

Tretower Castle was listed in 1403 as a defensible stronghold for Henry IV and in 1404 Sir James Berkeley successfully held off an attack by Owain Glyndŵr. The adjoining Court was once the home of the Vaughan family and the first Vaughan of Tretower was the son of Roger Vaughan of Bredwardine, who, with Dafydd Gam, was knighted by Henry V at the battle of Agincourt in 1415. It was at Tretower Court that the local archers assembled before marching off to fight at Agincourt.

Welshpool was devastated by Owain Glyndŵr in 1400. Its ancient name is Y Trallwng and it used to be the capital of the old Mid-Wales kingdom of Wenwynwyn (South Powys). In 1411 the vicar of St. Mary's and St Cynfelin's Church in Welshpool was Adam of Usk.

WEST WALES

Carmarthen Castle was the earliest home of the Princes of Deheubarth before they removed their seat to Dynefwr. It occupies an old Roman site on a rocky hill above the Tywi. It twice fell into the hands of Owain Glyndŵr and was finally demolished by Cromwell's men in 1648, although there was still sufficient of it left to be used as the County Gaol in 1792.

Carreg Cennen Castle is dramatically situated on the top of a one hundred metre crag above the Cennen valley and it has been described as the most romantic castle in Wales. It was the centre of the ancient commote of Is-Cennen and part of the kingdom of Deheubarth, which in ancient times had its seat at Dynefwr, near Llandeilo. On Henry IV's accession the castle became Crown property as part of the Duchy of Lancaster. Owain Glyndŵr's soldiers laid siege to this formidable castle in 1403, when it was held by John Scudamore. The siege lasted over a year and considerable damage was inflicted on the building, for there is a 1416 record of repairs being carried out to its walls, which had been 'destroyed and thrown down by rebels'. In 1842 a cannon ball weighing nearly nine pounds was found buried in the ground on the north side of the castle.

Cydwelli Castle in Glamorgan, was besieged by Owain Glyndŵr's forces in 1403, when they were assisted by soldiers from France and Brittany. The town was captured, but the castle held out for three weeks until it was relieved by an English army. During the siege, the gatehouse suffered extensive damage and the Lancastrian kings, Henry IV and Henry V, subsequently spent over £500 on its reconstruction

Dynefwr Castle was built by Rhodri Mawr in 870. He brought together under one rule the provinces of Ceredigion, Dyfed, Ystrad Tywi, Brycheiniog, Morgannwg and Gwent. Owain Glyndŵr attacked the castle in 1403 and caused considerable damage, but failed to capture it.

Dryslwyn Castle was once an important fortress standing on a hill halfway between Llandeilo and Carmarthen, but now only fragments remain. It was erected by one of the Dynefwr princes. When marching through this area, Owain Glyndŵr once spent a night here with Rhys ap Gruffydd, the warden of the castle. He captured this fortress in 1403.

Llanstephan Castle was taken by Owain Glyndŵr and held briefly. Sir John Pennes recaptured it in 1403 but shortly afte, he was taken prisoner by the Welsh. By 1408 Sir John Pennes was back in charge of the castle.

Milford Haven is one of the finest natural harbours in the world. A fjord penetrates inland for some twenty miles, with about ten miles of deep anchorage, varying in width from one mile to two miles. From here, Richard II set sail for Ireland in 1399. A French army sent to assist Owain Glyndŵr landed here in 1407 and later in the same century Henry Tudor landed here with his two thousand Norman and Breton fighting men under the command of Philibert de Shaunde.

Newcastle Emlyn was handed over to Owain Glyndŵr's forces in 1403 by Sioncyn ap Llywelyn, of his own free will.

St. Dogmael's Church is known as Llandudoch but the church is dedicated to St. Dogfael, a paternal cousin of St. David. The parish is said to be the birthplace of Owain Glyndŵr and there is also a tradition that he was buried in the valley of Wolfcastle.

Trefgarn Owen, in the parish of Brawd, is also called West Trefgarn and Trefgarn Castle. The name is derived from Owen ap Llywelyn, a lineal descendant of the Lord Rhys. Owen, who died without issue, had two nieces, the children of his brother Thomas, one of whom was the mother of Owain Glyndŵr, and from whom were descended the Newports, Earls of Bradford, who for many years held the manor of Trefgarn Owen. They had property in Pembrokeshire until the beginning of the nineteenth century. It is possible that Owain Glyndŵr was born here while his mother Helen, was visiting her parents.

SOUTH WALES

Abergavenny was sacked by Owain Glyndŵr in 1404. There is a tradition that his men were let into the walled town by a local lady, who sympathised with the uprising. She opened a gate at the end of Market Street at midnight and they came pouring in, to plunder and set fire to the town. The way into the town from that gate was thereafter known as 'Traitor's Lane.' Glyndŵr failed to take the castle, which was at that time held by Colonel James Proger.

In the Priory Church of St Mary can be seen the effigy and tomb of Gwladys (the daughter and heiress of Sir Dafydd Gam) and her second husband Sir William ap Thomas, who fought at Agincourt and later changed his name to Sir William Herbert of Raglan.

Abertridwr in the parish of Eglwysilan is where Sion Kent (John of Kent) is believed to have been born in the fourteenth century.

Caerffili Castle in mid Glamorgan, is the largest medieval fortress in Wales. It covers an area of more than thirty acres and was the first concentric castle to be built in Britain. The design is similar in many respects to the later concentric castles of Harlech and Beaumaris. It was captured by Owain Glyndŵr in 1403, but his occupation only lasted three months. Two years later, assisted by his French allies, he took the castle again, but it was abandoned by its Welsh garrison the following year. After that time it fell into decay. The castle is famous for its leaning tower, which is nearly twenty metres high and three metres out of perpendicular after being damaged by Cromwell's troops during the Civil War.

Campston Hill, above Monmouth in Gwent, is where a battle was fought between Owain Glyndŵr's retreating force and Prince Henry's men. The Welsh standard was captured and the bearer, Ellis ap Richard ap Howell ap Morgan Llwyd, was killed.

Cardiff Castle was built by Robert Fitzhamon on the site of a smaller Welsh fortress established by the Princes of Morgannwg. Owain Glyndŵr paid a visit to Cardiff in 1404 and caused much destruction to the town and part of the castle defences.

Castell Coch overlooks the Taffs Well Gorge, through which Owain Glyndŵr and his men passed when they came to ravage Cardiff and burn the palace of Llandaff.

Chepstow Castle in Gwent, was garrisoned in 1403 with twenty men-at-arms and sixty archers. This impressive garrison no doubt kept Owain's forces away, for Chepstow Castle was not attacked during the Glyndŵr uprising.

Coity Castle in the Vale of Glamorgan dates from the twelfth century and was once a very strong fortress. It resisted an attack by Owain Glyndŵr and endured a long siege in 1405. Parliament petitioned Henry IV to send a relief force. He sent orders to three loyal Bristol shipmasters - John Stevens, Thomas Sanders and John Drois - urging them to take food to the Coity garrison.

Craig y Dorth is a conical, tree clad hill between Monmouth and Cwmcarvan in Gwent. Here, in 1404, Owain Glyndŵr entrenched himself and fought off a royal force, which under the command of Richard Beauchamp, Earl of Warwick, had been sent to dislodge him. They fled to Monmouth with Owain's men in full cry behind them and were chased right up to the town walls.

Dinas Powis Castle was built on a very ancient site within the fortifications of an Iron Age hill fort. It was attacked by Owain Glyndŵr in 1403.

East Orchard and West Orchard Castles were built by the Berkrolles family to defend two large orchards. There is a popular tradition that Owain Glyndŵr came to East Orchard Castle, disguised as a harpist and accompanied by one of his followers who pretended to be a servant. Sir Lawrence Berkrolles invited them to stay the night. Over dinner that evening, he spoke with scorn of the scoundrel Glyndŵr and expressed the desire to have him in his clutches. When Owain 'the harpist' was about to depart the next morning, he produced his seal, which so frightened Sir Lawrence, that he was struck dumb and remained so for the rest of his life.

Llandaff, Bishops' Palace, near Cardiff, was burned by Owain Glyndŵr in 1402. All that remains of the castellated mansion and the house where the Archdeacon once resided, are the ruins of an early 14th century gatehouse. Following its destructiuon, Bishop Peveral decided to move the palace east to Monmouthshire. Twenty-one Bishops in succession had lived at Llandaff, so this was a big step. The Church already owned a house and land at Mathern near Chepstow, and this became the chosen location for a new palace of the Bishops of Llandaff. Mathern Palace was enlarged in 1410 by John de la Zouche. In 1706 the Bishops moved to a large house (now demolished) at Hardwick, near Chepstow. Then in the middle of the nineteenth century they returned to Llandaff and took up residence in a large mansion.

Maes y Gaer near Llanwynno, Mid Glamorgan, is where Owain Glyndŵr and part of his army once camped. They were opposed by some Glamorgan men and those who were slain in the conflict were buried in the fields of Tyle Fedw.

Monmouth Castle, in Gwent, is the birthplace of Prince Henry, the son of Henry Bolingbroke. He was born in the castle gatehouse on 16 September 1387.

Newport Castle, in Gwent never recovered from being sacked by Owain Glyndŵr, although some efforts were made to maintain it as a Royalist stronghold during the Civil War.

Pencoed Woods Cave, in South Glamorgan, is said to have been used by Owain Glyndŵr as a hiding place. It has even been suggested that he was buried inside this cave. In recent years two Cardiff historians have claimed that a coffin-shaped trench in the cave was an initial burial place of King Arthur.

Penllyne Castle, near Bridgend, was destroyed by Owain Glyndŵr and fragments of the old castle now form part of a stable block.

Pen Rhys, above Llwyn-y-Pia, in Mid Glamorgan, was once the site of a remote Cistercian monastic cell. Owain Glyndŵr is reputed to have presided at an Eisteddfod which was held there during his time. The event is preserved in the name of Pantsteddfa Farm to the south of Ystrad. During this period he was based for a while at Llantrisant, which was about eight miles away, across the hills, and many of his followers, led by Cadwgan, came from the Rhondda Valley. After the insurrection, the cell was dissolved and its possessions were sold by Henry V, in about 1415, as a punishment for supporting Owain Glyndŵr.

Skirrid Mountain Inn, near Llanfihangel Crucorney in Gwent, is said to be the oldest hostelry in Wales. It is said that Owain Glyndŵr once rallied his men on the cobbled courtyard. The inn was at one time used as a court house and sheep stealers were hung from an oak beam above the well of the staircase.

Stalling Down, near Cowbridge in Glamorgan, is also known as Bryn Owain and it is the site of a long and terrible battle fought between the forces of Glyndŵr and Henry IV. It lasted eighteen hours and Owain inflicted an appalling defeat on the King's army.

St George's Super Ely Castle was destroyed by Owain Glyndŵr and never rebuilt. A farmhouse now stands on the site.

Taffs Well, near Cardiff, was once renowned for healing rheumatism. Owain Glyndŵr is said to have paused here on his travels and washed in its medicinal waters.

Troy House, near Monmouth in Gwent, takes its name from the River Trothy which flows close to the mansion and the parish is called Mitchel Troy. According to Adam of Usk, a Scudamore of Troy was hanged at Shrewsbury in 1411 with other followers of Owain Glyndŵr. In the reign of Henry VII Troy House was the seat of William Herbert.

Usk Castle was attacked in 1405 by a Welsh force led by Gruffydd, Owain Glyndŵr's eldest son. But he was defeated and captured at a location known as Pwll Melyn which is situated a short distance to the north-east of the Castle. During the battle, Owain's brother Tudur, was killed.

HEREFORDSHIRE

Bredwardine Church contains an ancient tomb with an alabaster figure representing Sir Roger Vaughan the son-in-law of Sir Dafydd Gam. They both fell at Agincourt and were knighted by Henry V as they lay dying on the battlefield. Sir Roger Vaughan is shown wearing plate armour with his head resting on a helmet and his arms crossed on his chest. His widow, Gwladys, later married Sir William Herbert and she was buried with him at St. Mary's Church, Abergavenny.

Clifford Castle, near Hay-on-Wye, stands at a river crossing on the Wye. It was fortified by William Fitz-Osborn soon after the Norman Conquest and formed part of his chain of defences along the Wye and the Welsh Borders. It is famous as the home of the fair Rosamund, who was a mistress of Henry II. It was destroyed by Owain Glyndŵr in 1402.

Courtfield, near Welsh Bicknor, was originally known as Greyfield. The name was altered to Courtfield after Prince Henry had lived there as a child under the care of Lady Margaret Montacute. The building has been reconstructed since that time.

Croft Castle is situated five miles north-west of Leominster, just north of the B4362. It was the home of John Croft, who married one of Owain Glyndŵr's daughters. The Croft family were closely linked with the Mortimers, who were their neighbours, and the battle of Mortimer's Cross was fought on Croft land. In the fifteenth century the Croft family adopted the Welsh Wyvern crest, and the wounded black dragon was no doubt an allusion to the Glyndŵr descent and the fate of Owain himself. Inside the church of St. Michael, in the grounds of the castle, is a fine altar tomb of Sir Richard Croft (d. 1509) and his wife Eleanor who was a widow of Sir Hugh Mortimer. Now managed by the National Trust, the castle and church are open to the public on weekends (between April and October, 1.30 - 4.30 pm). In the park are avenues of Spanish chestnut, oak and beech. Within walking distance is an Iron Age hill fort which provides very fine views on a clear day.

Dorstone Castle in 1403 was in the charge of Sir Walter Fitzwalter who strengthened it for defence against Owain Glyndŵr. It still existed at the time of the Civil War (1645) but, apart from a large mound, has now disappeared completely.

Eccleswall Castle is now just an earthwork which can be seen near Eccleswall Court. It was one of the early homes of the great Talbot family, the Earls of Shrewsbury, and one of them fought with Henry V at Agincourt.

Ewyas Harold Castle was fortified against Owain Glyndŵr by Sir William Beauchamp. All that can be seen now is a tree-covered mound on the edge of the village.

Goodrich Castle stands above a ford known as Walesford or Walford and it was here that Henry Bolingbroke first heard the news that a son (the future Henry V) had been born to him at Monmouth Castle.

Goodrich Church is not far from Courtfield, where Prince Henry spent his childhood. The tomb of the Countess of Salisbury, who brought up Prince Henry, can be seen inside this church. It is an altar-tomb on the left hand side of the altar. It is a plain slab with small painted arches below, but there is no inscription or effigy.

Hereford Castle was established shortly before the Conquest. During the 13th century it was an important fortress but then went into decline. According to Leland it was once 'nearly as large as that of Windsor' and was 'one of the fairest and strongest in all England.' This seems hard to imagine now, for it has vanished completely. Even the mound on which the keep once stood has been levelled. It would seem that a large amount of the fortress was standing until 1746, when it was finally dismantled and the site turned into a park known as Castle Green. On the north side is Castle Pool, a remnant of the water-filled ditch which once protected the west, north and east sides of the castle. In the centre of the bailey a memorial to Lord Nelson was erected in the early years of the nineteenth century. Henry IV stayed at this castle on several occasions during his campaigns against Owain Glyndwr.

Huntingdon Castle stands in a commanding position on the border between England and Wales, overlooking the valley of Gladestry on its north side. To the west and north it was protected by a steep ravine and the south and east sides were moated with water supplied by the Bellowe stream It was erected in the early part of the reign of Henry III. When Henry Bolingbroke was created Earl of Hereford by Richard II, Huntingdon Castle became one of his possessions. But when he became Henry IV, he granted it to Edmund de Stafford, Duke of Buckingham. The defences of the castle were strengthened during the Glyndŵr uprising and in 1403 the custody of this castle was committed to Anne, Countess of Stafford, who had lost her husband at the battle of Shrewsbury. She appointed John Sment as Constable of the castle. Owain Glyndŵr passed this way after fighting the battle of Pilleth, but there is no record of him damaging this fortress. He merely drove away the cattle and took flour from the local mill, which was then burnt to the ground. In 1670 the keep was still standing, but the stone remnants are now much overgrown and exploration is very difficult.

Leominster derives its name from Leofric, Earl of Mercia, who founded a priory here in the eleventh century. He was the husband of Lady Godiva who made Coventry toll free by her ride round that town 'unclothed, save her chastity.' Edmund Mortimer was brought to Leominster after his capture at Pilleth and imprisoned for a short time in a building in Church Street. The Welsh force plundered the Priory Church and several manors in the locality.

Longtown Castle was built by the de Laceys. It was fortified against Owain Glyndŵr but not attacked.

Monnington Straddel, on the east side of the Golden Valley, is the site of a Manor House once the residence of Roger Monnington, who married Owain Glyndŵr's daughter Margaret, and it is here that Owain probably spent his last days. Near the present day Monnington Court, is a prominent fortified mound surrounded by a wet ditch. A stream runs through part of the ditch and was probably used as an outer defence to a crescent shaped bailey which lies to the west of the mound. The small hamlet of Monnington Straddel once had a church and a monastic fish pond which served the grange of Abbey Dore.

Much Marcle Church contains the tomb of Blanche Mortimer, which is of special interest because it bears the Mortimer arms. About fifty yards to the north-east of the church is a motte and bailey known as Mortimer's Castle.

Oldcastle, on the east side of the Black Mountains is where Sir John Oldcastle is reputed to have been born in 1360. He was elected as a knight of Herefordshire in the fifth year of Henry IV's reign. His grandfather, also called Sir John Oldcastle, was a Member of Parliament in the latter part of the reign of Richard II.

SHROPSHIRE

Battlefield Church, near Shrewsbury, was built over a large pit in which the men who lost their lives in the battle of Shrewsbury were buried. This is the only church in England that serves as a war memorial.

Clun Castle was built by Robert de Say, who held the district under Robert de Lacy of Ludlow, and it was probably completed at some time in the middle of the twelfth century. Today, all that remains are the gaunt square walls of the Norman keep, rising sheer from the moat. Owain Glyndŵr destroyed this fortress during his campaign in this area. Little was done to restore the castle after his visit.

Ludlow Castle was held by five generations of Mortimers and this fine fortress was more of a centre of power for them than their ancestral home of Wigmore.

Mortimer's Cross Mill, in the Lugg Valley, stands near the ancient battlefield of Mortimer's Cross. It contains an exhibition which tells the story of the battle which was fought here in 1461. It is open from April to September on Thursday, Sunday and Bank Holiday afternoons, 2.00 p.m. to 6.00 p.m.

Whitchurch Church contains the canopied tomb, with an effigy in full armour of John Talbot, the first Earl of Shrewsbury. He died in battle at Castillon near Bordeaux. His heart, discovered during the rebuilding of the church, was reburied in the south porch.

Wigmore Castle was the ancestral home of the Mortimers and it was once as important as Chepstow or Ludlow Castles. It was from Wigmore that the Mortimers set forth to conquer Radnor and Builth.

ACKNOWLEDGEMENTS

During my travels around Wales, researching and photographing the many locations featured in this book, I was given considerable assistance by farmers, house-owners and various people with a knowledge of local history and traditions.

Visits were also made to numerous libraries in all parts of Wales, where I always found the staff most helpful and enthusiastic about my project. In addition I was assisted in my research by Dr John Davies of Llandyssul and Paul Parry who both supplied useful information.

Jan Morris is a writer, whose work I have admired over many years and I am grateful to her for commenting on the original manuscript and writing a foreword. I am also grateful to Anne Waller for proof reading the new edition. Michael Blackmore is thanked for providing artwork and also MWL Ltd for their high quality printing.

RECOMMENDED READING

A History of Wales, Vol I and Vol 2, J.E. Lloyd.
A History of England under Henry IV, (4 Vols), James Hamilton Wyllie.
A Selected Bibliography of Owen Glyndŵr, David Rhys Phillips.
A Tour in Wales, Thomas Pennant.
Brut y Twysogion – The Chronicle of the Princes
Glyndŵr's Way National Trail Guide, David Perrott.
Henry V, R.B. Mowat.
Henry of Monmouth, J. Endell Tyler.
Henry IV, Parts I and II, William Shakespeare.
Henry V, William Shakespeare.
History of the County of Hereford, John Duncomb
History of Powys Fadog (6 volumes), J.Y.W. Lloyd.
Insurrection in Wales, D. Helen Allday,
Land of My Fathers, Gwynfor Evans
Memoirs of Owen Glendowe, T. Ellis.
Owen Glyndŵr, Arthur Gwilm Jones
Owain Glyndŵr, Prince of Wales, Ian Skidmore
Owain Glyndŵr's Way, Richard Sale
Owain Glyndŵr, Glanmor Williams
Owen Glyndŵr, J.D. Griffith Davies.
Owain Glyndŵr and the last struggle for Welsh Independence, Arthur Granville Bradley.
Owen Glendower, J.E. Lloyd.
Owain Glyndŵr & the War of Independence in the Welsh Borders, Geoffrey Hodges.
Prince Henry of Monmouth – His Letters and Dispatches during the War in Wales,
Royal Historical Transactions, new series, Vol IV, F. Solly Flood.
Richard II, William Shakespeare.
Shakespeare's History Plays, E.M.W. Tillyfor.
The Battle of Shrewsbury 1403, E.J. Priestly.
The Castles of Wales, Alan Reid.
The History of Wales, Owen Edwards.
The Revolt of Owain Glyndŵr, R.R. Davies
The Matter of Wales, Jan Morris
The Middle Ages, W.F. Bolton
Wales through the Age, (2 vols) A.J. Roderick.
Wild Wales, George Borrow.

INDEX

OTHER TITLES BY CHRIS BARBER

Walks in the Brecon Beacons
Exploring the Waterfall Country
Ghosts of Wales
Exploring the Brecon Beacons National Park
Exploring Gwent
Mysterious Wales
More Mysterious Wales
Cordell Country
The Romance of the Welsh Mountains
Hando's Gwent (Volume 1)
Hando's Gwent (Volume 2)
The Ancient Stones of Wales (Jointly with J.G. Williams)
The Seven Hills of Abergavenny
Journey to Avalon (Jointly with David Pykitt)
Arthurian Caerleon
Abergavenny in Old Picture Postcards
Portraits of the Past
Classic Walks in the Brecon Beacons National Park
Walks in Cordell Country
In Search of Owain Glyndŵr (Edition I)
Eastern Valley – The Story of Torfaen
Exploring Blaenavon Industrial Landscape World Heritage Site
Exploring Kilvert Country
Llanover Country